SERVING THE
SERVANT

DEVOTIONAL THOUGHTS ON THE GOSPEL OF MARK

Fred Donehoo

JOURNEYFORTH
Greenville, South Carolina

Library of Congress Cataloging-in-Publication Data

Donehoo, Fred, 1927-
Serving the servant : devotional thoughts on the book of Mark / Fred
Donehoo.
  p. cm.
Includes bibliographical references and index.
Summary: "Serving the Servant is a devotional commentary on the
book of Mark"—Provided by publisher.
ISBN 978-1-59166-917-3 (perfect bound pbk. : alk. paper)
1. Bible. N.T. Mark—Criticism, interpretation, etc. I. Title.
BS2585.52.D66 2008
226.3'077—dc22

                                                    2008030478

Cover Photo Credit: Craig Oesterling

The fact that materials produced by other publishers may be referred to in this
volume does not constitute an endorsement of the content or theological position
of materials produced by such publishers.

All Scripture is quoted from the Authorized King James Version unless other-
wise noted.

Serving the Servant:
Devotional Thoughts on the Book of Mark

Design by Nick Ng
Page layout by Kelley Moore

© 2009 by BJU Press
Greenville, South Carolina 29614
JourneyForth Books is a division of BJU Press

Printed in the United States of America
All rights reserved

ISBN 978-1-59166-917-3

15   14   13   12   11   10   9   8   7   6   5   4   3   2   1

*To my friend Dr. Robert M. Wood, who loves
the Word of God and who has paid his old
professor the ultimate compliment of learning
and practicing what he was taught*

CONTENTS

MARK 1   1

MARK 2   18

MARK 3   28

MARK 4   44

MARK 5   58

MARK 6   69

MARK 7   84

MARK 8   102

MARK 9   115

MARK 10   128

MARK 11   150

MARK 12   163

MARK 13   187

MARK 14   204

MARK 15   229

MARK 16   250

PREFACE

Serving the Servant is a journal of what I believe God has said to me through my daily reading of His Word. The idea of recording these thoughts was shared with me many years (about a half-century) ago by a man named Dale Simpson. I was reluctant to adopt this habit, for, as I told Dale, systematizing the blessings flowing from my addiction to the reading of the Word was just not my style. Dale challenged me to tell him what I had learned from the Scripture just a few days before, and I could not. He convinced me that it was an irresponsible waste of God's blessings not to preserve them for future enjoyment and edification and possible sharing with others.

Since we have been blessed (or cursed?) with computers and the Internet, sharing has become easier, though more time consuming. It has, nevertheless, been a great joy and blessing to share with others the things I believe God is saying to me through His wonderful Word. I am sharing with you through this book largely to convince some of you to follow my example. God loves all His children; He will speak to you just as He does to me. He knows your need just as He does mine. Please let me challenge you to begin recording what God says to you each day from His inerrant Word of Truth.

My own method of reading is to start at the beginning of a book of the Bible and read through. I resume reading each morning where I left off the previous morning. I look for a verse (or verses) whose meaning is clear to me and that applies to my own life and situation.

Sometimes I will stay with the same verse for several mornings; other times I may read many verses, looking carefully at each verse, before I come to the one that speaks to me. I recommend this approach since it helps us overcome our tendency to read the words and miss the meaning, as I have done so often in my school textbooks.

I should make clear that this is not a commentary on the book of Mark. On the other hand, it will naturally reflect my view of the book and its message in some ways. It will also reflect my interpretation and understanding of many individual passages of Scripture. Often, when I am reading a passage from the Bible, similar passages come to mind; I often cite these and sometimes quote them. In order to follow what I believe God has said to me, you may sometimes want to look up and read cited passages.

This little book is my personal thoughts, though it may speak to you even as it has to me. It may even say to you things that I have missed. God's Word is not mere raw material, which we may deconstruct and twist to suit our own convenience, but God knows each of us individually and can speak through His Word to each of us uniquely. Some of these observations have spoken to me in a general way, but many are very personal to me or my situation. I have included some of the latter, as there may be someone else to whom they may also speak and apply. My final warning would be that God's Word is not just a novel to be enjoyed or a theological treatise to be understood. My own experience says that the ultimate blessings come from reading the Word of God only as I then obey it exactly as it is written.

MARK 1

MARK 1:1–2A, 4

The beginning of the gospel of Jesus Christ, the Son of God; as it is written in the prophets . . . John did baptize in the wilderness, and preach the baptism of repentance for the remission of sins.

The message of the Gospel of Mark starts abruptly with the preaching of John the Baptist, but the message begins about the same as the Gospel message of Matthew (Matt. 3:1–2). The messianic genealogy and recognition in Matthew 1–2 are all introductory material for the message that now is the time and occasion for confession, repentance, and acceptance of the rulership of God over His chosen nation and in the individual lives of His chosen people.

Mark's message is clear: the problem is sin, and the solution is confession and repentance, expressed outwardly by baptism. While John's immediate audience was the Jewish nation and people, his good news is now universally available to all (Matt. 28:19), including you and me. The problems that bother me are caused by sin, and the solution is still honest confession and repentance.

MARK 1:4–5, 14–15

John did baptize in the wilderness, and preach the baptism of repentance for the remission of sins. And there went out unto him all the land of Judaea, and they of Jerusalem, and were all baptized of him in the river of Jordan, confessing their sins. . . . Now after that John was put in prison, Jesus came into Galilee, preaching the gospel of the kingdom of God, and saying, The time is fulfilled, and the kingdom of God is at hand: repent ye, and believe the gospel.

Like Matthew, Mark repeatedly describes the opportunity to allow God to rule one's life as "good news." Like Matthew, Mark also identifies the introduction to the good news closely with confession and repentance for sin.

This is a warning to me as a follower of Jesus for many years. Cultivating my relationship to Him into a rich fellowship with Him does not start with enjoying and indulging myself. What it calls for is acknowledging my unworthiness and accepting forgiveness as I change direction to obey Him (by the power of the Holy Spirit, v. 8).

I believe this also says something to me about sharing the good news with others. I need to avoid sugarcoating the gospel. Like John the Baptist, I need to be honest about the need to deal with the problem of personal sin through confession and repentance before experiencing God's forgiveness and enjoying God's fellowship.

MARK 1:4–5

John did baptize in the wilderness, and preach the baptism of repentance for the remission of sins. And there went out unto him all the land of Judaea, and they of Jerusalem, and were all baptized of him in the river of Jordan, confessing their sins.

Some years ago, I made a careful study, along with a good friend from the Restoration Movement, of the subject of baptismal regeneration. From our study of the Scripture, we concluded that baptism as a testimony to a believer's commitment was commanded of all Christians and that the command was to the church as well as to the individual. We also observed that the requirement of baptism before the indwelling of the Holy Spirit was restricted to Jewish believers only.

Apparently, baptism had become firmly fixed in Jewish thinking as a symbol of cleansing. For a person to submit voluntarily to the administration of baptism was to confess sinfulness and unclean-ness and a desire and intent to take a new direction for his life. For the ordinary Jewish citizen to accept baptism at the hands of John was to confess personal and national sin and prepare himself for participation in the kingdom (rulership) of the coming Messiah.

In the twenty-first century, this is a reminder that the only way to come into God's presence and present myself as an applicant for His rulership of my life is honest confession of my sinfulness and of my need for His power to change my direction so as to become what He created me to be, and to become an instrument of His grace in helping others to become reconciled to relationship and fellowship with Him. The only "I" who is eligible to come into His presence is the real "who I am," redeemed by the death of Christ for my sins.

MARK 1:8

I indeed have baptized you with water: but he shall baptize you with the Holy Ghost.

The Greek preposition *en* has a two-edged meaning in this verse. The prepositional phrases are translated "with water" and "with the Holy Spirit," but both are translations of the Greek preposition *en*. The primary meaning of *en*, of course, is not "with" but "in."

Here we have a beautiful confirmation of the clear biblical teach-ing concerning the practice of baptism by immersion "in" water. We also have a word picture of our special relationship to God the Holy Spirit. This relationship has been created and initiated for us by God the Son through His death for our sins. Jesus has died for our sins, and now stands before the Father as our intercessor so that God the Holy Spirit can come to live in us (John 14:17), but we also may now live our lives "in Him."

As I read, study, and obey the written word, inspired by the Holy Spirit, and as I allow Him to control my behavior, I am living "in Him." I am thus able to be used of the Holy Spirit of God to make the invisible God visible to my world.

MARK 1:10–11

And straightway coming up out of the water, he saw the heavens opened, and the Spirit like a dove descending upon him: and there came a voice from heaven, saying, Thou art my beloved Son, in whom I am well pleased.

John the Baptist was preaching "repentance for the remission of sins" (v. 4) and promising that Jesus would baptize human beings with (*en*) the Holy Spirit (v. 8). This becomes exciting and meaningful for me when I read the two words *beloved* (*agapetos*) and *well pleased* (*eudókesa*) in the verse above.

John was saying there is a repentance that is more than just regret, when we recognize that our "mistakes" are, in fact, sins against God. When thus recognized and confessed, they can be forgiven (remitted) by God Himself. We then are made eligible for the indwelling of God Himself in the power of the Spirit and the person of the Son (John 14:20). This makes it possible to surrender our self-will and allow the Holy Spirit to make us what God (Father, Son, and Holy Spirit) created us to be (Gen. 1:26: "Let us"). Then God the Father can see God the Son in our life by the power of God the Spirit and can say that we are "beloved" and He is "well pleased."

It would not be inappropriate to spend some time each day considering the fact that, because of the death of Jesus for my sins, I may confess my sinfulness, be forgiven, and become absorbed into the infinite love and harmony among the eternal Trinity. Awesome!

MARK 1:12–13

And immediately the Spirit driveth him into the wilderness. And
he was there in the wilderness forty days, tempted of Satan; and
was with the wild beasts; and the angels ministered unto him.

The "testing" (from *peirazomai*) of Jesus by Satan was arranged
by the Holy Spirit. Apparently the purpose of this testing was to
demonstrate Who Jesus was. This testing of Jesus proved that He
was (and is) God and absolutely could not be tempted to sin.

When God the Holy Spirit led God the Son into a time of testing, the results were a foregone conclusion. The sinless character
of Jesus was given the ultimate "stress test," as it was conducted
by Satan himself. In reality, of course, the character of Jesus was
actually "under stress" about as much as the Golden Gate Bridge
would be "under stress" with the passage of a child's tricycle over its
expanse.

The encouragement for me is this: Living in obedience to the
commands and principles of the Scriptures inspired by the Holy
Spirit, I must not be shocked to find myself sometimes placed under
great stress. To whatever extent that I will trust and be true and
obedient to His Word, this is not a test of me but of His truth,
His character, and His faithfulness. Of course, in whatever measure I depend on my own character or cleverness, I will fail the test.
In whatever measure I trust Him and His Word—to the extent
of simple obedience—there will be victory, blessing, and spiritual
growth.

MARK 1:14–15

Now after that John was put in prison, Jesus came into Galilee,
preaching the gospel of the kingdom of God, and saying, The time
is fulfilled, and the kingdom of God is at hand: repent ye, and
believe the gospel.

Now after John was put in prison, Jesus came to Galilee, preaching the gospel of the kingdom of God, and saying, "The time is

fulfilled, and the kingdom of God is at hand. Repent, and believe the gospel."

The introduction to the message of John the Baptist (Matt. 3:2, 8, 11; Mark 1:4; Luke 3:3, 8) includes the concept of repentance (*metanoeo* or *metanoia*), generally connected with the concept of rulership (*basileia* or *kurios*). The same is true for the introduction to Jesus' preaching as we see in these verses and in Matthew 4:17.

There is a reason these two concepts are connected at the very "beginning" (Mark 1:1) of the gospel message. God's truth for us as human beings begins with acknowledgment that we are headed in the wrong direction in life and need to make a 180-degree turn. Only with such an acknowledgment and turn may we experience the "kingdom of God." As an American, I have no personal experience with kings or kingdoms; I find it helpful—even necessary—to interpret *kingdom* as *rulership* and to make its application personal and individual. Acknowledging my sinful direction of life, which is self-will, opens for me the opportunity to accept the rulership of God's will. The good news is that by this surrender of control of my life I begin to move in the wonderful direction for which a loving God created me. Hallelujah!

MARK 1:16–17

> *Now as he walked by the sea of Galilee, he saw Simon and Andrew his brother casting a net into the sea: for they were fishers. And Jesus said unto them, Come ye after me, and I will make you to become fishers of men.*

As human beings created in God's image to be His stewards of the earth and its resources, these men were fully engaged in a legitimate activity as part of the earth's food chain. They were harvesting, "by the sweat of their face," a nutritious source of nourishment for human consumption. Jesus was calling them to the opportunity of a higher occupation. Instead of working with fish on behalf of the interests of human beings, they might now work with human beings on behalf of the interests of God Himself.

From this point on, they were no longer primarily interested in making their contribution to the purposes of God in the world by facilitating human physical life and health through providing physical food. They were to be enrolled in the learning and living experience of being instruments of God in facilitating human spiritual life and health through providing spiritual truth. This included their lives as evangelists, church planters, and teachers. One of the primary ways God used the apostles in "fishing for men" was in transmitting God's eternal truth to later generations through writing the New Testament.

If I make myself available to God for His will to be done in my life in this church age, He may or may not choose to use me in some legitimate occupation that contributes to the physical or mental welfare of the human race. On the other hand, He will most certainly employ me in His own way as part of His redemptive work and purposes for the spiritual benefit of the human race. I may become a "fisher of men." I suspect one of the best ways to be sure I do not miss my place in God's will and purposes is to read, believe, study, and obey the Scriptures written under His supervision by the first generation of fishers for men.

MARK 1:17–18

And Jesus said unto them, Come ye after me, and I will make you to become fishers of men. And straightway they forsook their nets, and followed him.

I suspect that before following Jesus in His peregrinations all over Galilee and much of Judea, the disciples went to their respective homes, packed a few things, and let their family and friends know what they were about to do.

The word translated *straightway* (*eutheos*) is used in Mark's short Gospel far more often than in the other Gospels. As I have looked at

Mark's use of the word, I have become convinced that his reference is less to time than to attitude. I do not think He meant for us to understand that they started moving without an intervening nano-second but that their decision and purpose were without hesitation. There were no second thoughts or inner debates. Immediately their settled purpose in life was to follow Jesus. Every subsequent decision and action were to be controlled by that purpose.

I suspect this is the thought behind James's insightful comments concerning the contrast between *patience* (stability or consistency) versus double-mindedness (James 1:4–8). I believe the Holy Spirit is using Mark to say to me, "If your controlling motivation in life is to be obedient to God, most of your everyday decisions are already made." I never again have to debate with myself about whether I will follow God's will or my own will; I have to be sure only that I know what God's will is and my decision is made. When Jesus says, "Follow Me," my automatic response should be to say, "Yes, Sir!"—and get moving.

MARK 1:21–22

And they went into Capernaum; and straightway on the sabbath day he entered into the synagogue, and taught. And they were astonished at his doctrine: for he taught them as one that had authority, and not as the scribes.

The Jewish people have always kept meticulous written records of their teaching, so we have a good idea just how the scribes of Jesus' day would have taught. The speaking or writing scribe would have felt obligated to quote an authority (who probably quoted earlier authorities) for any interpretation of Old Testament passages. Yet here was Jesus going directly to the Word of God itself (John 5:39) and apparently saying, "This is what it says, and this is what it means." The scribes would never have allowed an uneducated carpenter to do such a thing.

I am convinced that Jesus did not speak with "authority" as God the Son (which He was), but as a Jewish citizen. I believe Jesus "astonished" His hearers because He was saying, in effect, "God's Word was written for everybody; you have the right and responsibility to read it, interpret it, and obey its clear meaning for yourself."

I am responsible to approach God's Word with the settled intention of obeying it. If I do so, I have no need for the help of "experts" or "authorities" to find ways for me to hedge its meaning for my own convenience or indulgence.

MARK 1:21

And they went into Capernaum; and straightway on the sabbath day he entered into the synagogue, and taught.

This verse is a good illustration of the likelihood that *straightway* (*eutheos*) means "without hesitation" rather than "hurriedly." In this case, I think dynamically equivalent interpretations might even be "as usual," "automatically," or "of course." It was Jesus' custom, as a matter of principle, to attend Sabbath services in the synagogue. When the Sabbath morning arrived, He "immediately" got ready and went to the synagogue.

This is a good example for Christians. Sunday morning should see me in church unless I am providentially hindered. I doubt that Jesus ever attended a synagogue service where there were no hypocrites present. It is entirely likely that He listened many times to discussions and teaching that contained serious theological weaknesses—perhaps even heresy or some serious errors in Aramaic grammar. Nevertheless, when Sabbath came, Jesus was found, of course, going to synagogue services.

This is a good example for me (Heb. 10:25).

MARK 1:23–25A

And there was in their synagogue a man with an unclean spirit;
and he cried out, saying, Let us alone; what have we to do with
thee, thou Jesus of Nazareth? art thou come to destroy us? I know
thee who thou art, the Holy One of God. And Jesus rebuked
him.

There is much we don't know about "unclean" and "false" spirits
and demons. From this passage, however, we can see several things
clearly: (1) unclean spirits recognize the presence of Jesus; (2) they
don't like it; (3) their reaction to His presence is "Let us alone!"
(4) Jesus' response to their demand was not to acquiesce and let
them alone but to rebuke them.

If we are living and walking in obedience to Jesus, we will encounter those who resent His name, His presence, and His influence in
our lives and on our culture. Will my response be to acquiesce and
to be socially correct by avoiding offense? Or will I have the courage
to rebuke the evil of falsehood and uncleanness in relation to Jesus?

MARK 1:25–27

And Jesus rebuked him, saying, Hold thy peace, and come out of
him. And when the unclean spirit had torn him, and cried with a
loud voice, he came out of him. And they were all amazed, inso-
much that they questioned among themselves, saying, What thing
is this? what new doctrine is this? for with authority commandeth
he even the unclean spirits, and they do obey him.

The people in the synagogue perceived immediately that the
genuine spiritual power Jesus exercised was integrally related to His
doctrine. This is still true. Feelings and emotions that are gener-
ated and cultivated by artificial means of manipulation are often
unrelated to sound biblical teaching. The key to knowing whether
a person, a feeling, or an event is truly spiritual is a doctrinal test.
Real Christian spirituality is integrally and inseparably dependent
on genuine Christian theology.

Beloved, do not believe every spirit, but test the spirits, whether they are of God; because many false prophets have gone out into the world. By this you know the Spirit of God: Every spirit that confesses that Jesus Christ has come in the flesh is of God, and every spirit that does not confess that Jesus Christ has come in the flesh is not of God. And this is the spirit of the Antichrist. (1 John 4:1–3 NKJV)

MARK 1:30–31

But Simon's wife's mother lay sick of a fever, and anon they tell him of her. And he came and took her by the hand, and lifted her up; and immediately the fever left her, and she ministered unto them.

The literal meaning of the word here is that she was "burning with a fever." It seems that she was asleep or in some kind of stupor, as Jesus was said to have "aroused" her (from *egeiro*) before taking her hand. As He grasped her hand, the fever "immediately" ceased and she arose, refreshed, and with sufficient energy to serve them in some way.

When Jesus aroused her and grasped her hand, He was doing things easily understood and explained as purely natural phenomena. However, as Jesus' touch resulted in "immediate" cessation of fever, a miracle had clearly occurred in her body. Her "ministering unto them" straight out of a state of burning fever demonstrated the miraculous nature of her healing and was another miracle in itself.

God often works this way. In the midst of natural occurrences, a miracle may occur that cannot be legitimately explained in natural terms. I need to be found doing the things God would have me do in obedience to the commands and principles of Scripture and accomplishing thereby the things within my power to accomplish for Him. But I need also to be alert to the possibility He may choose to intervene miraculously and do things well beyond my natural abilities. These are opportunities to praise Him and give Him the glory.

MARK 1:33–35

And all the city was gathered together at the door. And he healed many that were sick of divers diseases, and cast out many devils; and suffered not the devils to speak, because they knew him. And in the morning, rising up a great while before day, he went out, and departed into a solitary place, and there prayed.

Jesus had been the focal point of very busy and draining activity during the previous afternoon and evening. After only a couple hours of rest, He roused Himself while the world slept to spend time alone in the peaceful and refreshing quiet of His Father's presence.

Good idea! Thank the Lord for the early morning hours. It isn't just the quiet or the isolation that refreshes the spirit. They do help, however, to appreciate and enjoy the one thing that always meets my every need, which is the reality of His loving presence.

MARK 1:37–38

And when they had found him, they said unto him, All men seek for thee. And he said unto them, Let us go into the next towns, that I may preach there also: for therefore came I forth.

Jesus had experienced a very busy Sabbath day, ministering and healing. After minimal sleep, He had aroused Himself to slip out and spend time alone with His Father. His privacy was interrupted by friends coming to inform Him that a popular and powerful healing ministry was waiting for Him back in town. In reply, Jesus said, "Let's go share the truth in other places."

I interpret Jesus' response to mean "I did not come just to heal many people in one place at a time, but to bring an important message everywhere I go." His message was, of course, "Repent of your sins, so you may be eligible to allow God to establish His kingdom (rulership) in your life" (Matt. 3:2; 4:17; Mark 1:15; 6:12; Luke 13:3, 5; Acts 17:30; 26:20). This exchange confirms the observation that His ministry of compassionate miracles was Jesus' presentation of

His credentials as Messiah so that people might hear and obey His message of repentance and obedience.

"From that time Jesus began to preach and to say, 'Repent, for the kingdom [rulership] of heaven is at hand'" (Matt. 4:17 NKJV).

This still applies to me today. God's supplying all my needs, His rich blessings on my life, the many answers to prayer—all these are the proofs of Who He is and how much He loves me. But their ultimate purpose is to give me confidence to trust Him to the point of confession of my sin and then of acceptance of His rulership by obedience to the commands of His Word.

MARK 1:40–41

And there came a leper to him, beseeching him, and kneeling down to him, and saying unto him, If thou wilt, thou canst make me clean. And Jesus, moved with compassion, put forth his hand, and touched him, and saith unto him, I will; be thou clean.

Jesus' miracles were an essential part of the presentation of His credentials as the Messiah. On the other hand, these healing miracles were not like official decrees handed down impersonally as demand for recognition. Jesus' response to the pitiful condition and the humble appeal of this man with leprosy was one of genuine, deep compassion. The Son of God did not step back and declare the man healed with a royal wave of the divine hand. Instead, Jesus instinctively reached out to touch the pitiful and "unclean" body of the deeply hurting human being kneeling before Him (Matt. 8:17; Heb. 4:15).

The leprous man had not felt a caring human touch since his symptoms had first been diagnosed. Had Jesus not actually healed the man, just that touch of genuine compassion alone would have met a deep inner need. If Jesus lives in me, my instinctive response to people in "unclean" conditions will be compassion for the human person. God's indwelling Holy Spirit does not blind me to the truth of God's Word concerning sin and its consequences, but He will affect my heart with the compassion of the Lord Jesus.

If I should find I do not feel compassion for human suffering, I have reason to question the reality of my walk with the Lord Jesus. I may need to cultivate a deeper fellowship with Him and His Spirit by reading, believing, and obeying His Word.

MARK 1:40–41

And there came a leper to him, beseeching him, and kneeling down to him, and saying unto him, If thou wilt, thou canst make me clean. And Jesus, moved with compassion, put forth his hand, and touched him, and saith unto him, I will; be thou clean.

The word translated *wilt* (*thelo*) means more than "OK, I will allow it." It carries the implication "It is what I want," even sometimes meaning "I am determined!"

It seems clear that one of the messages of this verse is that it is not God's automatic response to heal everyone who "asks in faith." I think there is, however, a deeper message. I see in this exchange the importance of bringing my petitions to God with the intention of bringing my desires into line with His desires rather than trying to get Him to bend to what I want. Of course I have natural desires, but they should not take priority over His will in my life. As I grow spiritually through my obedience to His Word, I am able to learn from actual experience what I can know "up front" through faith in His Word: in the long run, God's loving will for me is always better than my shortsighted desires.

"If you abide in Me, and My words abide in you, you will ask what you desire, and it shall be done for you" (John 15:7 NKJV).

When I recognize this truth, then I can pray, even as this leper did, "If it be Your will." I can know that, if it is not His will, it is not what I would really want. Experience teaches that God's will for me reflects His love for me, is guided by His infinite wisdom

and knowledge, is expressed in His inerrant Word, and it is exactly
what I want!

MARK 1:40–44

*And there came a leper to him, beseeching him, and kneeling
down to him, and saying unto him, If thou wilt, thou canst make
me clean. And Jesus, moved with compassion, put forth his hand,
and touched him, and saith unto him, I will; be thou clean. And
as soon as he had spoken, immediately the leprosy departed from
him, and he was cleansed. And he straitly charged him, and forthwith sent him away; and saith unto him, See thou say nothing to
any man: but go thy way, shew thyself to the priest, and offer for
thy cleansing those things which Moses commanded, for a testimony unto them.*

Moses had been led by God to designate the priests as official di-
agnostic physicians for determining the presence or absence of leprosy in any person (Lev. 13–14). Assumedly the man Jesus healed had
been declared leprous by those trained and designated to do so.

In demonstrating His messianic compassion and presenting His
messianic credentials through this miraculous healing, Jesus was
not interested in advertising His power to impress and attract large
crowds of people. He did, however, want to prove the reality of the
disease and the genuineness of the healing to avoid a charge that
either the disease or the healing was merely subjective and that no
"real" (i.e., physical) healing had occurred.

I believe this is always true. When God performs His work in
human lives, either physically or spiritually, it is real. It does not need
the crutch of an advertising campaign. When God does a work in or
through my life, its reality can stand the strictest scrutiny of any legitimate examination; it does not need the froth of self-serving publicity.

MARK 1:42–45

And as soon as he had spoken, immediately the leprosy departed from him, and he was cleansed. And he straitly charged him, and forthwith sent him away; and saith unto him, See thou say nothing to any man: but go thy way, shew thyself to the priest, and offer for thy cleansing those things which Moses commanded, for a testimony unto them. But he went out, and began to publish it much, and to blaze abroad the matter, insomuch that Jesus could no more openly enter into the city, but was without in desert places: and they came to him from every quarter.

When Jesus performed for the leper this wonderful and transforming miracle of healing, the leper's spontaneous response was to tell everyone about it. My first thought is that this is a wonderful example and the way I should react to God's blessing of salvation.

This leper had deliberately disobeyed Jesus' specific instructions to him. He apparently felt that his own passion to share was more relevant than the command of Jesus. The Holy Spirit points out to us that, in thus following the lead of his spontaneous enthusiasm instead of Jesus' instruction to obey the Word, the leper became a problem and a stumbling block to Jesus' further ministry.

Obedience to the Word of God pleases the Lord Jesus and facilitates His will for me and others more than trying to do things for God in my own ignorant (and disobedient) enthusiasm.

MARK 1:45

But he went out, and began to publish it much, and to blaze abroad the matter, insomuch that Jesus could no more openly enter into the city, but was without in desert places: and they came to him from every quarter.

Jesus was not seeking popularity as some of His followers assumed (vv. 36–37), nor did He want the advertising campaign the healed leper disobediently provided for Him (vv. 44–45). Nevertheless, even when consigned to "desert places," He was still Jesus; He still met people's needs. Though having to bypass locations where a healer would normally be found, and having to go to places that were inconvenient and unpopular, many needy people still sought out the real thing.

This is still true. Sometimes spiritually needy people must bypass the religious centers, activities, and movements based on popularity and advertising to find a genuine encounter with truth to meet their needs. The warning in this is that I should focus my life on having and sharing spiritual reality, not on offering a form of religion that may be more culturally popular and acceptable.

MARK 2

MARK 2:1–2

> *And again he entered into Capernaum after some days; and it was noised that he was in the house. And straightway many were gathered together, insomuch that there was no room to receive them, no, not so much as about the door: and he preached the word unto them.*

"And he preached the word [*logos*] unto them." There is no question that the compassionate healing ministry of Jesus was an important demonstration and credential of messianic identity. On the other hand, Jesus was not just a healer. He did not come to earth primarily to heal. Jesus came to earth to deliver a message.

My prayer time should not consist primarily of a list of my own needs—or even intercessory needs (vv. 3–5)—for Jesus to meet. My primary prayer activity should be my listening to His message from His Word.

MARK 2:3–5

> *And they come unto him, bringing one sick of the palsy, which was borne of four. And when they could not come nigh unto him for the press, they uncovered the roof where he was: and when they*

had broken it up, they let down the bed wherein the sick of the palsy lay. When Jesus saw their faith, he said unto the sick of the palsy, Son, thy sins be forgiven thee.

The paralytic clearly had a serious physical problem. He was aware of it. His four friends were aware of it. Jesus, of course, was also very aware of it. But when Jesus looked at the paralytic with eyes of compassionate discernment, He perceived that the paralysis was not his biggest problem. Jesus saw that there was a problem needing much more immediate attention and solution: the problem of the man's sin.

How are we any different? When I bring to Jesus a problem for which I need a solution that only He can supply, perhaps I should first acknowledge my sinfulness and confess my sins. When Jesus has freely forgiven my confessed sins (1 John 1:8–10), the way is cleared so that He may address whatever secondary problem I have brought to Him.

MARK 2:9–12

Whether is it easier to say to the sick of the palsy, Thy sins be forgiven thee; or to say, Arise, and take up thy bed, and walk? But that ye may know that the Son of man hath power on earth to forgive sins, (he saith to the sick of the palsy,) I say unto thee, Arise, and take up thy bed, and go thy way into thine house. And immediately he arose, took up the bed, and went forth before them all; insomuch that they were all amazed, and glorified God, saying, We never saw it on this fashion.

The "bed" on which the paralytic had made his unconventional entrance was really a stretcher. When Jesus spoke to him, he was healed. He had no more use for the stretcher. Why should he pick it up and carry it home?

He may have been told to retain possession of the stretcher as a reminder of where he had come from. Even though he could now walk about just as well as anyone else, he would always be a man who had once been paralyzed. The picture here, associated as it is with forgiveness of sins, may be of help to all of us. Having been forgiven of confessed sins, I am seen by God through the sacrifice of Jesus and accepted as totally forgiven. He no longer sees me as a sinner (Ps. 103:12). On the other hand, the fact is that I will never be a person who has never sinned. This plain fact should help me to be appropriately grateful and to continually praise God for the complete forgiveness that is mine through the death of Jesus in my place. Hallelujah!

MARK 2:15–16

> And it came to pass, that, as Jesus sat at meat in his house, many publicans and sinners sat also together with Jesus and his disciples: for there were many, and they followed him. And when the scribes and Pharisees saw him eat with publicans and sinners, they said unto his disciples, How is it that he eateth and drinketh with publicans and sinners?

Notice that the local religious leaders did not address their question to Jesus but to His followers. Can we detect here a criticism and an appeal to the disciples? Could the Pharisees be asking, "How can you loyal Jews follow this guy who does not conform to rules for living and worshiping God laid down by official religious leaders?"

Jesus was eating and associating with the tax collectors and sinners. Jesus did not collect taxes, and He did not sin. Jesus did not adopt their lifestyle to reach them, but He did eat with them and associate with them. The passage does not say that He sought them but that "they followed Him." Obviously, Jesus did not eat with them because they collected Roman taxes or because they sinned but because they were needy human beings made in God's image. Apparently, they were drawn to Jesus because He was willing to recognize and appreciate their God-created humanity while not muting the truth of their self-created sinfulness and their need for repentance.

If the Holy Spirit lives in me and I obey His Word, people may not like God's message in me but should recognize in me a respect and love for them that, at the very least, piques their interest.

MARK 2:16–17

And when the scribes and Pharisees saw him eat with publicans and sinners, they said unto his disciples, How is it that he eateth and drinketh with publicans and sinners? When Jesus heard it, he saith unto them, They that are whole have no need of the physician, but they that are sick: I came not to call the righteous, but sinners to repentance.

The Jewish people had a special hatred for fellow Jews who worked for the Roman "tax farmers." Tax farmers were private contractors who collected tribute from various non-Roman populations and usually hired local inhabitants to act as agents interfacing with the different ethnic groups. The Jewish people did not like paying taxes, but not just because of the money. They assumed that because they were the chosen people of God they were better than any other ethnic peoples and should not be paying tax to anyone. The Pharisees, having assumed the mantle of being religious examples and exercising religious discipline, especially rejected the Jewish tax collaborators as traitors against God.

The fact that Jesus, Who claimed to be the messenger of God, would associate with these tax-collecting traitors just did not compute with the Pharisees. In answering them, Jesus did not justify the tax collectors nor join them in their sin. He certainly did not adapt His message or lifestyle to make the tax collectors feel comfortable. What Jesus did was to make clear that sinners, which included tax collectors, who were willing to see themselves as sinners (Luke 18:13) were more eligible for the grace of God than religious people who thought they did not need the grace of God.

This should help me to keep my place in the "grace line" by remembering that is exactly where I belong. It might also help me to feel at home associating socially with other sinners while viably maintaining personal fellowship with God and living out the character and lifestyle of a child of God.

MARK 2:17

When Jesus heard it, he saith unto them, They that are whole have no need of the physician, but they that are sick: I came not to call the righteous, but sinners to repentance.

Jesus' primary call to mankind is not a call to noble sacrifice or effective service. Jesus is not recruiting strong soldiers and brilliant officers to fight His battles. Jesus' call is addressed only to self-acknowledged sinners, and it is a call to confess and repent.

This is certainly applicable in today's world and relevant for any individual living in our contemporary society. God's call is still a call to sinners to repent. God's call to me is still the call that first demands a self-examination on the basis of His Word (Ps. 119:9–11). Then it demands that I give up my own will and direction. Only then do I become available for His will to rule my life and to give me power to change my direction 180 degrees and move in His direction—the exact direction in which I was created to move.

MARK 2:17

When Jesus heard it, he saith unto them, They that are whole have no need of the physician, but they that are sick: I came not to call the righteous, but sinners to repentance.

When we are called by God, we are not righteous; we are not what God created us to be. We are in sin and must repent, totally reversing our direction and our lifestyle (2 Cor. 5:17) and beginning to live the sort of righteousness that has not previously characterized our life but has now been freely granted to us through the death of Jesus. This is the miracle of the tension and paradox of the Christian life: only the unrighteous are called, but they are called to become righteous!

I am to live the wonderful, self-disciplined, unselfish, and moral life for which God created me, but I must live it always in full view of the fact that I am not eligible or able to live this life except as I acknowledge that it is not natural to me and that I am unworthy of it.

MARK 2:19–20

And Jesus said unto them, Can the children of the bridechamber fast, while the bridegroom is with them? as long as they have the bridegroom with them, they cannot fast. But the days will come, when the bridegroom shall be taken away from them, and then shall they fast in those days.

Since Jesus is no longer here on earth, it is most appropriate for Christians to fast. We may fast to give attention to prayer and for various other reasons. These verses seem to indicate that one reason we fast is that He is no longer with us.

Whatever our reason for fasting on any given occasion, one element always present in our fasting should be the consciousness that He is not here. We fast to enrich our present fellowship with the absent Savior in anticipation of the day we shall be in His heavenly presence to feast on His love forever. Hallelujah!

MARK 2:21–22

No man also seweth a piece of new cloth on an old garment: else the new piece that filled it up taketh away from the old, and the rent is made worse. And no man putteth new wine into old bottles: else the new wine doth burst the bottles, and the wine is spilled, and the bottles will be marred: but new wine must be put into new bottles.

What Jesus was saying is complex, but it is not unclear. He was talking about the relationship between His ministry and message and God's truth received through the Old Testament. His questioners were trying to create a conflict between Jesus' message and that delivered through Moses and the holy prophets of the Old Testament (2 Pet. 1:20–21). In doing so, they identified their contemporary religious practices with God's eternal truth received from the writers of the Old Testament. The implication was that because Jesus did not conform to contemporary religious practices, He must be out of touch with God.

Jesus' reply indicated that His message was directly connected to God's eternal truth and was, in fact, the very development and fulfillment of that truth that they must recognize to be in harmony with God's work and purposes at that time and in the future.

The message for me is to keep in touch with God directly and not to depend for my spiritual reality on current and contemporary religious habits and practices dictated by any "official" religious leaders.

MARK 2:24, 27

And the Pharisees said unto him, Behold, why do they on the sabbath day that which is not lawful? . . . And he said unto them, The sabbath was made for man, and not man for the sabbath.

"The sabbath was made for man." God's law consists of "thou shalt" and "thou shalt not." When we keep God's law, it pleases God, but the law was not given for God's welfare; it was given for man's welfare. When God says, "thou shalt not," it is for our protection, and when He says, "thou shalt," it is for our fulfillment.

God's commandments, however, do not dictate every detail of life. While they are unambiguous, they are not exhaustive. They are of no use to a person who is not determined to apply his energy, focus, and God-given intelligence to living according to God's will. God's laws were given on the assumption that man wants to live to the fullest the life for which God created him.

Serious mental problems are experienced by some "religious" people who want to keep God placated but do not really mean to trust Him to the point of consistent obedience (James 1:8). Their problem is a guilty conscience. Such people welcome the services of "codifiers" such as the Pharisees. Codifiers are happy to supply detailed specifics concerning the meaning of God's law so that people might keep the rules without giving up self-will or self indulgence.

The first requirement for my living a truly fulfilled life is that I must decide definitively that I want to obey God because I trust His wisdom, His power, and His love for me. If this decision controls my attitude and actions, it drives me to read God's Word and to seek God's fellowship and presence so that I may know His will for me. It also frees my conscience so that I am no longer a guilt-ridden slave to the Pharisees' rules. When faced with decisions, I will always want to know what God's Word says and am not at all concerned about what the official religious leaders dictate. I do not need interpretations and excuses to help me get around God's Word because I will want to do what it says so that I may please Him.

MARK 2:25–27

> And he said unto them, Have ye never read what David did, when he had need, and was an hungred, he, and they that were with him? How he went into the house of God in the days of Abiathar the high priest, and did eat the shewbread, which is not lawful to eat but for the priests, and gave also to them which were with him? And he said unto them, The sabbath was made for man, and not man for the sabbath.

The Pharisees had appropriated the authority of the written Word of God to include their own self-serving interpretations of God's law (v. 24). They controlled people's behavior by laying on guilt trips when Jews did not follow the interpretations of the official religious leaders at all times. Jesus' disciples had eaten when hungry on the Sabbath, which was perfectly legal. The way they went about it, however, violated the Pharisees' interpretation of God's command against doing any business on the Sabbath. The Pharisees, then, were quick to upbraid Jesus for allowing His followers to break the Pharisees' standards for living the Jewish life.

Jesus' answer ignored their presumption and their sophistries and went directly to the heart of the matter. He used an illustration from God's Word demonstrating that an emergency need could take priority over a law given to cover everyday living. David's behavior in the illustrative incident actually violated a clearly written ceremonial law in order to preserve human life. Modern parallels include the violation of the speed limit laws by ambulances or the operation of hospitals on the Lord's Day.

This is strong support for obeying God's Word in all the normal circumstances by recognizing God's purpose in giving the law: human welfare and fulfillment living in God's world. Jesus recognized that purpose by allowing for genuine emergencies. This is not a license to ignore God's law for personal convenience or to accommodate any personal desires but is a warning not to get caught up in keeping the letter of the law in a way that ignores or excludes the purpose of God's laws.

MARK 2:27–28

And he said unto them, The sabbath was made for man, and not man for the sabbath: therefore the Son of man is Lord also of the sabbath.

The historical Jesus was (and is) God; He was (and is) also absolutely human in every way except sin (Heb. 4:15). This is part of the mystery of the eternal Trinity. Jesus described Himself in several ways, including "the Son of man." I do not believe He used this title randomly as a mere synonym for His name or for the first person singular. It was His way of helping us distinguish between His roles as man and as God.

Jesus did not authorize His disciples to pluck the grain on the Sabbath in His role as God as if He were above the law because of His deity. After all, the Old Testament law is God's law; when God became man, He kept His own laws for man. Jesus had pointed out that the disciples were not really breaking God's law but only violating the religious leaders' misinterpretation of the law. What they were doing, they had a right to do as Jews and as human beings, and Jesus allowing them to do it was acceptable and legitimate human behavior within God's law.

I have found a tendency (and a temptation) on the part of those of us serving the Lord to excuse ourselves from careful keeping of God's commands on the basis that God's work takes priority, so it is OK for God's servant to ignore the rules. I should remember that all things are under God's control, and an important part of my testimony as God's representative is punctilious keeping of God's commandments. If this was true for Jesus as God the Son, it is most certainly true for me.

If Jesus were alive today, would He break the speed limit laws—and would He encourage His followers to do so (Rom. 13:1)? And if I should do so, may I claim authority as a "spiritual leader"?

MARK 3

MARK 3:1–2, 5

> And he entered again into the synagogue; and there was a man there which had a withered hand. And they watched him, whether he would heal him on the sabbath day; that they might accuse him. . . . And when he had looked round about on them with anger, being grieved for the hardness of their hearts, he saith unto the man, Stretch forth thine hand. And he stretched it out: and his hand was restored whole as the other.

"That they might accuse Him." We live in a day when many people watch Christian behavior and listen to Christian messages for the sole purpose of finding some way to criticize them and some excuse to ignore them. I must decide whether I will be careful and politically correct in what I say and how I say it or whether I will live and speak God's truth without compromise.

I am quite sure when Jesus entered the synagogue He knew that He was being watched for this very purpose (v. 5). What was His response? While Jesus was aware of their "hardness [*porosei*] of heart" and it grieved Him, He executed without hesitation the ministry for which He had come. Jesus knew He would be criticized by the official religious leaders and, while He was saddened by their callousness and profound spiritual insensitivity, He went right ahead with His ministry.

Good example! I believe I should follow it.

MARK 3:1–2

And he entered again into the synagogue; and there was a man there which had a withered hand. And they watched him, whether he would heal him on the sabbath day; that they might accuse him.

The opponents of Jesus, most of them religious leaders (v. 6), assumedly had the full use of both arms and both hands. It appears their hearts were not at all moved in sympathy for this man who had to go through life with the use of only one hand. The entire physical world in which he lived and functioned was organized on the assumption that everyone had two working hands; he continually had to adjust, adapt, or be left out. The religious critics of Jesus didn't care! There is no evidence they had made any attempt to help the man with the withered hand deal with his need. Apparently, in fact, they were glad there was someone with a problem in the synagogue service that day so they would have an excuse to criticize Jesus.

I need to beware that I do not join the Pharisees. When I see someone doing something that seems to be helping people, but not doing it "the right way," what is my response? Do I sympathize with those in need and appreciate the efforts of those trying to meet the need, or do I mostly apply my superior knowledge to analyze their mistakes and to criticize them to others. This is important in a world where lots of sincere but ignorant or immature people are doing lots of really dumb things.

In God's work I think there is a principle involved here. If God allows me, as His follower, to see other Christians doing wrong things, or doing things in wrong ways or from some wrong motives, I think He is commissioning me to pray for them. My observations about their wrong actions, methods, or motives should be shared with God first, possibly directly with those persons who are responsible for the mistakes, but never with anyone else (Matt. 18:15–17). I appreciated the response of a parachurch organization for whom I did some work many years ago when their methods were criticized by others. Their response was "Our methods may be imperfect, and we are willing to learn and improve, but in the meantime, we like the way we are doing it imperfectly a lot better than the way our critics are not doing it at all."

MARK 3:1–3, 5B

And he entered again into the synagogue; and there was a man there which had a withered hand. And they watched him, whether he would heal him on the sabbath day; that they might accuse him. And he saith unto the man which had the withered hand, Stand forth. . . . He saith unto the man, Stretch forth thine hand. And he stretched it out: and his hand was restored whole as the other.

This man entered the synagogue with a debilitating and disfiguring problem. He left without the problem, completely restored. I feel sure He knew that the religious leaders were watching Jesus and that Jesus would be criticized, ostracized, and persecuted if He offended official religious leadership by healing on the Sabbath. The man with a withered hand realized also that he himself could be ostracized and excommunicated if he identified himself with the Lord Jesus in any way.

Jesus did not make it easy for the man with the problem. First, He required that he step out from the crowd. Then He told him to hold out his disfiguring problem for everyone to see. The man's problem was solved only after he publicly and completely identified himself with Jesus by obedience to His words in the presence of the religious leaders and of the whole congregation.

Good example! I should make it my practice to obey the Word of God completely and unashamedly. Even though it may offend official religious leadership. This may be the way of healing for my problems and of restoring me to the joy of being all I was created to be.

MARK 3:4–5

And he saith unto them, Is it lawful to do good on the sabbath days, or to do evil? to save life, or to kill? But they held their peace. And when he had looked round about on them with anger, being grieved for the hardness of their hearts, he saith unto the man, Stretch forth thine hand. And he stretched it out: and his hand was restored whole as the other.

Verse 5a should, I believe, be translated, "He surveyed all of them [*periblepsamenos*] with great emotional intensity [*orges*], being overwhelmed with sadness for them [*sullupumenos*] upon seeing the callousness [*porosei*] of their hearts."

I suspect one of the things that saddens God most profoundly is our response when He wants to share with us the deep sense of hurt He feels in the face of human needs. When we callously and self-centeredly resist sharing His burden, He is deeply (*orges*) grieved for us (*sullupumenos*). We resist allowing our emotions to be in tune with His because we are unwilling for His hurt to affect our deep inner feelings. Instead, we trivialize our real emotions by attaching our superficial "passion" to our own programs and ambitions. Little wonder that He is saddened for us.

Perhaps I need to make my heart as well as my hands available to the influence of the word of God and the Spirit of God so that His power on behalf of human needs may replace my effort to influence people for my own programs.

MARK 3:5–6

And when he had looked round about on them with anger, being grieved for the hardness of their hearts, he saith unto the man, Stretch forth thine hand. And he stretched it out: and his hand was restored whole as the other. And the Pharisees went forth,

*and straightway took counsel with the Herodians against him,
how they might destroy him.*

"How they might destroy Him." Jesus had done absolutely nothing to the Pharisees or Herodians. Their bitter opposition to Him had to do entirely with how He was relating to other people. He healed them. They came to Him to have their problems solved, and they remained to listen as He taught them the truth of God.

But in the minds of the Pharisees and the Herodians, Jesus was threatening them. Their very existence and identification as Pharisees and Herodians was dependent on influence over the lives of others. In their mind, Jesus was building an "empire" of influence through meeting people's needs, physically and spiritually. This was a great threat to the empires of influence of the Herodians and Pharisees, which were built on telling people how to live their lives, politically and spiritually.

If God the Holy Spirit truly ministers through me, God expects me not to be surprised or upset when attacked by people who are threatened. They are not my problem, and I may endure their criticisms, opposition, and even persecution with calm equanimity as long as my conscience is clear about my being in God's will.

MARK 3:6

*And the Pharisees went forth, and straightway took counsel with
the Herodians against him, how they might destroy him.*

"How they might destroy Him." The truth Jesus taught had tremendous power to attract and influence people. The Herodians and Pharisees found this threatening. Their interest was not in the truth He taught but in the power He exercised.

The written Word delivered by Moses and other Old Testament writers had an amazing power to attract and influence people because it was (and is) God's eternal truth. This power of God's truth was the basis for authority exercised by the Pharisees, who were the responsible stewards of God's Word. Any legitimate power exercised by the Herodian party was based on the simple truth that unregenerate man needs an orderly system of government control. Order and control among men require the granting of adequate power to those responsible for such order.

The unfortunate fact is (1) truth possesses power to attract and influence people, but (2) where there is power, it also attracts people who are far more interested in exercising power than speaking truth, with the result that (3) teaching God's truth often offends and threatens those who have usurped legitimate power to advance their own self-serving agendas.

Jesus did not let this inhibit Him in speaking the truth of God. Neither should I.

MARK 3:6

And the Pharisees went forth, and straightway took counsel with the Herodians against him, how they might destroy him.

Herodians represented a civil government the Pharisees resented as illegitimate. The Pharisees represented a religious system the Herodians considered fanatical, irrational, and rebellious. By merely teaching the truth of God, Jesus threatened entrenched authority in both realms.

Organized Christianity has always had problems harmonizing the necessary authority of a civil government (Rom. 13:1) with the absolute authority of God. Caesaropapism in Eastern churches and the "Two Swords" theory of the state church in Western thinking were attempts to deal with this tension. The "wall of separation" dogma of our own day is a perversion of the concept of a "voluntary church," introduced into American life through the influence of early Baptists such as John Leland of New England and Virginia.

The truth is that God is still God Almighty. The civil state should function according to God's laws for the state just as much as the individual human being should function according to God's plan for man and the church should function according to God's New Testament pattern for His church. This is no less true when it is unpopular with contemporary Herodians and Pharisees. I am authorized by God to speak and teach this biblical truth even though it does not harmonize with the popular modern concept of the democratic secular state and is offensive to the claims of some hierarchical churches and officials. I should never be surprised to see natural enemies join hands to resist the truth of God; it has ever been so.

MARK 3:7–10

> But Jesus withdrew himself with his disciples to the sea: and a great multitude from Galilee followed him, and from Judaea, and from Jerusalem, and from Idumaea, and from beyond Jordan; and they about Tyre and Sidon, a great multitude, when they had heard what great things he did, came unto him. And he spake to his disciples, that a small ship should wait on him because of the multitude, lest they should throng him. For he had healed many; insomuch that they pressed upon him for to touch him, as many as had plagues.

"Who Jesus was" to the people of His local area of Galilee spread in all directions so that "Who Jesus was" as a healer of many sorts of diseases and as a teacher of intriguing truth about God became known in many other places. "Who He was" was becoming firmly established everywhere. But this had to do only with what people knew and thought of Him. Reputation is not the whole of reality. Sometimes it has little relation to reality. Likewise, popularity often is unrelated to truth.

Jesus had a boat prepared as a possible escape from the unreal and incomplete world of popular ministry. All that He was to the people of Galilee and many surrounding areas was superficial. It had to be rooted in the real truth of "Who He was" as God. Jesus regularly left the artificial world of relationships (to people) in order to relax in "Who He really was" in relation to God the Father.

As His follower, I can learn from this to ignore the shallow emphasis of this age on relationships—and on popularity and success.

I must remember that relationships are never a part of the definition of who I really am. Who I am in relationships and in ministry may be a pale and fairly reliable reflection of who I really am in relation to God, but it is never the real thing. The only legitimate "significant other" for me as a Christian is God Himself.

MARK 3:7

But Jesus withdrew himself with his disciples to the sea: and a great multitude from Galilee followed him, and from Judaea.

As I read the Gospels, I am repeatedly struck with how often Jesus walked away from the opportunity to minister to large crowds to commune with His Father or to communicate with His close disciples. People sought Him and He ministered to their needs, but He rarely sought the crowds in order to minister to them. He never advertised nor did He ever offer popular entertainment to draw people to Himself.

This may speak to the way God directed the organization of ministry in the church in Acts 6. It seems clear that there were specific persons designated and equipped to minister directly to the needs of people, while those responsible for leadership in sharing God's truth were expected to spend their time and give the primary focus of their life "continually to prayer and to the ministry of the word" (Acts 6:4).

This also says something to me about my own priorities.

MARK 3:11–12

And unclean spirits, when they saw him, fell down before him, and cried, saying, Thou art the Son of God. And he straitly charged them that they should not make him known.

Apparently the assignment God the Son had given Himself in coming to earth included a thorough and scriptural presentation of His undeniable credentials as Messiah. The Gospels, especially

Mark, seem to indicate He planned to complete this while remaining under the radar screen of the Jewish religious leaders' opposition until God's time for His Passover sacrifice of Himself for our sins.

It is axiomatic that Satan would oppose, as best he could, any of God's plans and purposes. When unclean spirits cried out that Jesus was God Himself, Jesus exercised His divine authority by ordering them not to reveal Who He was. I think this says that God, in His wisdom, does not always carry out His will by making a big splash in the eyes of man.

I think this can be a warning to know and obey God's Word to remain in God's will and be usable in carrying out God's purposes. I do not want to be an obstruction to God's work and an instrument of Satan's purposes by pushing my own ministry agenda or schedule.

MARK 3:11–12

> And unclean spirits, when they saw him, fell down before him, and cried, saying, Thou art the Son of God. And he straitly charged them that they should not make him known.

Is it possible that the cry of the unclean spirits was one of amazement and surprise? Could they have meant, "You are God Almighty; what are You doing here? You are supposed to be in heaven, basking in the glorious majesty of deity and holiness; so what are You doing slumming down here among these sorry and sinful human beings? We consider this to be our territory."

This highlights the stark contrast between the total hatred and lack of respect Satan has for all human beings and the self-sacrificing love and pity God has for sinful humanity. It is to the great amazement of Satan, his unclean spirits, and all those whose minds he influences that Jesus, God the Son, actually became a man and died for the sins of the human race. This simple fact, nevertheless, is the kernel of Christian truth and is the key to reality for every individual human being. When first recognized, this fact seems awesome and strange, yet it somehow makes everything in life fall into place and make sense. Hallelujah!

MARK 3:13–14

And he goeth up into a mountain, and calleth unto him whom he would: and they came unto him. And he ordained twelve, that they should be with him, and that he might send them forth to preach.

The order of Christ's purposes for His apostles in verse 14 is consistent with the meaning of the reflexive voice of His call and their response described in verse 13.

First, Jesus called them to Himself. His first call was not to preach, to serve, to go or to witness but to Himself.

Second, they came to Him (*pros auton*); they did immediately not go forth; they went to Jesus first.

Note then, His very first purpose for calling the apostles (*apostolous* = "sent forth") was not to send them forth, but "that they should be with Him."

Only after being with Him were they ready to be sent to preach.

I will never know God's will for what I should do in His world until I am surrendered to His will for who I should be in His presence (Rom. 12:1–2).

MARK 3:13

And he goeth up into a mountain, and calleth unto him whom he would: and they came unto him.

The words *unto him* in the KJV and *Him* in the NKJV are in italics to indicate that the word *him* (in the objective or dative) is not in the original text. I appreciate the careful accuracy of these two translations in contrast to most modern idiomatic "translations" that twist Scripture to fit an interpretation. However, in this case the meaning "unto Himself" is clearly found in the use of the middle voice (*proskaleitai*) of the verb meaning "to call forth" (*proskaleo*).

The personal meaning of the use of this verb in this voice in this context is critical to an understanding of my relationship to the purposes of God: God's primary call to me is not to service but to Him. There is no such thing as a call to ministry until I have established a relationship with Him and cultivated that relationship into such a vital fellowship with Him that I am surrendered to His will in everything I do (Rom. 12:1) and think (Rom. 12:2).

I must know Him intimately before I can know myself genuinely. Only then can I have any idea how He calls me, and equips me, to serve Him. I will never know what God wants me to do until I have answered His call to know who He wants me to be in relation to Himself.

MARK 3:14, 19B–21

> *And he ordained twelve, that they should be with him, and that he might send them forth to preach . . . and they went into an house. And the multitude cometh together again, so that they could not so much as eat bread. And when his friends heard of it, they went out to lay hold on him: for they said, He is beside himself.*

Those close to Jesus felt sure they understood Him and were sure they knew what was best for Him. They had cast themselves in the role of stewards of His affairs. They felt it necessary to intervene and to protect Him from His own foolish mistakes and delusions as He carried out the will of His Father ministering to people.

When these sorts of things happen to me, I assume I may ignore the friendly advice of my own people. When given questionable helpful advice by those who have appointed themselves to manage my affairs, I should first check myself to make absolutely sure I am following the will of God as it has been revealed in the Word of God. But having done this, I may then ignore other voices and go about my business in obedience to God's Word and in harmony with God's will.

MARK 3:21, 31, 35; 3:22–25

> *And when his friends heard of it, they went out to lay hold on him: for they said, He is beside himself. . . . There came then his brethren and his mother, and, standing without, sent unto him, calling him. . . . For whosoever shall do the will of God, the same is my brother, and my sister, and mother. . . . And the scribes which came down from Jerusalem said, He hath Beelzebub, and by the prince of the devils casteth he out devils. And he called them unto him, and said unto them in parables, How can Satan cast out Satan? And if a kingdom be divided against itself, that kingdom cannot stand. And if a house be divided against itself, that house cannot stand.*

Jesus' response to the scribes is sandwiched into the middle of His response to His genetic family. I do not believe this intertwined juxtaposition is accidental. The Holy Spirit has arranged it for some reason. I see here the greater strength and deeper reality of the household of faith built on trusting obedience to the kingdom (*basileia* = "rulership") of God as compared to the household of genetic relationships.

There is an interesting implication many modern psychologists seem to have missed. Jesus appears to imply that a household built on genetic and emotional relationships, but lacking a defining structure of authority, is open to attack and potentially subject to defeat and dissolution. The "kingdom" of the home must prepare itself to resist the "strong man" of sinful human nature—reinforced by the surrounding heathen culture—by channeling God's authority into the structure of the family.

The lesson is that becoming an effective part of God's spiritual family only started with rebirth at the time of my salvation. To be a part of a family that stands under all circumstances of life, I must be also part of a "kingdom." I must obey the Word of the head of the family.

MARK 3:22–23, 27

And the scribes which came down from Jerusalem said, He hath Beelzebub, and by the prince of the devils casteth he out devils. And he called them unto him, and said unto them in parables, How can Satan cast out Satan? . . . No man can enter into a strong man's house, and spoil his goods, except he will first bind the strong man; and then he will spoil his house.

The word *demons* (NKJV) appears to be used in the New Testament synonymously with "unclean spirits" and "false spirits." They are identified as agents of the Devil (accuser), who is Satan (adversary). The clearest identifying indicator of these demon spirits is found in 1 John 4:1–3. There they are called by the term "false spirits," meaning they teach falsehood and oppose truth. The particular falsehood with which they are associated is denial of the basic theological truth of Christianity: the identification of the historical Jesus as God Himself in human flesh.

Mark 3:27 was one of three parables (v. 23) Jesus used to illustrate the falsehood of the scribes' charge against Him (v. 22). Here Jesus said unclean spirits must be defeated (*diaparsai* = "plundered") by a superior power. This means unclean spirits can be defeated by a cleansing spirit, false spirits by the power of truth, and the adversarial accuser by the power of God Himself.

The beauty of these truths, here illustrated by Jesus in parables, is most clearly stated by John in 1 John 4:4: "Ye are of God, little children, and have overcome them, because greater is he that is in you, than he that is in the world." Hallelujah!

MARK 3:22

And the scribes which came down from Jerusalem said, He hath Beelzebub, and by the prince of the devils casteth he out devils.

"The scribes which came down from Jerusalem." These representatives of the institutional religious establishment found Jesus meeting people's needs and teaching them the truth about God. But

He was doing so without having applied for permission and authorization through proper institutional channels. As the representatives of the religious authority responsible for the truth of God, their position was "Anyone teaching about God without our permission is against God." In other words, "Anyone presuming to teach about God without our institutional OK is an enemy of God."

As responsible spiritual leaders, they had twisted the truth 180 degrees. They thought that whatever they taught as true was to be accepted as the word from God. They did not recognize their awesome responsibility to make sure anything they taught lined up with the eternal and unchanging written Word of God.

The scribes thought that spiritual truth was resident in religious institutions and therefore was dispensed by them to individuals. They did not grasp the fact that God created man in His own image and desires fellowship with individual human beings. God has communicated spiritual truth about an eternal and unchanging God through His unchanging written revelation addressed to individuals. Jesus was teaching the people of God straight out of God's Word in the Old Testament without the need for institutional sponsorship. God has indeed ordained religious institutions, but their purpose is to serve individual followers of God, not vice versa.

MARK 3:28–30

Verily I say unto you, All sins shall be forgiven unto the sons of men, and blasphemies wheresoever they shall blaspheme: but he that shall blaspheme against the Holy Ghost hath never forgiveness, but is in danger of eternal damnation: because they said, He hath an unclean spirit.

The occasion for Jesus' statement concerning the "unforgivable sin" was the accusation that the message and ministry of Jesus were motivated and empowered by evil. The definition Jesus gave to the "unforgivable sin" seems to be that it is the rejection of the ministry and message of God's Holy Spirit.

The essence of the message of God to man—the gospel—starts with confession of sin and repentance (Luke 24:47) in preparation for accepting God's rulership. This is true of the message of John the Baptist (Matt. 3:2; Mark 1:4, 15; 2:7; Luke 3:3, 8; Acts 13:24; 19:4), of Jesus (Matt. 4:17; 9:13; 11:20; Luke 5:32; 13:3), of the apostles (Mark 6:12), of Peter (Acts 2:38; 3:19; 5:31; 11:16–18; 2 Pet. 3:9), of Paul (Acts 17:30; 19:4; 20:21; 26:20), and, of course, of John the apostle (1 John 1:8–10).

The ministry of God the Holy Spirit to the world in this age is very specifically described by the Lord Jesus in John 16:8–10. He is here to convict of sin, of the need for accepting God's standards of right and wrong, and of the inevitability and importance of coming judgment. It is the rejection of this message—the gospel—that is final and will not be forgiven. In a very real sense, it is denying the need for forgiveness for which there is no forgiveness.

It is important that I read, study, and believe the Holy Spirit's book so I will not be caught up in the thinking of my age (Rom. 12:2) and call evil good and good evil, thus rejecting the truth and importance of the Holy Spirit's message for me and for those around me.

MARK 3:33–35

> And he answered them, saying, Who is my mother, or my brethren? And he looked round about on them which sat about him, and said, Behold my mother and my brethren! For whosoever shall do the will of God, the same is my brother, and my sister, and mother.

"How to know the will of God" is a topic that can always provoke an interesting discussion. Claims that "God led me to . . ." or "I felt it was God's will that . . ." will often elicit the very critical question "How can I know God's will?"

In these verses, Jesus indicates that my doing His will is a matter of great importance as it makes me in some special way a member of His intimate family. This passage puts the finger directly on a key element in knowing God's will. In defining His "family," Jesus pointed to those who were seated about Him and listening to His words. This means the very first step in knowing the will of God is to listen to Him; this means reading His Word. And if I really want to know His will for me, I will study His words very carefully and try to obey His Word exactly. Knowledge of the will of God in specific details of my life is built on having an intimate family relationship that comes only to those who "sit about Him," absorbing His words in order to do His will.

Family relationship does not guarantee mind reading. Nevertheless, real intimate family relations built on long habits of knowing and doing what pleases one another often lead to the automatic understanding of what to do in new and unanticipated situations. In this same way, being absorbed in reading, studying, and obeying God's Word on a regular basis will never leave me puzzled about God's will in any situation that arises.

MARK 4

MARK 4:1–2A, 35–36A

And he began again to teach by the sea side: and there was gathered unto him a great multitude, so that he entered into a ship, and sat in the sea; and the whole multitude was by the sea on the land. And he taught them many things by parables. . . . And the same day, when the even was come, he saith unto them, Let us pass over unto the other side. And when they had sent away the multitude, they took him even as he was in the ship.

In these verses, we see Jesus once again abandoning the opportunity for increased popularity and for a widening ministry among people who sought Him and admired Him. Jesus had no animus toward the crowds beside the sea. There was no hatred or choosing sides involved in His move. He simply moved His venue of ministry according to His own perfect plans and purposes.

Jesus knew He had other places to be (5:1), other needs to meet (5:2), specific other ministries to perform (5:8), and other lessons to teach (4:33–34) and demonstrate (4:38–41) to His close disciples. He was already sitting in the boat beside the sea, teaching those on the shore, so He simply commanded His disciples to launch the boat out into the open sea.

There are things God's Word commands me to do that no doubt fit exactly into His perfect plans and purposes but that I do not always understand, sometimes do not agree with, and occasionally do not want to do. Wisdom on my part would dictate that I obey God's perfect commands and trust Him to meet my own needs while He carries out His plans and purposes through me in His own time and in His own way.

MARK 4:2–3, 13–14

And he taught them many things by parables, and said unto them in his doctrine, Hearken; Behold, there went out a sower to sow. . . . And he said unto them, Know ye not this parable? and how then will ye know all parables? The sower soweth the word.

"How then will you [understand] all parables?" The parable of the sower sowing "the word" (*ton logon*) was Jesus' explanation of why He taught in parables.

What Jesus taught was God's truth. To help people understand God's truth, Jesus employed illustrations from real life with which His hearers were familiar. The truths Jesus taught and all the illustrations He used were effective in communicating with people genuinely interested in knowing God's truth for real life. At the same time, they remained a mystery to religious bureaucrats and others whose life priority was not on God and whose frame of reference was not real life. It is probably significant that Jesus' illustrations came from the worlds of natural phenomena and daily tasks. All His literary references were from the Word of God in the Old Testament, and none of His proof texts came from traditional or contemporary commentarial authorities. The parable of the sower as explanation for the use of parables is a perfect illustration.

The "sower" broadcasts the same quality of truth to every listener. The results of the sowing—in real life—varied widely. This variation was not caused by any difference in the straightforward method of distributing the word (*logon*) but was in the attitude of the hearers! I should keep my priorities on God's truth and His world of reality if I am to live the life in the real world for which He lovingly created and redeemed me.

MARK 4:3–4, 14–15

Hearken; Behold, there went out a sower to sow: and it came to pass, as he sowed, some fell by the way side, and the fowls of the air came and devoured it up. . . . The sower soweth the word. And these are they by the way side, where the word is sown; but when they have heard, Satan cometh immediately, and taketh away the word that was sown in their hearts.

"By the way side" literally means "along the path" or even "in the middle of the road." This seed did not fall on ground prepared for cultivation but on soil compressed and perhaps gullied by traffic. Jesus explained to His disciples that this represented persons not prepared to listen and learn the truth. Their hearts and minds were hardened and misshapen by the constant pounding of false ideas and were resistant to considering the real possibility of any spiritual change or growth.

Satan easily snatched away any consideration of real truth because the persons represented by the wayside never accepted responsibility for internalization and spiritual growth. They knew that new and different facts had been presented to them, and they were willing to profess interest or even acceptance but were unwilling to change their worldly lifestyle to fit God's truth.

As I read God's Word, I must accept it as God's truth and be willing for it to change the way I think, the way I live, and the way I worship. If my life is a "wayside," then my tastes, habits, and lifestyle are not radically changed by the gospel. This may mean that the seed of real truth has been snatched away. I may need to do some radical plowing to prepare the soil of my worldly lifestyle for openness to change so that a new lifestyle conformed to the Word may grow in my life.

MARK 4:5, 16–17

And some fell on stony ground, where it had not much earth; and immediately it sprang up, because it had no depth of earth. . . . And these are they likewise which are sown on stony ground; who, when they have heard the word, immediately receive it with glad-ness; and have no root in themselves, and so endure but for a time: afterward, when affliction or persecution ariseth for the word's sake, immediately they are offended.

"Stony ground" does not mean that the soil was full of rocks. It refers to a shallow layer of arable topsoil lying over a shelf of rock or hardpan. It is in the nature of a little seed to develop adequate roots downward before sending a shoot upward through the surface of the ground. When, however, this downward root development is arrested by the hardpan or stone sill, the plant shoots upward prematurely and without an adequate root support and nourishment system. Judging by appearance, this crop seems to be earlier and healthier than that planted in deeper and richer soil. As time goes on, though, and the plants receive the warming heat of the sun from above, but inadequate moisture and nourishment from below, they wither and die.

Jesus compared this to the person who appears to embrace the Christian message with enthusiasm on account of some of its pleasant and enjoyable aspects but is shallow of character and unwilling to make permanent and enduring commitments. Such a person often appears outwardly to be a precociously maturing Christian, making great strides in spiritual growth and church activities. When it appears, however, that true Christianity will demand a high level of commitment, obedience, and lifestyle change, such a person either drifts away or becomes offended and quits in a huff.

There is a lesson here for me. I know by faith that God's Word is true and that He loves me. I read and obey His Word, not because I always like everything it says to me but because it is always true. God's Word often requires of me a level of commitment to obedience that demands faith in the character of God and in His willingness to plant in me His faithful character even as He has created me in His image.

MARK 4:7, 18–19

And some fell among thorns, and the thorns grew up, and choked it, and it yielded no fruit. . . . And these are they which are sown among thorns; such as hear the word, and the cares of this world, and the deceitfulness of riches, and the lusts of other things entering in, choke the word, and it becometh unfruitful.

This is about weed seeds. It is another vivid illustration from familiar things in real life. One of the most important activities in gardening or farming is weeding.

Jesus' word picture illustrates the fact that our relationship to God has to compete with other interests, and our obedience to His Word has to compete with other desires and values. One of the purposes of the many "thou shalt nots" found in the Bible is to guide us in weeding our lives.

Solving the weed problem involves (1) cultivating, watering, and feeding the good plants, and (2) killing the weeds. If I cultivate my relationship with God by my consistent fellowship with Him through His Word, it is easier to keep my priorities straight and the weeds under control through obedience to His "thou shalt nots."

MARK 4:8, 20

And other fell on good ground, and did yield fruit that sprang up and increased; and brought forth, some thirty, and some sixty, and some an hundred. . . . And these are they which are sown on good ground; such as hear the word, and receive it, and bring forth fruit, some thirtyfold, some sixty, and some an hundred.

"Sprang up, increased, and produced" (NKJV). In the Greek, the word *increased* (*auxanonta*) is preceded by *and*, replaced in the NKJV by a comma. The "and" (*kai*) is used here in an augmentative sense, especially as *auxanonta* is followed by three successively increasing numbers, each separately introduced by *en*. There is an implication here that plants in certain "good" soils supported a second and third harvesting.

This certainly speaks to me as an older Christian called to several different ministries over the course of the years. These verses may say that if I am truly willing to be "good soil," I may continue to be used of the Lord for His purposes in some way or another as long as I live.

MARK 4:21–23

And he said unto them, Is a candle brought to be put under a bushel, or under a bed? and not to be set on a candlestick? For there is nothing hid, which shall not be manifested; neither was any thing kept secret, but that it should come abroad. If any man have ears to hear, let him hear.

There is a mixing of metaphors here, but it is made clear by sorting it out in the context. As these word pictures follow the parable of the sower, it seems obvious the light of the lamp in verse 21 is God's Word (v. 14) sown in the soil of human hearts. The first lesson here for me is that God's Word is not given just to illuminate the inside of the overturned bushel basket of my spiritual or church life. The truth of God's Word is to be illustrated by my life in such a way that it touches and illuminates everything within my line of sight.

The metaphor of hearing reinforces this truth. What I hear from God through His Word should permeate all my thinking about everything. Only as my understanding is dominated by the truth of His Word can I evaluate accurately all the things I see in God's world and discern the pattern of God's working among the plethora of various facts and impressions with which my mind is bombarded.

MARK 4:23–25

If any man have ears to hear, let him hear. And he said unto them, Take heed what ye hear: with what measure ye mete, it shall be measured to you: and unto you that hear shall more be given. For

he that hath, to him shall be given: and he that hath not, from him
shall be taken even that which he hath.

Verse 25 does not change the subject, which is still "having ears
to hear." Jesus is saying here that if I am willing to hear what God
is saying by using His Word as my interpreting criterion when ob-
serving any information or ideas, I will then be enabled to see and
understand more and more. On the other hand, if I am not willing
to employ the Word of God as my measuring rod, then the clarity
which would have been available to me will be taken away. Then, any
increase in information and ideas will only confuse me. Ideas and
information that could have been the means of seeing God's hand at
work in my world and circumstances become instead only sources of
puzzlement and sometimes even excuses for denying God's truth.

I doubt there is such a thing as secular facts, and I am not sure
there is such a thing as secular learning, but I am sure that a secular
motive for learning will often lead to a misunderstanding of the true
meaning of things. On the other hand, I believe this verse promises
that if I have a sincere desire to learn God's Word and obey God's
will, I may increasingly develop a clearer and clearer understanding
of everything in my world.

MARK 4:24

And he said unto them, Take heed what ye hear: with what mea-
sure ye mete, it shall be measured to you: and unto you that hear
shall more be given.

This can be, and probably should be, translated, "The measure
by which you measure shall be measured." This means that the standard by which I judge what I will listen to and the standards by
which I evaluate what I hear will be laid down beside God's standards and judged by comparison with God's truth. This fits the context perfectly.

It behooves me to be familiar with God's standards, to expose my "hearing" only to things consistent with His truth, and to act only in accordance with His Word.

MARK 4:26–28

And he said, So is the kingdom of God, as if a man should cast seed into the ground; and should sleep, and rise night and day, and the seed should spring and grow up, he knoweth not how. For the earth bringeth forth fruit of herself; first the blade, then the ear, after that the full corn in the ear.

It is significant that Jesus pointedly said, "He himself does not know how," and followed by saying, "For the earth yields crops by itself." This reminds me of the amusing fact that government agricultural experts now discourage use of the term *farmer* and have replaced it with the word *producer*. I suppose these status-conscious bureaucrats think the word *farmer* is demeaning.

This change, of course, is ridiculous. God is the producer; the farmer is the facilitator. Historically, the word *farmer* has not been limited to agriculture. It has been used in many contexts to refer to persons facilitating accomplishment on behalf of, and by the power of, a higher authority. Roman equestrians, for instance, who took a private contract to collect taxes on behalf of the Roman government were called tax farmers.

Jesus' emphasis here reminds me that any true spiritual accomplishment in which I may be involved is done on the authority of, by the power of, and according to the Word of, God alone. My role is to facilitate His work by acknowledging His authority, depending on His power, and obeying His Word.

MARK 4:28

For the earth bringeth forth fruit of herself; first the blade, then the ear, after that the full corn in the ear.

Jesus had introduced this little parabolic illustration by saying it had to do with God's rulership over the entire agricultural process (v. 26). He then pointed out that man has an important role, but only as a facilitator of God-controlled processes and under God's authority (vv. 26b–27). Verse 28 reinforces the point of the parable by describing an orderly process of growth, controlled by a predetermined calendar as it moves inexorably toward a predetermined goal.

If I expect to carry out my part as a facilitator effectively, I must have a clear understanding of the process and the calendar of God's operations. The farmer must know the processes of botanical growth in order to know when to sow (v. 26), when to "lay by" (v. 27), and when to harvest (v. 29). My only textbook of information and instruction for carrying out my role as a facilitator of God's spiritual processes is the Bible. To know what to do and when to do it, and to know what is and is not my responsibility, I must be a diligent student of God's Word. After that, of course, I must obey its instructions.

MARK 4:30–32

And he said, Whereunto shall we liken the kingdom of God? or with what comparison shall we compare it? It is like a grain of mustard seed, which, when it is sown in the earth, is less than all the seeds that be in the earth: but when it is sown, it groweth up, and becometh greater than all herbs, and shooteth out great branches; so that the fowls of the air may lodge under the shadow of it.

Jesus is once again talking about the "kingdom (rulership) of God" in the individual believer (Luke 17:21). When Jesus spoke about the kingdom of God, it was never a political, social, or even religious organization. It was an inner commitment of obedience to the rulership of God in the life of the individual.

These verses speak, then, about the awesome possibilities that lie within a genuine commitment to obedience to the Word of God—consistently carried out. To the secular or "religious" mind, the idea of one individual obeying rigidly the words of an ancient book may seem like a peculiar quirk without a shred of importance and no significant place in the real (i.e., physical) world. The Scriptures, however, are loaded with illustrations of the shallowness of such a view from Noah all the way through Paul (Heb. 11).

This invitation is open to all, including me. If I simply obey God's Word, good things begin to grow within me that defy all logic (Phil. 4:7) and inform my peace, my joy, and even my thinking and understanding processes (Rom. 12:2) so that everything in life begins to be seen in its true light and finds its proper place in God's all-encompassing truth. Besides, I may never know what other persons and events God may choose to influence or support in some way through my simply obeying His Word.

MARK 4:33–34, 38

> And with many such parables spake he the word unto them, as they were able to hear it. But without a parable spake he not unto them: and when they were alone, he expounded all things to his disciples. . . . And he was in the hinder part of the ship, asleep on a pillow: and they awake him, and say unto him, Master, carest thou not that we perish?

Jesus taught by using parables and by explaining the parables. His disciples recognized Him and addressed Him as their teacher (*didaskalos*). Yet until the coming of the Holy Spirit, they did not really understand His teaching (John 14:25–26; 16:13) so that they might pass it along in writing to the church (John 15:26–27; 17:20; 2 Pet. 1:15–21).

On the surface, there appears to be a conflict between Jesus' command not to call anyone teacher (*didaskalos*; Matt. 23:8) and Paul's inspired statement that some of us are given the gift of teachers (*didaskalous*; Eph. 4:11). The answer to the apparent problem is in Jesus' statements that He, "the Christ," is our teacher (Matt. 23:8) and that the Holy Spirit would inspire the disciples to relay Jesus' teaching to us (John 15:26–27; 17:20; 2 Pet. 1:15).

If I have the gift of pastor and teacher, my responsibility lies in being as sure as I can that those I am called to teach know clearly what the written Word of God says. If I do this, I do not need to add anything but prayer (Acts 6:4). God the Holy Spirit is responsible to lead people in applying His Word to their lives (John 16:8–13). I need to resist the temptation to "convict" people concerning how to live the Christian life. If I prayerfully teach God's Word, the Holy Spirit will interpret it to the hearers; He does not need for me to try to lay guilt trips on them.

MARK 4:37–40

> *And there arose a great storm of wind, and the waves beat into the ship, so that it was now full. And he was in the hinder part of the ship, asleep on a pillow: and they awake him, and say unto him, Master, carest thou not that we perish? And he arose, and rebuked the wind, and said unto the sea, Peace, be still. And the wind ceased, and there was a great calm. And he said unto them, Why are ye so fearful? how is it that ye have no faith?*

"How is it that ye have no faith?" Faith is not a magic wand by which we control what God does; living faith in God will control what we do—and don't do (James 2:20). The disciples had awakened Jesus and sternly rebuked His lack of concern for their welfare (*ou melei soi 'oti apollumetha*). When Jesus asked about their lack of faith, He meant, "Why didn't you trust God instead of waking Me up to nag Me and blame Me for your fears?" He was rebuking something the disciples actually did based on their lack of faith in God.

I need to remember that "Trust and Obey" is a fine hymn, but it is a redundancy. If I trust God, I will obey God's Word; if I do not obey, I have no right to claim to trust. If I have true, living faith in God, it will affect my fears and my peace, but it will also determine what I say and what I do—and don't do.

MARK 4:37–40

And there arose a great storm of wind, and the waves beat into the ship, so that it was now full. And he was in the hinder part of the ship, asleep on a pillow: and they awake him, and say unto him, Master, carest thou not that we perish? And he arose, and rebuked the wind, and said unto the sea, Peace, be still. And the wind ceased, and there was a great calm. And he said unto them, Why are ye so fearful? how is it that ye have no faith?

This parable is addressed directly to all Christians, including me. The people in the ship were Jesus' closest disciples. They were the ones who knew Him best and had committed themselves to be His followers. Yet, when their circumstances became threatening, they panicked.

I think the lesson for me is that when I am in the ship with Jesus, surrounding circumstances are not my problem. My assignment is to be sure my focus is on being in the ship with Him. The threatening circumstances are His department.

MARK 4:39–40

And he arose, and rebuked the wind, and said unto the sea, Peace, be still. And the wind ceased, and there was a great calm. And he said unto them, Why are ye so fearful? how is it that ye have no faith?

I don't know whether this would say anything to anyone else, but I found it meaningful and reassuring. There appears to be a direct correspondence between the two commands of Jesus to the wind and the two questions He asked the disciples.

Jesus' first command to the wind was "Peace (*Siopa*)!" The word means literally to "be mute," or unable to speak. A dynamic translation might have Jesus saying, "Shut up!" Jesus' second command was "Be still (*Pephimoso*)!" This command meant "be muzzled!" Where the first command of Jesus meant the wind must cease its noisy threatening, the second meant it was to lose its power to "bite," or to carry out its threat by actually harming (drowning) the disciples.

Correspondingly, Jesus' first question was "Why are you so fearful?" He implied they should not have dreaded the blustering and fearful threat of the noisy wind. His second question implied the reason they had no need to fear. Jesus asked, "How is it that you have no faith?" They should have had faith in God's power over the wind, His loving concern for His followers, and His wisdom in timely meeting all their needs. They should have recognized that they were never at the mercy of the wind and water except by permission of God, Who held the leash and muzzle over all their circumstances.

This speaks to me as a child of God. Fear and dread have no place in my heart or mind as I am the object of the loving care of the almighty God of the universe. Hallelujah!

MARK 4:39

And he arose, and rebuked the wind, and said unto the sea, Peace, be still. And the wind ceased, and there was a great calm.

When Jesus rebuked the wind, the sea did not merely return to its normal state, which would be described in NOAA jargon as a light chop. No, what it did was suddenly assume a most unusual aspect, a "great calm" (*galene megale*). The state of agitation of the Sea of Galilee (or almost any fairly large body of water) does not range from a norm of calm through various states of disturbance. The norm is nearly always a light chop; a period of absolute calm is not only not its normal state but also a highly rare state. It most certainly would not happen suddenly in the midst of a violent storm.

This double miracle of Jesus teaches me more than just His power over the world's weather. The normal state of the human heart in this fallen world is most certainly not "calm." The norm for the average human heart is dissatisfaction. Most of us are at least a little agitated or concerned about one thing or another most of the time. This physical miracle of Jesus speaks also of the possibility of a spiritual occurrence that is equally rare and of equally miraculous proportions. God the Holy Spirit tells me through Paul of the ready availability at all times of a miraculous attitude of mind that defies all human psychological analysis and approaches a state of absolute calmness (*galene megale*) in my heart. Hallelujah!

MARK 4:40–41

> *And he said unto them, Why are ye so fearful? how is it that ye have no faith? And they feared exceedingly, and said one to another, What manner of man is this, that even the wind and the sea obey him?*

An interesting contrast is seen here in the use of two different Greek words translated by the same English word.

Jesus asked His disciples, "Why are you so fearful?" The word used here, *deiloi*, which means "to dread," is always used with a negative connotation, and is sometimes translated "cowardice" or "timidity." On the other hand, the word used when the disciples are said to have "feared exceedingly" is *ephobethesan*, from *phobeo*, which is sometimes used, as it is here, to describe a response of a reverential awe.

Deilos, then, is an adjective, and describes a negative attitude, reflecting a weakness of character, while *phobeo* is a verb and describes a response or reaction to a specific person, object, or situation. It is often used in the positive sense of reverence and respect.

As a child of God, my spiritual growth should include overcoming any tendency to be a fearful person. My confidence in the reality of God's love for me will make it totally unrealistic ever to be fearful. I may enjoy God's peace that passes all human understanding at all times and in all circumstances (Phil. 4:7). I may always be a peaceful, optimistic person with a naturally positive and cheerful outlook on life. Hallelujah!

MARK 5

MARK 5:2, 7–8

And when he was come out of the ship, immediately there met him out of the tombs a man with an unclean spirit . . . and cried with a loud voice, and said, What have I to do with thee, Jesus, thou Son of the most high God? I adjure thee by God, that thou torment me not. For he said unto him, Come out of the man, thou unclean spirit.

I do not join those who become obsessed with knowing all about unclean spirits, but this incident tells us several obvious things. Unclean spirits appear to be fixated on death (v. 3), they refuse to be bound by any kind of restraint, (vv. 3–4), and they possess self-destructive tendencies (vv. 5, 13). They appear to be quite willing to worship God in their own way (v. 6), but the verses above show us that unclean spirits consider themselves victims of torment when expected to obey a command of the Son of God.

I need to remember that it is a privilege for God to direct my life. I should not only obey His Word but should do so with great joy and thankfulness for God's direction in my life. Grudging and complaining obedience to Him is characteristic of an unclean spirit.

MARK 5:13B, 15–17

And the unclean spirits went out, and entered into the swine: and the herd ran violently down a steep place into the sea, (they were about two thousand;) and were choked in the sea. And they that fed the swine fled, and told it in the city, and in the country. And they went out to see what it was that was done. And they come to Jesus, and see him that was possessed with the devil, and had the legion, sitting, and clothed, and in his right mind: and they were afraid. And they that saw it told them how it befell to him that was possessed with the devil, and also concerning the swine. And they began to pray him to depart out of their coasts.

These Jewish farmers and villagers noted two results of Jesus' ministry among them: (1) a man was freed of an unclean spirit, and (2) an unclean herd of swine was destroyed. They apparently placed no value on the man who was freed but were so concerned for the swine that they begged Jesus to leave (lest they lose more hogs?).

They had greater concern for animals than for a human being. Their value system was incapable of appreciating the eternal beauty of a human freed to begin the process of becoming all he was created to be in the image of God. Instead, they were greatly exercised over the danger of animals being destroyed just to benefit a human being. These people would have made wonderful environmental and pro-choice activists.

I need to resist the temptation to accept popular politically and socially correct values that exalt the creature above the creator (Rom. 1:25) and His work in human beings who are created in His own image.

MARK 5:15A, 18–19

And they come to Jesus, and see him that was possessed with the devil, and had the legion, sitting, and clothed, and in his right mind . . . And when he was come into the ship, he that had been possessed with the devil prayed him that he might be with him. Howbeit Jesus suffered him not, but saith unto him, Go home to thy friends, and tell them how great things the Lord hath done for thee, and hath had compassion on thee.

When God's truth entered the life of this man, it affected his behavior: instead of his shouting and gesticulating, he was sitting quietly and listening. It affected his appearance: he was wearing adequate clothing (contra. Luke 8:27). It affected his intellect: he was in his right mind. It affected his emotions and interests: he pleaded (*parekalei*) with Jesus for permission to spend all his time with Him.

When the truth of Christianity impacts my life, it makes powerful differences in many ways. On the other hand, genuine Christianity does not consist entirely (or even primarily) of any one of its effects. It does not consist exclusively of intellectual accomplishment theologically nor of experience emotionally nor of change in appearance and behavior. The core of genuine Christianity is that it is the eternal truth concerning God, man and the universe. God and His truth exist independently of man's participation. Christianity, along with everything else in the universe, is centered in God and His truth, not in man and his experience.

It is precisely because God's truth does not need my response that it demands a response. No response to God's truth is not possible. No response to God is a response because He is eternal truth (John 14:6). It is a privilege to respond to the gospel and then to order my life according to God's Word.

Whether therefore ye eat, or drink, or whatsoever ye do, do all to the glory of God. (1 Cor. 10:31)

MARK 5:18–20

And when he was come into the ship, he that had been possessed with the devil prayed him that he might be with him. Howbeit Jesus suffered him not, but saith unto him, Go home to thy friends, and tell them how great things the Lord hath done for thee, and hath had compassion on thee. And he departed, and began to publish in Decapolis how great things Jesus had done for him: and all men did marvel.

The words translated "thy friends" is difficult to translate into understandable English. It is much broader and less specific than "friends." It means, literally, "those of you." It can mean friends, family, acquaintances, fellow citizens, those of similar social or ethnic background, or even official civil or religious authorities of one's native town or parish.

Jesus was telling him to present himself as both a witness and an evidence of God's power ("how great things") and love ("compassion on thee") to those who had known the man before. These people could see and evaluate the measure and quality of difference in the man's own life (v. 20). This man was not sent on a preaching mission but on a presentation and explanation mission (cf. Matt. 8:4; Mark 1:44; Luke 5:14).

One of the things this says to me is that when I tell people how great God's power and love are, they should be able to look at my life and see the proof of my words.

MARK 5:22–23, 35–36

And, behold, there cometh one of the rulers of the synagogue, Jairus by name; and when he saw him, he fell at his feet, and besought him greatly, saying, My little daughter lieth at the point of death: I pray thee, come and lay thy hands on her, that she may be healed; and she shall live. . . . While he yet spake, there came from the ruler of the synagogue's house certain which said, Thy daughter is dead: why troublest thou the Master any further? As soon as Jesus heard the word that was spoken, he saith unto the ruler of the synagogue, Be not afraid, only believe.

Jairus had already clearly expressed confidence in Jesus' ability to heal his little daughter when she was "at the point of death." Those who came from his house indicated that Jairus's belief should now be canceled because the little girl was dead. Jesus' response to this message was a double imperative: (1) "Do not be afraid," but (2) "only believe." The use of the word *only* (*monon*) seems to indicate that the change in circumstances should not affect the quality of trust or the adding of an element of fear. Adding fear to belief makes belief tentative; it cancels out the absolute character of true confidence and trust. Jesus was saying, in effect, "You believed I could heal her when she was at the point of death; continue to believe that I can heal her if she is actually dead."

Jairus's expression of belief that Jesus could heal his daughter was absolute. His belief that Jesus would heal her was more tentative because he felt it depended on Jesus' response to his appeal by coming to his house and laying His hands on the little girl. All Jesus was asking of Jairus on receiving news of his daughter's death was that he not waver in his absolute confidence that Jesus could heal if He chose to do so.

As I think about how this applies to me, I am encouraged to maintain an absolute faith that God has the power to do what I pray for, the wisdom to know whether it is good for me, and the love to do what is the very best for me. This is all I really need to cancel all my fears. I am not authorized to believe He will always do exactly what I ask for; that is not faith; that is presumption. All I need is to know He cares and that He can and will answer my prayer in the way that is best for me.

MARK 5:24, 31, 37, 40, 43A

And Jesus went with him; and much people followed him, and thronged him. . . . And his disciples said unto him, Thou seest the multitude thronging thee, and sayest thou, Who touched me? . . . And he suffered no man to follow him, save Peter, and James, and John the brother of James. . . . And they laughed him to scorn. But when he had put them all out, he taketh the father and the mother of the damsel, and them that were with him, and entereth in where the damsel was lying. . . . And he charged them straitly that no man should know it.

The verses above illustrate the fact that Jesus repeatedly and consistently emphasized spiritual truth and physical reality to the exclusion of popularity, advertising, and image. We find Him again and again meeting individual needs but avoiding the crowds and the popularity that others would have sought. This is so clear in Mark's Gospel that modern scholars have invented terms for it, such as "the messianic secret" and the "secrecy motif."

God's work is always concerned with truth and reality, and it does not need to be puffed up with advertising and image building. If I seek to know God, walk with Him, and obey His Word, then He will accomplish His will in and through me without my having to promote or glorify myself or my ministry in any way.

MARK 5:25–29

And a certain woman, which had an issue of blood twelve years, and had suffered many things of many physicians, and had spent all that she had, and was nothing bettered, but rather grew worse, when she had heard of Jesus, came in the press behind, and touched his garment. For she said, If I may touch but his clothes, I shall be whole. And straightway the fountain of her blood was dried up; and she felt in her body that she was healed of that plague.

The contrast in meaning between the word translated "suffered" and the word translated "touch" is striking. Apparently, this woman had suffered much actual physical pain (*pathousa*, from *pascho*) from the treatments of the physicians. When she came to Jesus, however, she simply "touched" ('*epsato*, from '*apto*) His garment and became whole.

Since there are at least a half-dozen Greek words translated "touch" in English in the New Testament, the one used to describe what happened here is significant. '*Apto* is the word used when a burning lamp or candle is used to ignite another that is unlit. There passes a significant change of condition from one to the other without diminishing the power of the donor lamp while initiating fulfillment of the legitimate purpose of the receiving lamp. What a beautiful and accurate picture of the healing (from *sozo*) that entered the life of this woman from her faith-touch of Jesus' garment.

When I have used up all the natural means for being the whole person I was created to be, I may "touch" Jesus through His Word and experience the solution to my problem.

MARK 5:27–31

> *When she had heard of Jesus, came in the press behind, and touched his garment. For she said, If I may touch but his clothes, I shall be whole. And straightway the fountain of her blood was dried up; and she felt in her body that she was healed of that plague. And Jesus, immediately knowing in himself that virtue had gone out of him, turned him about in the press, and said, Who touched my clothes? And his disciples said unto him, Thou seest the multitude thronging thee, and sayest thou, Who touched me?*

This is just one more incident emphasizing the personal and individual nature of God's interest in relating to the human race. This woman did not come to Jesus through an organization, nor in any public way. In her desperation, she went directly and very privately (indeed secretly) to the Lord, and He recognized her and met her need.

While Jesus promises to honor voluntary concerted prayer (Matt. 18:19–20), He does not require any joint effort or human intercession to meet an individual human need. I can pick up a private "hotline" and talk to Him anytime.

> *Behold, I stand at the door, and knock. If any man hear my voice and open the door, I will come in to him, and will sup with him, and he with me. (Rev. 3:20)*

MARK 5:30

And Jesus, immediately knowing in himself that virtue had gone out of him, turned him about in the press, and said, Who touched my clothes?

I hope this doesn't seem too complicated, abstruse, and unrelated; I found it exciting. The word translated as "virtue" (*dunamin*, from *dunamis*) is defined in Greek dictionaries and lexicons in almost the same words as physicists define the term *energy*. *Dunamis* is the ability to perform work or to bring about positive change. What Jesus perceived in Himself was not a diminution in total power but an emission of creative power.

When the Scripture says God "rested" on the seventh creative day, it included His institution of the law of the conservation of energy. Either at that time, or perhaps after the fall or the great flood, He also instituted the law of entropy. I believe God Himself is exempted from both of these laws.

Most of the time, when He hears our prayers, or is aware of our problems, God accomplishes what is best for us through natural means. The sovereign God usually will accomplish His supernatural will through His natural laws. On the other hand, God Himself is not limited to such means. On those occasions when He chooses to do so, God may accomplish His will through suspension and overriding of any of the natural laws, which He Himself has ordained. God Himself can insert His supernatural or creative law on behalf of His purposes in the lives of His children. Whenever He deems it necessary, God can override all the natural circumstances surrounding me to protect and bless me—supernaturally. Hallelujah!

MARK 5:31

And his disciples said unto him, Thou seest the multitude thronging thee, and sayest thou, Who touched me?

The disciples saw only the thronging multitude. They apparently did not grasp the possibility of one individual "unclean" person gaining wholeness by an individual and personal touch of faith while the throng surged along virtually unaffected by the presence of the power of almighty God in their midst. I recognize that it is politically correct in contemporary evangelical circles to deprecate "Lone Ranger" Christianity and instead to emphasize the importance of institutional and corporate fellowship and worship. This attitude, of course, is endorsed with special vigor by those with a vested interest in Christian institutions.

I agree with those who criticize Christians for leaving a local congregation because they are not "being fed." Yet the ones doing the criticizing will often encourage this very attitude. They do this by implying that one's personal relationship to God cannot be maintained at its ideal level independent of one's corporate and institutional Christianity. The implication is that the spiritual life of the congregation is primary and personal spiritual life is dependent and secondary.

I believe it was most fortunate for the woman with the issue of blood that she had not heard and accepted this sort of propaganda. I consider it a privilege to walk with God personally in gratitude for His blessings. If I enjoy daily fellowship with Him by saturating myself in His Word, then when I obey His command to assemble (Heb. 10:25) with a local congregation, I may have something to share and may make a contribution to corporate spiritual life. I believe the Christian life should be more than just accepting the feeding formula of the church and burping my complaints on others.

MARK 5:33–34

> *But the woman fearing and trembling, knowing what was done in her, came and fell down before him, and told him all the truth. And he said unto her, Daughter, thy faith hath made thee whole; go in peace, and be whole of thy plague.*

"The whole truth" (NKJV). These verses could easily be interpreted to say that from this woman's telling Jesus the whole truth flowed (1) faith, (2) wellness (from *sozo*), (3) peace, and (4) healing (*'ugies*).

Could this mean that when I wonder why I lack faith or need rescue or do not have inner peace or am plagued with affliction, I may need to examine whether I have been totally honest with God?

MARK 5:34

> *And he said unto her, Daughter, thy faith hath made thee whole;*
> *go in peace, and be whole of thy plague.*

When Jesus said, "Your faith has made you well," He was not speaking of "faith" as a medical instrument, prescription, or placebo. He meant that faith is the means of appropriating the power to be made whole.

This woman was made well not because she had faith but because she placed her faith in Jesus. After all, she had previously had faith in a series of physicians and this faith had brought her only suffering and pain. It was when her faith was placed where faith belongs in a world created by God that she began to enjoy the wholeness of being all she was created to be.

This is a universal principle. I believe that my faith for anything and everything that is right for me may be safely placed in God and nowhere else. Everything I really need to be fulfilled in my God-assigned role in life comes from the hand of God and fits into the biblical pattern of God's will for me.

MARK 5:35

> *While he yet spake, there came from the ruler of the synagogue's*
> *house certain which said, Thy daughter is dead: why troublest*
> *thou the Master any further?*

The word translated "troublest" (*skulleis*) is a strong word with a broad range of meanings in various contexts. In the common language of Jesus' day, it could mean anything from "flay" to "harass" to "annoy." The assumption on the part of Jairus's household was that coming to heal the sick daughter was a burden or a chore for Jesus. Since the daughter had died, therefore, they felt Jesus should be relieved of the responsibility of this burden He had assumed.

Apparently, they did not grasp the reality of the character of Jesus. When asked by Jairus to heal his little daughter, Jesus' sense of compassion, both as man and as God, was stirred with a strong desire to relieve the painful agony in the heart of this synagogue ruler. Jesus' move toward the place and act of miraculous healing was not a chore for Him, or even "part of a day's work." Jesus was motivated by a powerful drive to accomplish this act of compassion.

What an encouragement! God may sometimes allow my heart to feel pain so that I will turn to Him. I may then receive the comforting relief and encouragement I desire to have and He desires to give me. Then I can, in turn, look forward to enjoying the opportunities God sends my way to comfort others even as He has comforted me.

> *Blessed be the God and Father of our Lord Jesus Christ, the Father of mercies and God of all comfort, who comforts us in all our tribulation, that we may be able to comfort those who are in any trouble, with the comfort with which we ourselves are comforted by God. (2 Cor. 1:3–4 NKJV)*

Mark 6

Mark 6:1–3

And he went out from thence, and came into his own country; and his disciples follow him. And when the sabbath day was come, he began to teach in the synagogue: and many hearing him were astonished, saying, From whence hath this man these things? and what wisdom is this which is given unto him, that even such mighty works are wrought by his hands? Is not this the carpenter, the son of Mary, the brother of James, and Joses, and of Juda, and Simon? and are not his sisters here with us? And they were offended at him.

These people knew all about Jesus and His background. They believed that knowing Jesus' past gave them complete understanding of all His character and potential. They believed that one could only be whatever his father had been. The idea that a carpenter presumed to be a theologian upset them; that function was reserved for those officially appointed because of family connections and education.

In fact, individual human potential actually is controlled within parameters defined by genetics and experience (nature and nurture). What the people of Nazareth did not know was that being God made a qualitative difference. Who Jesus was could not be understood by these Galilean villagers, who knew only His carpenter training and were unaware of the long night hours Jesus spent in communion with His Father.

This should be an encouraging word for every Christian. If my life can be explained by my genetics and experience, then I have not been staying in touch with the almighty creator God as I am privileged to do as His child. Perhaps I have been believing my psychology books instead of reading my Bible. If I walk with my heavenly Father through His Word, there should be important aspects of my life that cannot be understood or explained by my inheritance, education, or experience.

"Therefore if any man be in Christ, he is a new creature" (2 Cor. 5:17; cf. Gal. 6:15).

MARK 6:4

But Jesus said unto them, A prophet is not without honour, but in his own country, and among his own kin, and in his own house.

Verse 4 is Jesus' commentary on what occurred in verses 2–3. He used three specific words to describe those who would not acknowledge God's prophet. Spiritual aspects of people's lives can never be properly evaluated—or even recognized—by those who judge by geography (*patridi*), ethnicity (*suggeneoi*), or family connections (*oikia*).

Since we live in the world and among people, it is most natural—and usually accurate—to judge one another on the basis of worldly criteria and human characteristics. These evaluative criteria, however, fail to take into account the most important dimension of human existence, which is the spiritual. Accepting Jesus' sacrifice for our sins and living according to His Word to please Him will make a radical and qualitative difference in our experience of life. It should also make a difference in our lifestyle in the world. Yet those who know us best will not perceive the real meaning of this lifestyle change if they lack spiritual sensitivity. Their understanding and explanation regarding Christian attitudes, habits, tastes, and decisions will be completely off the wall.

When those we know and love totally misjudge us and when they fail to accept our witness to Christian truth, it can be very disappointing. What happened in "his own country," and Jesus' comment on it should help us deal with these experiences. It should help us mature spiritually to live our lives "as unto God" and no longer "as unto other people." Too often we think our lives are defined by worldly accomplishments and recognitions or by our human relationships. This is not true! Real life for me is truly defined by only one relationship. All the other factors in life, including all my worldly accomplishments and human relationships, must be subsidiary to my relationship to God. Until this is true, I can never be His "prophet" and live the life for which His wisdom has designed me, His power created me, and His love redeemed me.

MARK 6:5–6

And he could there do no mighty work, save that he laid his hands upon a few sick folk, and healed them. And he marvelled because of their unbelief. And he went round about the villages, teaching.

How could Jesus, being God, lack the power (from *dunamis*) to do mighty works? God is still God Almighty, but in choosing to make us in His own image, He granted us the right to make decisions and choices regarding our own relation to God, His world, and His ways. These Galilean villagers were willing to know Jesus as a friend Whom they admired and liked but were not willing to believe in Him as God.

God has placed in our hands the ability to frustrate His loving desire to pour out His grace upon us and bless us (Gal. 2:21). We can frustrate His grace the same way as the Galileans in Jesus' own country: we do it by our unbelief (*apistian*). We should trust God's grace to care for us while we, in turn, obey and please Him. Instead, we assume responsibility to care for ourselves and even try to impress Him (and one another) with how well we can take care of His business. Little wonder we frustrate His grace and then have to invent terms such as *stress, burnout, worry,* and *depression* to describe our own frustration. We need to replace our unbelief with trust. This comes from getting to know Him as God through our obedience to His Word instead of just knowing Him as a familiar friend like the people of his own country.

MARK 6:7, 12–13, 37

> *And he called unto him the twelve, and began to send them forth by two and two; and gave them power over unclean spirits. . . . And they went out, and preached that men should repent. And they cast out many devils, and anointed with oil many that were sick, and healed them. . . . He answered and said unto them, Give ye them to eat. And they say unto him, Shall we go and buy two hundred pennyworth of bread, and give them to eat?*

The disciples had just returned from a wonderful preaching mission during which they had been instruments of many divine miracles. They knew Jesus could perform the miraculous and He could do it through them. Yet when commanded to do what only God could accomplish, instead of making themselves available for trusting obedience, they proposed plan B. At the same time, they clearly indicated that plan B would not really work and hinted they should return to the disciples' plan A, which was to send the people away to get their own food (v. 36).

When God commands me to do something, my response should be "Yes Sir," followed by looking to His Word for specific orders and then carrying them out (vv. 38–40).

MARK 6:7, 12–14

*And he called unto him the twelve, and began to send them forth
by two and two; and gave them power over unclean spirits. . . .
And they went out, and preached that men should repent. And
they cast out many devils, and anointed with oil many that were
sick, and healed them. And king Herod heard of him; (for his
name was spread abroad:) and he said, That John the Baptist was
risen from the dead, and therefore mighty works do shew forth
themselves in him.*

The original Greek does not have the words "of him" in verse
14. What Herod heard was that Jesus' disciples were combining the
performance of great miracles with a message of repentance for sin.
It was this that stirred up his guilty conscience concerning John the
Baptist. Herod had executed John, knowing that he was not only an
innocent man but a prophet of God (v. 20).

This was a typical human reaction and response. The difference
between the created image of God in us and our actual motives and
behaviors is often brought to our attention by the Holy Spirit and
our conscience (John 16:8). Sometimes the very sin by which we
have tried to solve or eliminate a problem becomes our biggest problem. Counselors and psychologists often find people fixated on any
subject related to the area of their sin.

I need always to remember that the only effective way to solve
and eliminate problems is to go all the way back to my sin and confess it as sin, along with all the subsequent sinful cover-ups and
excuses. Then I can receive and accept God's full free forgiveness
(1 John 1:8–10). Hallelujah!

MARK 6:7

*And he called unto him the twelve, and began to send them forth
by two and two; and gave them power over unclean spirits.*

Jesus did not call the twelve disciples to go out, nor did He call
them to have cleansing power in an unclean world. The prepositional

prefix is clear in emphasizing that the call was to come to Him. How He might direct them to serve at that time or in the future was not a part of the call. They were called to Jesus. It was only after they had answered that call that He began to direct and empower them for specific ministries.

The Twelve did not have a permanent call to go two by two about Galilee. This was only a temporary assignment for those who answered the call to come to Jesus and spend time with Him. The apostle James was later directed to lead the church and then to submit to martyrdom. Peter was led to preach primarily to the Jews (Gal. 2:7), was also directed to open the gospel to the Gentiles, and apparently was later led to go to Rome and also submit to martyrdom. John was led to spend a long and productive life and ministry in Ephesus, a long way from Galilee. Other disciples were led and directed to their various types of ministries. None had a permanent call to a particular function or place, but all had the call to relationship, fellowship, and obedience.

This focus and flexibility is still required by God. His primary and enduring call is to a relationship and fellowship with Himself. After I know Him and walk with Him, I am expected to be available for His leading and direction. It is God's prerogative to send me when, where, and as He wills to do whatever He commands and empowers me to do.

MARK 6:12

And they went out, and preached that men should repent.

Once again, we see that the introduction to the message we call the gospel, or "good news," for both Jews and Gentiles, is the word *repent* (cf. Matt. 3:2, 11; 4:17; 11:20; Mark 1:4, 15; Luke 3:3–5; 16:30; 24:47; Acts 2:38; 3:19; 5:31; 11:18; 13:24; 17:30; 19:4; 20:21; 26:20; Heb. 6:1; 2 Pet. 3:9). There is no shortcut gospel by way of our own self-improvement or pleasant experiences into the kingdom of God. The only way in is by personal repentance for personal sin.

Jesus did not suffer persecution, torture, and death because I needed a boost or deserved a blessing. I come to God as a repentant sinner or I do not truly come to God at all. God's loving arms are wide open to me, but God's holiness rejects both a self-sufficient and a casual attitude. The blood of Jesus will wash away the filth of my sins but will not mix with the oil of my pride and self-indulgence.

MARK 6:17–18

For Herod himself had sent forth and laid hold upon John, and bound him in prison for Herodias' sake, his brother Philip's wife: for he had married her. For John had said unto Herod, It is not lawful for thee to have thy brother's wife.

The life and ministry of John the Baptist were inextricably linked with the coming of God the Son to be the solution of the sin problem for all mankind. In this capacity, John recognized no alternative to identifying with God's truth in all areas of life. He accepted his responsibility to speak out for God with special emphasis on subjects of special sacredness to God, such as home and marriage. The facts that his was not a popular view and that speaking out threatened his welfare and his very life were not relevant. Being true to God and His truth was all important.

This is still expected of anyone accepting a position in God's ministry. I should speak and I should live consistent with God's standards in every area of my life if I have accepted a position of responsibility in His work.

MARK 6:20–23

For Herod feared John, knowing that he was a just man and an holy, and observed him; and when he heard him, he did many things, and heard him gladly. And when a convenient day was come, that Herod on his birthday made a supper to his lords, high captains, and chief estates of Galilee; and when the daughter of

> the said Herodias came in, and danced, and pleased Herod and
> them that sat with him, the king said unto the damsel, Ask of me
> whatsoever thou wilt, and I will give it thee. And he sware unto
> her, Whatsoever thou shalt ask of me, I will give it thee, unto the
> half of my kingdom.

Herod reminds me of some contemporary American Christians. He was fascinated with the things of God. God's truth piqued his curiosity and had great appeal for his naturally emotional and superstitious nature. On the other hand, he had no intention of ever allowing the godly and disciplined life habits of God's humble prophet, John the Baptist, to affect his own self-glorifying attitudes or his self-indulgent lifestyle.

God's highest will for me is far more likely to lead me to follow the example of John the Baptist than that of Herod.

MARK 6:27–28

> And immediately the king sent an executioner, and commanded
> his head to be brought: and he went and beheaded him in the
> prison, and brought his head in a charger, and gave it to the dam-
> sel: and the damsel gave it to her mother.

What a disgraceful and ignominious end for the life of God's chosen herald for His coming Messiah. Surely God could have seen to it that John would have enjoyed some kind of reward for His faithfulness to such an important and noble task. To lose his life at an early age by execution and to have his head presented to an angry, vengeful and totally immoral woman just does not seem exactly appropriate. But, then, the disgraceful crucifixion of God's Son by petty, jealous religious leaders was not right either.

God had things happen in this way and be recorded for us for several reasons. First, they are a warning to us regarding the likely reception we may receive when we represent the truth of God. Angry, vengeful people still try to eliminate those who speak and live the truth concerning the contrast between sinful behavior and the standards of God's Word. Petty religious leaders still attempt to crucify those who threaten their popularity and bureaucracy.

In addition, God means for His Word to haul us up short from time to time in our smug and triumphalistic efforts to bring in His kingdom on earth to our own glory. Those of us who claim to be God's servants need to be reminded that our earthly lives are at His disposal to be used according to His will. And His will may be to consume our lives in pointing the world to eternal and heavenly values as well as teaching and exampling His Word on earth. After all, the terms "kingdom of God" and "kingdom of heaven" appear sometimes to be used synonymously. A happy ending is not required for my earthly pilgrimage; this is only chapter 1. If I am truly God's servant, I can trust Him to write the script, knowing that if I am God's servant, I am about eternal business and God will more than right all wrongs according to His own eternal calendar.

> *For our light affliction, which is but for a moment, worketh for us a far more exceeding and eternal weight of glory; while we look not at the things which are seen, but at the things which are not seen: for the things which are seen are temporal; but the things which are not seen are eternal. (2 Cor. 4:17–18)*

MARK 6:30–31

> *And the apostles gathered themselves together unto Jesus, and told him all things, both what they had done, and what they had taught. And he said unto them, Come ye yourselves apart into a desert place, and rest a while: for there were many coming and going, and they had no leisure so much as to eat.*

The apostles, of course, were all excited about their successful ministry and recounted it all (*panta*) to Jesus and to one another. Jesus recognized that their successful ministry was a natural result of, and secondary to, their time alone with Him (see v. 7). Now a time of getting away from ministry opportunities and from "prospects" to be alone with Him was essential for any further effective spiritual service for God.

Jesus commanded the apostles to get away to a "deserted place" (*eremon topon*) and to spend time with Him meeting their own needs. They had started their successful service for Him in this way, and His command to them was to follow up their successful ministry in the same way.

The lesson is obvious. My relationship to God is primary. My service and my ministry are secondary and derivative. I do not need to be controlled by guilt to exhaust myself by doing things for God. His instructions are to spend time with Him and then to serve at His command.

MARK 6:32–34

> *And they departed into a desert place by ship privately. And the people saw them departing, and many knew him, and ran afoot thither out of all cities, and outwent them, and came together unto him. And Jesus, when he came out, saw much people, and was moved with compassion toward them, because they were as sheep not having a shepherd: and he began to teach them many things.*

Jesus took His disciples away for an important retreat after their challenging and successful preaching tour. As they reached their destination, a *huge* crowd was waiting for Him. These were not physically needy people seeking healing; they had walked the long way around the lake to what they knew was His favorite retreat to listen to His teaching. Jesus' response was to be "moved with compassion" (*esplagchisthe*). He then began to teach these presumptuous interrupters as wandering sheep who desperately needed His guidance.

What would my response have been? I am afraid I would not have been moved with compassion. I may have been moved with annoyance and resentment. I would certainly have been moved with problem-solving creativity in seeking a way to ditch this crowd of interlopers and get away to a different site.

Is it possible that my response to annoying, unplanned demands for ministry could be an index to how much I am filled with the

Spirit of Jesus? Am I really available for God to work through me on His schedule when it interrupts my schedule? When I encounter spiritually needy people seeking guidance, do I respond with compassion, even when it interrupts my carefully laid personal plans? What would Jesus do?

MARK 6:38–43

He saith unto them, How many loaves have ye? go and see. And when they knew, they say, Five, and two fishes. And he commanded them to make all sit down by companies upon the green grass. And they sat down in ranks, by hundreds, and by fifties. And when he had taken the five loaves and the two fishes, he looked up to heaven, and blessed, and brake the loaves, and gave them to his disciples to set before them; and the two fishes divided he among them all. And they did all eat, and were filled. And they took up twelve baskets full of the fragments, and of the fishes.

When I am careful to follow God's biblical directions and principles in obtaining and using the things I need to sustain life, then I can trust them all into His hands. As I allow Him to handle all the breaking, I may submit them to Him to bless them. When I do this, I always find all I need to maintain my ministry to others and to meet my own needs.

MARK 6:39–40

And he commanded them to make all sit down by companies upon the green grass. And they sat down in ranks, by hundreds, and by fifties.

Everybody else was either deeply concerned or totally unaware there was an impending problem. When Jesus took over, He had things done in a controlled, calm and orderly manner, in anticipation of good things happening to solve the problem.

When I truly let Him take over my life and I make it my business just to obey His Word, that's the way things are: calm, orderly, and optimistically expecting Him to meet my needs—which, of course, He always does.

MARK 6:41

And when he had taken the five loaves and the two fishes, he looked up to heaven, and blessed, and brake the loaves, and gave them to his disciples to set before them; and the two fishes divided he among them all.

"He looked up to heaven." In all places where the Bible indicates a direction for heaven, it is always up. When the Scriptures refer to heaven as "up," it is based on the fact that the earth is round and it is spinning and God is teaching us that He is everywhere.

I find that when praying alone, I usually instinctively look up rather than bowing my head. If I am praying in this way, and simultaneously a Christian in China is praying in the same posture, we are, astronomically speaking, looking in opposite directions. Likewise, when I pray at 3 a.m. and 3 p.m. the same day I will be looking in opposite "directions." This is OK. God really is everywhere! I can always look up and always find Him there. Hallelujah!

MARK 6:45–46

And straightway he constrained his disciples to get into the ship, and to go to the other side before unto Bethsaida, while he sent away the people. And when he had sent them away, he departed into a mountain to pray.

On a few occasions Jesus spoke directly to His Father in the presence of others, but nowhere in Scripture do I find Jesus leading His disciples or followers in public worship of God. Jesus' times of communion and communication with His Father were almost always personal and private.

Jesus' time with His disciples, His followers, and with the curious crowds was spent in meeting needs and teaching God's truth. If I am God's child, it seems reasonable to follow the example of God's only begotten Son if I wish to bear a "family resemblance" to my heavenly Father.

MARK 6:45–48A

And straightway he constrained his disciples to get into the ship, and to go to the other side before unto Bethsaida, while he sent away the people. And when he had sent them away, he departed into a mountain to pray. And when even was come, the ship was in the midst of the sea, and he alone on the land. And he saw them toiling in rowing; for the wind was contrary unto them.

The disciples were involved in the real world. They struggled as a team in a relationship of close cooperation as they faced together a very real problem. I am sure not one of them was shirking his responsibility to make a contribution to solving the problem. Very slowly and painfully (*basanizomenous*) they were accomplishing just a little real progress against the very real problem they were facing.

Jesus, on the other hand, was off by Himself on a mountain doing nothing but praying.

And yet . . .

Jesus, alone with His Father, was the One Who saw what was going on in the real world and was able to do something about it. This is not unusual. More things really are wrought by prayer than this world dreams of.

MARK 6:48A, 51

And he saw them toiling in rowing; for the wind was contrary unto them. . . . And he went up unto them into the ship; and the wind ceased: and they were sore amazed in themselves beyond measure, and wondered.

If you have ever tried to row a rowboat or canoe against the wind, you know how frustrating it can be. Such rowing can become very difficult long before whitecaps appear, especially in a commercial fishing boat big enough to hold twelve to fifteen men. It would make a big difference (and a big impression on these rowers) for the wind to cease. John even says they came "right away" (*eutheos egeneto*; John 6:21) to the land where they were going. This was probably not a miracle of movement by Jesus but indicates that what had been an arduous and demanding task became easier for these experienced fishermen when the wind died down.

Sometimes God performs miraculously those things that are totally impossible for us—such as the feeding of the five thousand. At other times He performs miracles that make it easier for us to do those things He expects us to do in obedience to Him (v. 45). It is OK for me to ask Him to make the job go smoothly as I do my part by obeying His Word.

MARK 6:49–50

But when they saw him walking upon the sea, they supposed it had been a spirit, and cried out: for they all saw him, and were troubled. And immediately he talked with them, and saith unto them, Be of good cheer: it is I; be not afraid.

The word translated "Be of good cheer" (*tharseite*) means "have courage" or "be confident." When Jesus said, "Have courage" and "Do not be afraid," He was using a typical Hebrew thought and speech pattern. He said precisely the same thing in two different forms as a sort of couplet. In this case, Jesus gave a specific command in both positive and negative terms. To be confident and courageous is exactly the opposite of being afraid. The connecting phrase, which explains and justifies the commands, is "It is I" (*ego eimi*).

The presence of Jesus should have been recognized by the disciples as inconsistent with fear and as a reliable source of confidence and courage. This is still true for me today.

Mark 6:51–52

> *And he went up unto them into the ship; and the wind ceased: and they were sore amazed in themselves beyond measure, and wondered. For they considered not the miracle of the loaves: for their heart was hardened.*

These disciples had recently been used as God's instruments to perform many types of miraculous healings. They had seen Jesus feed over five thousand people with a little sack lunch. And they had just watched Him strolling on the surface of the lake. Why would they be amazed when He made the wind to cease? The answer to the question is given right along with the description of the conundrum (the Bible is the best and most reliable commentary on itself): "because their heart was hardened" (*peporomene*).

Whenever this word is used to describe the mind, it means dull or lacking intelligence, but here it describes the disciples' hearts. It does not describe their thinking ability but their attitude as dull and lacking in understanding. Their lack of learning had nothing to do with intelligence, and everything to do with mindset. They were unwilling to recognize and deal with their spiritual ignorance.

My hope is that I may be so saturated with God's Word that I have a learning attitude for God's truth. I want to recognize my spiritual ignorance and have whatever native intelligence God has given me activated into spiritual effectiveness by an educable heart.

MARK 7

MARK 7:1–3

> *Then came together unto him the Pharisees, and certain of the scribes, which came from Jerusalem. And when they saw some of his disciples eat bread with defiled, that is to say, with unwashen, hands, they found fault. For the Pharisees, and all the Jews, except they wash their hands oft, eat not, holding the tradition of the elders.*

The Pharisees were not impressed with the fact that Jesus taught God's Word with great patience and compassion (6:34), that He miraculously fed thousands (6:41–44), or that He was healing hundreds, perhaps thousands (6:55–56). These Pharisees were accustomed to doing things in a certain way, which they enjoyed and found fulfilling.

They were unwilling to listen to a message not brought to them on their own terms. In order to reach the Pharisees, Jesus would have had to change His ministry and message to speak to them within their own culture. Jesus' message, however, was just not consistent with their self-glorifying and self-indulgent lifestyle, and He did not teach His disciples to adapt to the Pharisees' ways so as to communicate with them (v. 5). This led to their ignoring the message and criticizing the messenger.

This still happens. God's message must be communicated in clear understandable terms, but the message of God's Word does not change to fit unregenerate self-indulgent and self-glorifying lifestyles, even those of religious leaders such as the Pharisees. The Pharisees were religious leaders, but they were not truth seekers. I want to be flexible within the parameters of God's Word but discerning about pressure to change God's message and ministry to pander to fleshly pride and inflexibility.

MARK 7:3–5

For the Pharisees, and all the Jews, except they wash their hands oft, eat not, holding the tradition of the elders. And when they come from the market, except they wash, they eat not. And many other things there be, which they have received to hold, as the washing of cups, and pots, brasen vessels, and of tables. Then the Pharisees and scribes asked him, Why walk not thy disciples according to the tradition of the elders, but eat bread with unwashen hands?

The Jewish hand washing taught by the Pharisees had nothing to do with cleanliness. The ritualized motions they performed with their hands (or cups, pitchers, etc.) with water did nothing to the dirt on their hands. What it did was to make them feel more spiritual and religiously pure because it was what their religious leaders taught and practiced.

Jesus, of course, taught His disciples to deal with truth rather than subjective feelings in the physical world as well as in the realm of the Spirit. I need to be sure I do not fall into the pharisaical trap of judging spiritual reality by my emotions rather than by the Word of God.

MARK 7:5–7

Then the Pharisees and scribes asked him, Why walk not thy disciples according to the tradition of the elders, but eat bread with unwashen hands? He answered and said unto them, Well

hath Esaias prophesied of you hypocrites, as it is written, This
people honoureth me with their lips, but their heart is far from
me. Howbeit in vain do they worship me, teaching for doctrines
the commandments of men.

"'This people honoreth me with their lips, but their heart is far
from me.'" Isaiah's prophecy was certainly true in Jesus' day; there
are times when it appears to be true today as well. One cannot always discern the location of the heart of religious leaders by listening to what their lips say.

Jesus, however, went on to put His finger on the crux of the problem, which gives a clue to discernment. The Pharisees were "teaching for doctrines the commandments of men." One cannot judge
the heart's location by how often or eloquently church people speak
with their lips about God, God's will, God's work, worshiping God,
witnessing for God, and so forth. The key to discerning where their
heart is lies in discovering the source of their doctrinal teaching.
Is their teaching based on pragmatism, human logic, intellectual
pride, worldly wisdom, human tradition, or human ambition? Or
is it always based on a careful and prayerful study of the Word of
God?

I need to check myself in this regard. Do I consistently teach and
live according to the commands and principles of God's Word, or do
I attempt to use His Word to serve human goals, human traditions,
or human desires and ambitions?

MARK 7:5

Then the Pharisees and scribes asked him, Why walk not thy
disciples according to the tradition of the elders, but eat bread with
unwashen hands?

The Pharisees were not concerned for the truth of God's Word
but for the practices and interpretations handed down by their parents and religious teachers.

We live in a dynamic time with regard to Christian teaching. Many Christians resist unscriptural novelties in belief and practice and cling to the teaching of their parents and leaders who were godly believers and teachers of God's Word. The question arises "Do they hold sound doctrinal positions because these positions are biblical or because they are familiar?" On the other hand, many evangelicals in America are in the third or fourth generation of receiving from their forebearers a lot of unscriptural religious tradition in place of biblical truth. No matter what we have been taught, our criterion for accepting or rejecting any spiritual idea or practice should always be God's Word.

My concern is for my own beliefs and practices, and when appropriate, for those of persons for whose ministry I am responsible. I should be careful always to follow clear biblical truth rather than mere tradition. Administrative, pedagogical, and personnel decisions must never be made on the basis of "what are others doing or saying?" but always on the basis of "what is consistent with biblical truth and principles?"

MARK 7:6–7

> *He answered and said unto them, Well hath Esaias prophesied of you hypocrites, as it is written, This people honoureth me with their lips, but their heart is far from me. Howbeit in vain do they worship me, teaching for doctrines the commandments of men.*

We live in a day when evil is becoming flagrant, open, and in many ways dominant in the culture of our country. Many Christians become discouraged and wonder where God is when we pray for things to get better and they just seem to get worse and worse.

These verses point out that (1) things were much the same in Jesus' day, and (2) God had anticipated it and was still in charge. Isaiah had prophesied specific details concerning the rejection of God's truth by His people, the substitution of human opinion for God's Word by the religious leaders, and the total rejection of God's

Messiah. God knew ahead of time these things would happen and used them for His glory and for the blessing of all people. Rejection of Jesus as Messiah and the apparent triumph of evil laid the basis for the church and for the gospel for all nations.

This should be a word of encouragement for me. God has not abandoned His people. I do not need to engage in unrealistic triumphalism to recognize that God will be true to His Word. God anticipates all Satan's moves and ultimately God will not be defeated. He uses even the appearance of defeat to bring glory to Himself and blessing to His people. God is still in charge and my own faithfulness to Him will not go unrewarded. He is always present in the storm. He controls the future and He gives inner peace in all circumstances.

MARK 7:7–9

> *Howbeit in vain do they worship me, teaching for doctrines the commandments of men. For laying aside the commandment of God, ye hold the tradition of men, as the washing of pots and cups: and many other such like things ye do. And he said unto them, Full well ye reject the commandment of God, that ye may keep your own tradition.*

Three times in this short passage—in rapid succession—the real nub of the Pharisees' problem was revealed. First, Jesus quoted the problem from Isaiah. Then He stated the problem and illustrated from the ceremonial rinsing of cooking vessels. Then He stated it once again as introduction to another illustration from the law of Corban He was about to explain.

Jesus pointed out the underlying reason the Pharisees always seemed to be in opposition to Him: They had rejected the Word of God. As substitute for respect and obedience in relation to God's Word, they demanded obedience to their own decrees and rules. Their reference and authority for these demands was not the teaching of Holy Scripture but only the opinions of their predecessor religious leaders: "the tradition of the elders" (v. 5).

In searching for guidance in living and teaching the Christian life, I want to be able to find God's truth in God's Word. I do not want to be satisfied with the opinions of quoted experts, either contemporary or ancestral.

MARK 7:10–12

For Moses said, Honour thy father and thy mother; and, Whoso curseth father or mother, let him die the death: but ye say, If a man shall say to his father or mother, It is Corban, that is to say, a gift, by whatsoever thou mightest be profited by me; he shall be free. And ye suffer him no more to do ought for his father or his mother.

The word *Corban* was a transliteration into Greek (and English) of a Hebrew word used often in the books of Leviticus and Numbers. It referred to the sacrificial offerings brought to the altar in the tabernacle (and later the temple). In later Hebrew practice, the word referred to any offering, in money or in kind, made in support of the operation of the temple complex and the priesthood. By Jesus' day, the word had come to refer also to the temple treasury itself.

Apparently, the religious leaders had come up with an arrangement similar to our modern IRS regulations. This allowed a Jewish worshipper to make a "gift" to the temple treasury during his lifetime and continue to use it until his death, when it became the property of the temple. In this way, any personal property, such as a house or the corpus of some other form of investment, could be declared "Corban," so the real estate itself or the principal of the investment became off limits for personal disposal or inheritance purposes. The hypocritical members of the religious hierarchy protected their rights in the subject property by making it illegal to reduce its value even to obey the Old Testament command to honor one's parents (Exod. 20:12; 21:17; Deut. 5:16; cf 1 Tim. 5:8).

I feel sure it is OK to take advantage of all the government rules that are legal and appropriate to save money to have more to give to God's work. On the other hand, as I return God's tithe and make gifts to His work, I want to be a cheerful giver with my thoughts on

God and His work and not on IRS rules and my own advantage. I also need to be a discerning investor and not be taken in by religious leaders concerned primarily with their own financial and ego interests.

MARK 7:10–12

For Moses said, Honour thy father and thy mother; and, Whoso curseth father or mother, let him die the death: but ye say, If a man shall say to his father or mother, It is Corban, that is to say, a gift, by whatsoever thou mightest be profited by me; he shall be free. And ye suffer him no more to do ought for his father or his mother.

The thrust of this passage is to underscore the fact that God's Word, including His moral law, is still the absolutely reliable guide to appropriate, moral, and fulfilling human life on earth. In this case, Jesus emphasized the superiority of God's written Word over the derivative and contradictory "interpretations" of the rabbis.

We read in Paul's epistles, especially Romans and Galatians, that we must trust the death of Christ as sufficient to pay the penalty we have earned by breaking God's law (Rom. 3:23–28). It is clear we must not trust our own ability to keep the law for our salvation (Rom. 7:18). Salvation comes by accepting and placing our faith in Christ's death for our sins. But this by no means abrogates God's moral and social law as an expression of God's holiness and of His standard for the behavior of human beings created in His image (Matt. 5:17; Rom. 7:12).

As a Christian, I am saved by grace from the punishment I deserve for breaking God's law. Nevertheless, I may still profit immensely from reading and studying God's law as found in God's Word. I can find great fulfillment in obeying the commands of my Creator, who is also my loving heavenly Father.

MARK 7:13A

Making the word of God of none effect through your tradition.

We live in a day when fewer and fewer Americans have an appropriate respect for wisdom and structures accumulated through life experience by preceding generations. In Jesus' day, things were just the opposite. People restricted their thinking and living strictly within the parameters dictated by religious authorities. Obeying a different authority or thinking with originality or creativity were sins.

When Jesus appealed to the religious power structure to return to the original written Word of God, those in positions of power were threatened. Ultimately, they found it necessary to eliminate Him by crucifixion in order to maintain the social and political stability on which their exercise of power depended.

Ironically, these very religious leaders were the preservers and stewards of the written Word of God, which alone can afford the reliable stability and meaningful purpose for a fulfilling human life and a stable civilization. It is only the Word of God to which I can turn to protect me against the stultifying worship of tradition or the meaningless worship of self-indulgence.

MARK 7:13A

Making the word of God of none effect through your tradition.

Jesus was consistent and "stubborn" about putting the authority of God's Word above all other authorities, traditions, and opinions. Jesus had just quoted from Isaiah, who predicted that God's people would continue to be religious but reject the Word of God. He then described examples of the Pharisees' error in accepting and enforcing institutional religious rules in clear conflict with the commands of God's Word. Verse 13 sums up the point Jesus was making.

Many of the Pharisees were sincere in thinking they were just following good common-sense clarifications and codifications of God's Word handed down to them from their forebears or shared with them by well-known contemporary experts. Their problem was that they did not saturate themselves in God's Word as their final authority against which to check and compare all their teaching and practice.

This is a good warning. What I do and what I teach as a good way to live the Christian life or practice Christian ministry should always be checked against God's Word, no matter how good the authority or successful the practitioner who has suggested or decreed a given belief or practice.

MARK 7:14–16

And when he had called all the people unto him, he said unto them, Hearken unto me every one of you, and understand: there is nothing from without a man, that entering into him can defile him: but the things which come out of him, those are they that defile the man. If any man have ears to hear, let him hear.

Jesus both introduced and followed the summary statement of principle in verse 15 with a charge to pay close attention to this statement. Jesus considered it a critical truth, especially because He used the words *all* (*panta*) and *every one* (*pantes*) in verse 14 and *if any man* (*ei tis*) in verse 16.

In its context, Jesus was correcting the tendency of the Pharisees and their followers to cancel out the meaning of God's Word by substituting the opinions of religious leaders. But Jesus' pithy statement laid the responsibility for their life choices and lifestyle right within themselves. Each of these verses clearly teaches individual personal responsibility for human attitude and behavior.

We live in a day and in a culture that does not like this principle from God's Word. I am allowed to blame almost any sinful attitude or action on my environment. I am assured that my sins are caused by things from without that defile me. The responsibility for changing the environment lies with those in authority. Irresponsible sinful behavior goes hand in hand with centralization of authority.

But God's Word says, "No, your sin is from within you; you are responsible."

MARK 7:17–23

> And when he was entered into the house from the people, his disciples asked him concerning the parable. And he saith unto them, Are ye so without understanding also? Do ye not perceive, that whatsoever thing from without entereth into the man, it cannot defile him; because it entereth not into his heart, but into the belly, and goeth out into the draught, purging all meats? And he said, That which cometh out of the man, that defileth the man. For from within, out of the heart of men, proceed evil thoughts, adulteries, fornications, murders, thefts, covetousness, wickedness, deceit, lasciviousness, an evil eye, blasphemy, pride, foolishness: all these evil things come from within, and defile the man.

In His explanation to His disciples, Jesus corrected the erroneous view of naturalism and materialism. Our human bodies are an important part of who we are, but they are not all there is. The reality of our essential core identity is our spiritual personhood.

My physically intangible and invisible, but very real, spirit is responsible for controlling the structure and dynamic of my physical life in this world. Jesus explained, in His answer to the request of the disciples, the principle He had just enunciated in verse 15 of personal individual responsibility. He even listed a variety of specific sinful behaviors and attitudes that I may not blame on my background, environment, or circumstances. The Lord emphatically denied a basic premise of situation ethics and victimology.

MARK 7:20–23

> And he said, That which cometh out of the man, that defileth the man. For from within, out of the heart of men, proceed evil thoughts, adulteries, fornications, murders, thefts, covetousness, wickedness, deceit, lasciviousness, an evil eye, blasphemy, pride,

foolishness: all these evil things come from within, and defile the man.

This passage gives anyone believing God's Word a golden opportunity to grasp the difference between the meaning of the words *normal* and *average*. The world's use of statistics denies that there is any difference because the world does not recognize a designer and creator. For instance, the norm in educational statistics actually means average and equals the mean, median, or mode derived from a sample and applied to a population.

Too often, Christians think of a normal person as being pretty good with a few faults and problems. A person whose attitude and lifestyle are consistently spiritual or selfless is considered to be above the norm. A person who is consistently malevolent and destructive is considered below the norm morally.

The truth is just the opposite. This statement of Jesus, taken along with other Scriptures (Gen. 6:5; 8:21; Gal. 5:19–21), seems to indicate that everyone in this fallen world has the potential to sin every sin. On the other hand, human beings are created in the image of God. This image has been thoroughly defaced but not erased by the fall. Every Christian, designed and created in the image of God and redeemed and indwelt by the Holy Spirit, potentially may (and actually should) be a living example of the sublime character of God (Rom. 12:1–2).

This means I must deal daily with two challenges. First, I must honestly accept the fact of my own potential for selfishness, evil, and sin. Then, I must not be satisfied with an average Christian life but must be willing to strive for God's high standard of normal:

I beseech you therefore, brethren, by the mercies of God, that you present your bodies a living sacrifice, holy, acceptable to God, which is your reasonable service. (Rom. 12:1–2)

MARK 7:21–23

For from within, out of the heart of men, proceed evil thoughts,
adulteries, fornications, murders, thefts, covetousness, wicked-
ness, deceit, lasciviousness, an evil eye, blasphemy, pride, foolish-
ness: all these evil things come from within, and defile the man.

Once again we are faced with the word *heart* (*kardia*) in the New
Testament. This is not the same meaning we attach to the word in
modern usage. For Jesus, the heart was not the seat of the emotions or feelings but of the will, the attitude, or the mindset. The
evil things listed in verses 21–22 are potentially my natural reaction
to life situations unless I base my life on obeying the Scriptures and
depending on the power of the indwelling author of the Scriptures,
God the Holy Spirit.

MARK 7:25–26

For a certain woman, whose young daughter had an unclean
spirit, heard of him, and came and fell at his feet: the woman was
a Greek, a Syrophenician by nation; and she besought him that he
would cast forth the devil out of her daughter.

There is much we do not know about demons. God does not tell
us much because we do not need to know much. People who are fixated on the demoniac seem to waste a lot of good time, energy, and
focus that could be used in more productive ways. But a few things
seem to be clear from Scripture, and God means for us to know
these things. False spirits are discerned by their flawed theology
(1 John 4:1–3), outward behavior, including violence (Mark 5:1–5,
13), lack of self-control (Mark 9:18–22), nudity (Mark 5:15; Luke
8:35), and, as in this case, "uncleanness."

This passage, among others, identifies demons as unclean spirits.
Peoples with no Jewish or Christian background appear to recognize a natural state or condition called "uncleanness" and identify
it with falsehood, with evil, and with various sexual impurities and
perversions (Rom. 1:15–32).

Modern moral relativism, by denying the validity of value judgments found in God's Word, identifies itself with the cause of the very evil it denies exists. I need to be willing to avoid those things that God's Word calls evil. I also need to be willing to oppose them, even though it is much more popular in contemporary society to call good "evil" and evil "good." (Isa. 5:20).

MARK 7:26–29

The woman was a Greek, a Syrophenician by nation; and she besought him that he would cast forth the devil out of her daughter. But Jesus said unto her, Let the children first be filled: for it is not meet to take the children's bread, and to cast it unto the dogs. And she answered and said unto him, Yes, Lord: yet the dogs under the table eat of the children's crumbs. And he said unto her, For this saying go thy way; the devil is gone out of thy daughter.

Why did Jesus say that "for this saying" the daughter was healed? A study of individual healing miracles of Jesus described in the Gospels shows that He most often responded to an act or expression of helplessness and dependence, coupled with absolute confidence in His ability (e.g., Mark 2:3–5; 5:25–42; 9:14–29; John 5:5–9).

If I have a problem that needs to be solved, I first acknowledge my desperate helplessness to solve it myself. After that, I turn to Him, knowing He can handle the problem any way He pleases. After I have done these two things, I can relax because I know that whatever He does is what will be best for me.

MARK 7:27–29

But Jesus said unto her, Let the children first be filled: for it is not meet to take the children's bread, and to cast it unto the dogs. And she answered and said unto him, Yes, Lord: yet the dogs under the

table eat of the children's crumbs. And he said unto her, For this
saying go thy way; the devil is gone out of thy daughter.

We live in a time when immature self-centeredness is encouraged. Much of this is hype to separate people from their money. We are told by advertisers to "follow your own dream," to seek for an "experience" or a "feeling" that satisfies you, to demand your "rights," to choose "what is right for you," and to get whatever "you deserve." Jesus did not work this way! Jesus was prepared to give people all kinds of wonderful blessings they did not deserve after they acknowledged that they did not deserve them.

As a Christian, I need to avoid giving people the impression that God showers His blessings on me because I deserve them. Just the opposite is true; God showers His blessings on me because I honestly confess that I do not deserve them. Likewise, when I share the gospel message with others, I must not yield to the temptation to follow modern advertising techniques and pander to their childish tastes and demands in order to reach them for Christ.

MARK 7:29–30

And he said unto her, For this saying go thy way; the devil is gone
out of thy daughter. And when she was come to her house, she
found the devil gone out, and her daughter laid upon the bed.

We live in a world where many things are presented as true that turn out to be false. One of our most respected professions is that of the advertiser, which far too often involves the skill of presenting a symbol of the real thing that is illusory. Among America's most celebrated celebrities are actors, a class of people whose only demonstrated skill is pretending to be someone they are not. Even those whose profession is reporting information, or news, are best known for spin and other forms of lying.

The word of Jesus was the Word of God. The things He said were true! They always turned out to be just as He said they were. The Bible is the Word of God. Whatever it says is true and always turns out to be just the way things are. The Bible is my only absolutely reliable guide to knowing what is true (and doing what is true). Little wonder that for many centuries, Christian theology, based on the Word of God, has been called "the queen of the sciences."

MARK 7:32–33

And they bring unto him one that was deaf, and had an impediment in his speech; and they beseech him to put his hand upon him. And he took him aside from the multitude, and put his fingers into his ears, and he spit, and touched his tongue.

The word meaning "from" (*apo*), used as a prefix, is repeated as a separate preposition to emphasize the clear separation of this healing miracle from any audience. This is further reinforced by the phrase translated "aside" (*idian kat'*), better translated "by himself."

Jesus met peoples' needs because they had needs, and His reaction was in response to that need. He did not do miracles just to show off His power or to showcase His compassion. Many of His miracles were in private, and all but a few were on behalf of individuals. It is true that His miracles were signs, or credentials, of his messiahship and deity, but the very fact that they reflected His divine love as well as His divine power underscored the purpose for His coming.

In the present church age, God's work is primarily private, personal, and individual. The universal display of His power and glory is for the future and belongs to His second coming. I do not need to get caught up in the current fad of triumphalism and self-glorifying and self-indulgent mass "ministry" in the contemporary church.

MARK 7:33–34

And he took him aside from the multitude, and put his fingers into his ears, and he spit, and touched his tongue; and looking up to heaven, he sighed, and saith unto him, Ephphatha, that is, Be opened.

It may be significant that Jesus touched the man's ears before He touched his tongue. I believe it is necessary for God to open my ears to His Word before He opens my mouth to speak for Him.

MARK 7:35, 37

And straightway his ears were opened, and the string of his tongue was loosed, and he spake plain. . . . And were beyond measure astonished, saying, He hath done all things well: he maketh both the deaf to hear, and the dumb to speak.

"He hath done all things well" (*kalos*). This statement was made by those who observed the deaf and dumb man after His healing and who spread the word. It underscores and supports the description of the miracle in verse 35: "and he spoke plainly" (*orthos*). Jesus not only gave this man the physical ability to hear but also gave the ability to understand what he heard when he had never heard a word in his life. He also gave him the ability to speak and be understood when he had never spoken in any language before (Acts 2:4, 7–12).

Jesus was not only the God of real physical miracles but also the creator God of effective communication. When I share biblical and spiritual truth with others, I (1) have an obligation to speak in their language clearly in a way consistent with the truth of God, but (2) I am dependent on God the Holy Spirit to communicate the full spiritual meaning of the message.

This is consistent with the responsibility assumed by the apostles themselves when they assigned the first deacons to care for neglected congregation members. The apostles said on that occasion, "We will give ourselves continually to prayer and to the ministry of the word" (Acts 6:4). My ministry responsibility is to stick to God's

Word, but it also means I am first to saturate my ministry with prayer so that the author of the Word, the Holy Spirit, may communicate its true spiritual meaning to others.

MARK 7:35

And straightway his ears were opened, and the string of his tongue was loosed, and he spake plain.

"And he spake plain" (*orthos*). This man had been deaf as well as mute. He had never heard anyone say anything. Furthermore, he had never had any practice in speaking. Yet, when Jesus healed him, he immediately spoke plainly, clearly, and correctly.

God created the human race to be communicators and gave us the gift of language. I find repeated reminders in Scripture that God expects me—as a very minimum—to use total honesty, clarity, and precision in spoken and written communication. He also enjoys creativity and beauty in the use and appreciation of His gift of language. If I am guilty of carelessness, dishonesty, slovenliness, and laziness in the use of language, I have sinned against the creative love of God and have insulted His image in me.

MARK 7:37

And were beyond measure astonished, saying, He hath done all things well: he maketh both the deaf to hear, and the dumb to speak.

The deaf man received from Jesus a healing touch to his ears so that he could hear and a miraculous touch to his brain so that he could understand what he heard. His mouth received a healing touch so that he could speak, and his brain was miraculously affected, so that he could communicate in the local language.

My mental powers alone cannot "hear" significant spiritual truth from God; I am dependent on God the Holy Spirit to "open my ears" to the meaning of His Word. Likewise, while I am responsible to hone and develop my communication skills and to share God's truth, I am dependent on Him to effect successful transmission of His truth to others.

MARK 8

MARK 8:2, 6–10

I have compassion on the multitude, because they have now been
with me three days, and have nothing to eat: . . . and he com-
manded the people to sit down on the ground: and he took the
seven loaves, and gave thanks, and brake, and gave to his disciples
to set before them; and they did set them before the people. And
they had a few small fishes: and he blessed, and commanded to set
them also before them. So they did eat, and were filled: and they
took up of the broken meat that was left seven baskets. And they
that had eaten were about four thousand: and he sent them away.
And straightway he entered into a ship with his disciples, and
came into the parts of Dalmanutha.

Only Mark and Matthew relate the feeding of four thousand,
while all four Gospels mention the feeding of the five thousand. The
four accounts of the two feedings have several significant things in
common. The place was far away from any source of food (Matt.
14:13; 15:33; Mark 6:33; 8:4; Luke 9:12; John 6:3). After the miraculous feeding, Jesus sent the multitudes away (Matt. 14:23; 15:39;
Mark 6:45; 8:9) and either entered into a boat and departed (Matt.
15:39; Mark 8:10) or went away alone to pray (Matt. 14:23; Mark
6:46; John 6:15).

These miracles occurred when no nonmiraculous way was available for Jesus to express His compassion on the multitude. A miracle was a necessity or the need would go unmet. Our normal needs under normal circumstances can be handled by us, using normal methods, within our power following godly principles. God's miracles come through when His compassion and power and wisdom deem it necessary. The other observation was that Jesus left the scene immediately after the miracle. While Jesus became popular, He did not do things for the purpose of becoming popular or of advertising His power or His message. John, in fact, tells us that Jesus purposely avoided the opportunity to turn the miracle of feeding into political power (John 6:14–15).

If I go about my business, taking responsibility for myself and expressing compassion for others in ways within my means, God will come through with miracles when they are really needed. There will be opportunities to express God's compassion through work and words without my seeking notoriety or popularity.

MARK 8:11–12, 15

And the Pharisees came forth, and began to question with him, seeking of him a sign from heaven, tempting him. And he sighed deeply in his spirit, and saith, Why doth this generation seek after a sign? verily I say unto you, There shall no sign be given unto this generation. . . . And he charged them, saying, Take heed, beware of the leaven of the Pharisees, and of the leaven of Herod.

Immediately following the feeding of the four thousand, the Pharisees demanded from Jesus a "sign from heaven." Apparently, His teaching God's truth to the multitudes and His miraculously meeting their needs did not qualify as a sign from heaven confirming Jesus' divine mission. This, of course, was quite consistent with their primary problem, which Jesus repeatedly defined as placing their top priority on methods of practicing religion rather than on reading and obeying God's Word. Jesus' teaching God's truth and practicing God's compassion did not meet their demand for an exciting religious experience.

It seems significant that Jesus thought it necessary to warn His own disciples to beware of adopting the same attitude that blinded the Pharisees. I should take this seriously for myself. The Pharisees were "seeking [*zetountes*] from Him a sign from heaven," and Jesus refused to accommodate them. I also am under no obligation to pander to "seekers" after spectacular religious displays and exciting experiences.

MARK 8:15–21

> *And he charged them, saying, Take heed, beware of the leaven of the Pharisees, and of the leaven of Herod. And they reasoned among themselves, saying, It is because we have no bread. And when Jesus knew it, he saith unto them, Why reason ye, because ye have no bread? perceive ye not yet, neither understand? have ye your heart yet hardened? Having eyes, see ye not? and having ears, hear ye not? and do ye not remember? When I brake the five loaves among five thousand, how many baskets full of fragments took ye up? They say unto him, Twelve. And when the seven among four thousand, how many baskets full of fragments took ye up? And they said, Seven. And he said unto them, How is it that ye do not understand?*

"And do ye not remember?" As it turned out, they remembered exactly how many baskets of bread they had collected. The memory of these young disciples was just fine on numbers involved in their ministry. Yet they were so concerned about not having enough bread, they missed Jesus' point about the danger of thinking like the Pharisees, who were so fixated on worship methods and ministry details that they failed to see the far greater importance of the Word of God.

"For laying aside the commandment of God, you hold the tradition of men—the washing of pitchers and cups, and many other such things you do" (NKJV). He said to them, "All too well you reject the commandment of God, that you may keep your tradition . . . making the word of God of no effect through your tradition which you have handed down. And many such things you do" (Mark 7:8–9, 13 NKJV).

MARK 8:17–18

> *And when Jesus knew it, he saith unto them, Why reason ye, because ye have no bread? perceive ye not yet, neither understand? have ye your heart yet hardened? Having eyes, see ye not? and having ears, hear ye not? and do ye not remember?*

These young fishermen could see and hear perfectly well. As Jesus' closest followers, they were quite sure they understood and appreciated Him and His ministry. How sad it must have made Jesus to see how much they thought they knew and understood and how little they really knew. In our modern world, where outward material things change so rapidly while real inner truth remains stubbornly constant, lots of young Christians seem to have the same problem as the disciples. It is still sad to see, especially in young religious leaders.

Jesus' response to the problem was patience. He continued to teach by word and example and to pray for them (Luke 22:32). Good example for me.

MARK 8:17

> *And when Jesus knew it, he saith unto them, Why reason ye, because ye have no bread? perceive ye not yet, neither understand? have ye your heart yet hardened?*

Jesus used the metaphor of leaven to warn His disciples against the attitude of the Pharisees, which put religiously correct behavior ahead of God's Word. The disciples did not get it. Jesus indicated that the reason for their confusion was an attitude or mindset that was "petrified" (*peporomene*).

Apparently they did not grasp the true meaning of Jesus' teaching and compassionate miracles any better than the Pharisees did (v. 11). Their minds were not ready to accept the truth that Jesus was God with the implication that therefore they should always trust Him and obey Him.

As a child of God through the sacrifice of Jesus for my sins, I can see His miracles through His Word and always accept the kingdom (rulership) of God in every aspect of my life.

MARK 8:22–25

And he cometh to Bethsaida; and they bring a blind man unto him, and besought him to touch him. And he took the blind man by the hand, and led him out of the town; and when he had spit on his eyes, and put his hands upon him, he asked him if he saw ought. And he looked up, and said, I see men as trees, walking. After that he put his hands again upon his eyes, and made him look up: and he was restored, and saw every man clearly.

The more time I spend in contact with Jesus, the more I see everyone more clearly.

MARK 8:22–26

And he cometh to Bethsaida; and they bring a blind man unto him, and besought him to touch him. And he took the blind man by the hand, and led him out of the town; and when he had spit on his eyes, and put his hands upon him, he asked him if he saw ought. And he looked up, and said, I see men as trees, walking. After that he put his hands again upon his eyes, and made him look up: and he was restored, and saw every man clearly. And he sent him away to his house, saying, Neither go into the town, nor tell it to any in the town.

Too often, when people beg us (*parakalousin*) to do something others cannot do (or cannot do as well), we take it as a sign of how important we are. We then proceed to use the occasion to demonstrate our importance to as large an audience as possible. On the other hand, we find Jesus going again and again and yet again away from the admiring crowds in order to meet someone's needs privately.

I should be more responsive to people's real needs and more poised to help individuals than I am to showcase my abilities. The reality of private spiritual substance over public religious symbolism is basic to true Christian ministry.

MARK 8:29–30

And he saith unto them, But whom say ye that I am? And Peter answereth and saith unto him, Thou art the Christ. And he charged them that they should tell no man of him.

In today's evangelical religious world, Jesus would never become a recognized name or a person of importance. He betrayed here a complete lack of appreciation for the prime importance of name recognition.

Jesus did a wonderful job discipling His followers, teaching God's truth, and compassionately meeting people's needs. On the other hand, He apparently did not realize how essential it was to let people know Who He was. He never quite grasped the critical nature of such matters as building His image and of making a big public impact.

Today, Jesus' name and likeness would never be used in advertising great conferences, "experiences," and "happenings." After all, He never had an advance man, an advertising budget, entertaining Christian "artists," and a skillful "worship leader" for His ministry.

What a pity!

MARK 8:29–31

And he saith unto them, But whom say ye that I am? And Peter answereth and saith unto him, Thou art the Christ. And he charged them that they should tell no man of him. And he began to teach them, that the Son of man must suffer many things, and be rejected of the elders, and of the chief priests, and scribes, and be killed, and after three days rise again.

He said to them, "But who do you say that I am?" Peter answered and said to Him, "You are the Christ." Then He strictly warned them that they should tell no one about Him. And He began to teach them that the Son of Man must suffer many things, be rejected by the elders and chief priests and scribes, be killed, and after three days rise again.

"He strictly warned them that they should tell no one about Him" (NKJV). How does this harmonize with the Great Commission in Matthew 28:19–20 and Acts 1:8? There are clear indications that the contexts are different.

In Mark 8, Jesus was talking to His closest disciples before His death and resurrection. In the last chapter of Matthew, He was talking to His followers after accomplishing (Luke 9:31) all the purpose for which He had come. During Jesus' lifetime, His purpose was to present Himself and His credentials as the prophesied Messiah— knowing He would be rejected. His disciples' purpose was to minister in His name to reinforce this presentation (e.g., Mark 6:7ff.) and to listen and learn. They were not charged with any polemical responsibility to convince people Who He was or to "sell" Him as the Messiah.

In Mark 8, Jesus was teaching Old Testament truth and performing physical miracles. In Acts 1, He was preparing His followers to receive the Holy Spirit and thus be enabled (and commanded) to live a spiritual life and share spiritual truth with others.

My charge, living in the church age, is (1) to accept and receive the Holy Spirit by accepting God's forgiveness for my sins through the death of Christ, (2) to be filled with the Holy Spirit, the author of both Old and New Testaments (Eph. 5:18), (3) to live the Spirit-filled life (Eph. 5:19ff.), and (4) to obey God's leading in sharing God's truth with other people (Acts 10:19–20).

I should read the Bible regularly and study it carefully to discern its meaning and the progression and sequence of God's working in history. This will help me to recognize that Christianity is the truth concerning God, man, and the universe for all eternity and is based on historical truth, not contemporary feelings or opinions.

MARK 8:31–32

And he began to teach them, that the Son of man must suffer many things, and be rejected of the elders, and of the chief priests, and scribes, and be killed, and after three days rise again. And he spake that saying openly. And Peter took him, and began to rebuke him.

Jesus knew He was not just predicting the future and talking theologically. He knew that He personally was going to suffer these unimaginable tortures and indignities. Yet He could talk about them calmly with His disciples—who were not able to accept them calmly. Facing the persecution, torture, and death did not make a dent in His inner calm and peace because He knew there was also a resurrection. He knew God was still in charge and the ultimate purpose for everything in God's plans and God's will was under perfect control by God's wisdom and God's love.

This is still true. Situations of overwhelming difficulty and potential fearfulness cannot touch my inner peace as long as I am careful to be always in God's will. God is in charge of all events, and His purposes for me are all controlled by His love for me.

MARK 8:33–34

But when he had turned about and looked on his disciples, he rebuked Peter, saying, Get thee behind me, Satan: for thou savourest not the things that be of God, but the things that be of men.

And when he had called the people unto him with his disciples also, he said unto them, Whosoever will come after me, let him deny himself, and take up his cross, and follow me.

Several translations indicate a paragraph break between verses 33 and 34. I do not believe it belongs there. Verses 34–38 are a further explanation of Jesus' rebuke of Peter in verse 33 for Peter's behavior and attitude in verse 32 in reaction to Jesus' statement in verse 31.

Jesus gave the disciples an accurate prediction of His coming rejection, torture, crucifixion, and resurrection. Peter saw these things only from a worldly point of view and entirely missed the fact and meaning of the resurrection. He quickly corrected Jesus, telling Him not to talk so pessimistically about His future. What Peter did not grasp was that when experiences that are "bad things" from a selfish and worldly point of view come from the hand of God, they are really "good things" and will always accomplish the greater glory of God and the greater blessing of His people.

Visualizing, verbalizing, and honestly facing the future surrendered to the will of God cannot be pessimistic, regardless of what the future holds. To follow our own dreams is counterproductive and self-destructive when our dreams of fulfillment and success are based on our worldly standards of self-indulgence and self-glorification. The way of real fulfillment will be to "deny self" and "come after" Jesus with complete faith that God's will is the way of true fulfillment, no matter what it looks like from a selfish and worldly point of view. After all, His will is always based on His greater wisdom and His infinite love.

MARK 8:33

But when he had turned about and looked on his disciples, he rebuked Peter, saying, Get thee behind me, Satan: for thou savourest not the things that be of God, but the things that be of men.

A dynamic but accurate translation of the Greek for "Get behind Me" (*'upage opiso*) is "Back off!" (cf. Luke 4:8). Jesus plainly rebuked Peter but in doing so also identified the ultimate source of Peter's attitude or mindset.

The motivation behind Peter's correction of Jesus' negative attitude toward His future was not concern for Jesus nor friendly encouragement toward a more positive mindset. Rather it was Peter's desire to project a vision of fulfillment measured entirely by human and worldly standards of success. Jesus' response indicates that the source of this mindset is Satan himself. The entire New Age movement with its desire to control one's future according to one's own dreams by visualizing and verbalizing good things is not merely self-centered but is a part of the satanic kosmos and has no place in the life and ministry of a child of God.

Satan's program since the Garden of Eden has been encouraging self-indulgence in defiance of the Word of God. His method has often included "convenient" interpretations of God's Word to cater to human desires (Gen. 3:1–5; Matt. 4:5–6). My natural human ego and selfishness need constantly to be reminded that God's Word and God's will must take precedence in all decisions and actions. Self-worship = Satan worship.

MARK 8:34–35; 9:2

> *And when he had called the people unto him with his disciples also, he said unto them, Whosoever will come after me, let him deny himself, and take up his cross, and follow me. For whosoever will save his life shall lose it; but whosoever shall lose his life for my sake and the gospel's, the same shall save it. . . . And after six days Jesus taketh with him Peter, and James, and John, and leadeth them up into an high mountain apart by themselves: and he was transfigured before them.*

How many times in my contemporary world do I read, view, and hear the lie that to "find happiness" I must "follow my dream"? That is not what Jesus said. And it is not true!

Jesus said clearly that I may find the real life for which I was designed, created, and redeemed only when I deny my own dreams of self-indulgence and self-glorification and follow Him. As if to illustrate how this works out, the very next thing the Holy Spirit directed Mark to write after Jesus' saying "follow me" was what happened when Peter, James and John followed Him up the mountain "apart by themselves." They were given a glimpse of the glory of Jesus Himself and heard the Word of God testify to Jesus' identity as God.

If I truly follow Jesus in trusting obedience and listen to the voice of God through His Word (apart, by myself), the primary vision that will control me and fulfill me is not a visualization of my own dreams but a truer view of Him and His glory. Only when I lose myself and my "life" in Who He is will I find my own real life.

MARK 8:34–35

And when he had called the people unto him with his disciples also, he said unto them, Whosoever will come after me, let him deny himself, and take up his cross, and follow me. For whosoever will save his life shall lose it; but whosoever shall lose his life for my sake and the gospel's, the same shall save it.

I am not at all sure that the words *also* (NKJV) or *along with* (NIV) should have been inserted in verse 34. They are not in the Greek (*ochlon sun tois mathetais autou*). The context would better justify the dynamic translation (interpretation) "He called to Himself the people who were with His disciples."

The New Testament does not teach that Christianity has cognoscenti like the Gnostics or superior vocational religious classes like hierarchical denominations. God deals with human beings as individuals, and His will for and relationship with each person are unique to that person. After all, the Lord Jesus could not only observe distinct behavioral responses to His teaching but also knew the unique attitudinal response of every individual (John 2:25). Jesus often took His disciples aside for teaching and for experiences not involving others.

Jesus was talking directly and specifically to those people who were "with His disciples" (*sun tois mathetais autou*). The teaching about denying oneself and totally obeying the will of God found in the following verses (34*b*–37) was intended only for those who were already demonstrating a special interest in what Jesus did and said by accompanying His disciples in following Him. He warned them that following Him called for total commitment. He wanted them to know that being curious, or even "deeply interested" (Acts 17:21, 32–33), would not prepare them to be all they were meant to be in relation to Him and His ministry.

I should take this message seriously for myself and share candidly with those who may be "seekers" after "experiences" with God.

MARK 8:34–36

And when he had called the people unto him with his disciples also, he said unto them, Whosoever will come after me, let him deny himself, and take up his cross, and follow me. For whosoever will save his life shall lose it; but whosoever shall lose his life for my sake and the gospel's, the same shall save it. For what shall it profit a man, if he shall gain the whole world, and lose his own soul?

Jesus is warning me about living the only life God gave me with the aim of being a great success in the eyes of the world, even of the "Christian world." If I should do so at the expense of never becoming exactly that person God created and redeemed me to be, it would be an inexpressible waste, ultimately disappointing both to me and to God.

This may mean I should stop up my ears to the voice of my own desires, plans, dreams, and ambitions and open them to the Word of God as I make it my primary business in life to follow Jesus.

MARK 8:36–37

For what shall it profit a man, if he shall gain the whole world, and lose his own soul? Or what shall a man give in exchange for his soul?

The word translated "soul" (*psuche*) means roughly "life" and has some of the same problems of multiple meanings as the English word *life*. Depending on the context, *psuche* can mean physical life (the union of "soul" and body), spiritual life (the union of the "soul" with God), or biographical life (how I choose to live my "life").

In this context, I believe "soul" is a legitimate translation because *psuche* appears to refer to both spiritual and biographical life. In these verses, I am asked to compare the opportunity for an intimate personal relationship with God with the frustrating search for fulfilling relationships that characterizes most people's lives. I am also asked to face the fact that God, Who lovingly created me, knows far better than I how best my time and energy should be invested during my time here on earth.

Logically, the answers all seem very obvious. The real life choices are mine to make (and to live with).

MARK 9

MARK 9:1

> *And he said unto them, Verily I say unto you, That there be some of them that stand here, which shall not taste of death, till they have seen the kingdom of God come with power.*

Having heard and read several explanations of this verse, I checked a modern commentary and found that it listed six distinct interpretations of its meaning.

My own reaction to it is conditioned by my belief that the words translated "kingdom" (*basileia* and cognates) in the New Testament do not refer to an institution but to the acceptance of the rulership of God in the personal individual life. While its meaning may include the little foretaste of Christ's glory given three of the apostles on the mountain (vv. 2–8), its primary reference is to the coming of the Holy Spirit to live in believers after the death and resurrection that Christ was to "accomplish" (Luke 9:31). The "power," then, would be the power of the Holy Spirit, which makes it possible for a person to be truly ruled by God in his personal life. This understanding is certainly consistent with the immediately preceding context (Mark 8:34–37).

It is still true that I am the one who must make the decision to turn control of my life over to the One Who designed and created it.

But I have the assurance that the power to overcome my natural but self-destructive tendencies toward self-indulgence and toward self-glorification is available if I will accept it in trusting obedience.

MARK 9:2

> *And after six days Jesus taketh with him Peter, and James, and John, and leadeth them up into an high mountain apart by themselves: and he was transfigured before them.*

As I skimmed this verse in the Greek, I was struck by the word translated "transfigured" (from *metamorpho*). This word is found only four times in the New Testament. Twice it refers to Jesus' transfiguration (cf. Matt. 17:2), and twice it refers to the change occurring in the individual Christian as we commit ourselves to obey God. The most familiar occurrence is in Romans 12:2, where we are exhorted to commit the use of our bodies as a sacrifice to God so that our minds may be "transfigured" (*metamorphousthe*) from following the thoughts, tastes, and attitudes of the contemporary world (*aioni touto*) around us and develop totally new (*anakainosei*) thoughts, tastes, and attitudes.

This is encouraging and inspiring. If I am willing to present my body to God and allow Him to control my mind, my whole mental outlook, my attitudes, my mindset, and my tastes will be "transfigured" in the same way Christ was changed before the disciples on the Mount of Transfiguration.

> *And do not be conformed to this world, but be transformed by the renewing of your mind, that you may prove what is that good and acceptable and perfect will of God. (Rom. 12:2 NKJV)*

MARK 9:2–4

> *And after six days Jesus taketh with him Peter, and James, and John, and leadeth them up into an high mountain apart by themselves: and he was transfigured before them. And his raiment*

*became shining, exceeding white as snow; so as no fuller on earth
can white them. And there appeared unto them Elias with Moses:
and they were talking with Jesus.*

"He was transfigured before them." In this transfiguration of
His appearance, Jesus did not change His real identity. He did not
suddenly become "more God" than He was before. The transfiguration revealed to the disciples only a small glimpse of what had been
true of Jesus from all eternity (John 8:58).

Jesus was the God of Moses while Moses was alive on earth
(Heb. 3:3–6). This was not the first time Moses had talked with
Him. They had had many conversations (Num. 12:8), beginning
with one beside a bush (Acts 7:31–33). Jesus was the God Who
answered Elijah when Elijah called for fire from heaven (1 Kings
18:36–38) and again when he had called for rain (1 Kings 17:1;
18:41–45). Jesus had talked personally with Elijah in a "still small
voice" (1 Kings 19:12).

Jesus is always the almighty God of the universe; He is always
the One Who loves me and watches over me. What He chooses for
me is always best for me. What I need to do is to follow Him up the
mountain like Peter, James, and John did ("apart by themselves") so
that I may get a glimpse of the reality of Who He always was and
eternally is.

MARK 9:2–6

*And after six days Jesus taketh with him Peter, and James, and
John, and leadeth them up into an high mountain apart by themselves: and he was transfigured before them. And his raiment became shining, exceeding white as snow; so as no fuller on earth
can white them. And there appeared unto them Elias with Moses:
and they were talking with Jesus. And Peter answered and said
to Jesus, Master, it is good for us to be here: and let us make three*

tabernacles; one for thee, and one for Moses, and one for Elias.
For he wist not what to say; for they were sore afraid.

It was obvious that God was doing something unusual. Peter did not know what was going on, but he felt that, as a follower of Jesus, he ought to do something appropriate. As a minister of Jesus (Mark 6:7–13), Peter decided that he ought to create some sort of worship experience. Having attended the Feast of Tabernacles ("booths"; Lev. 23; Num. 8) in Jerusalem and seeing what a great success it was, Peter decided it would be good to imitate that success right where he was.

Sometimes it is hard, as a conscientious Christian, to recognize that there are times when we can be blessed and can be a blessing by saying and doing nothing but waiting on God to do His work on His schedule (Acts 1:6–8). Blessed are those who, having nothing to say, say nothing. I always need God's arm around my shoulder—and then, on occasion, like Peter, I also need His hand over my mouth.

MARK 9:2

And after six days Jesus taketh with him Peter, and James, and
John, and leadeth them up into an high mountain apart by them-
selves: and he was transfigured before them.

Jesus, of course was—and is—God. Everything He did and said demonstrated that He was the Jewish Messiah and that He was God Himself. Yet the disciples, His closest human acquaintances, had not fully perceived Who He was. In the transfiguration, He gave three of them a glimpse and proof of the reality they had missed (cf. 2 Pet. 1:16–18). This was the kind of experience He had flatly refused to give the self-important religious leaders (Mark 8:11–12).

I believe the application to me in my day was defined by Jesus in the context of His establishment of apostolic authority in the Last Supper conversation and prayer in John 14–17 (John 17:20). There is a special blessing promised to me as I give top priority in my life to studying the life and teachings of Jesus and His apostles under the guidance of God the Holy Spirit (John 20:29; 2 Pet. 1:14–15). By faith I may experience the same type of revelatory transfiguration as Jesus' closest apostles. As I saturate myself in His Word and truly make Him the Lord of my life, I may see the "historical Jesus" as He really was—and is: God Almighty in human flesh.

MARK 9:5–7

And Peter answered and said to Jesus, Master, it is good for us to be here: and let us make three tabernacles; one for thee, and one for Moses, and one for Elias. For he wist not what to say; for they were sore afraid. And there was a cloud that overshadowed them: and a voice came out of the cloud, saying, This is my beloved Son: hear him.

Moses and Elijah were among the greatest religious leaders of all time. They served God faithfully and effectively in their own day and among their own people. The Jewish people idolized them and often referenced them (or their interpreters) as the ultimate authorities in spiritual and theological matters. Peter reflected this view and the voice of God corrected him.

The Word of God is still the final authority on Who Jesus is. And Jesus alone is worthy of worship. It is good to appreciate and respect those who serve God and interpret His Word, but final answers are not found by consulting well-known religious authorities. Ultimately, I must find the answers to life's questions by reading, believing, and carefully obeying God's Word. This is just as true for me as it was for Peter.

MARK 9:9–10

And as they came down from the mountain, he charged them that they should tell no man what things they had seen, till the Son of man were risen from the dead. And they kept that saying with themselves, questioning one with another what the rising from the dead should mean.

"Questioning what the rising from the dead meant" (NKJV). After all, this was a pretty bizarre saying, and Jesus often spoke in symbols and parables (Matt. 13:34). What they found out later was that this statement meant exactly what Jesus said. God, of course, is the master of language; He invented it. In communicating spiritual truth to men, He knows how to use symbols, metaphors, similes, and parables anytime they are appropriate to His purpose (Matt. 13:11–16).

As I read God's Word, however, I find that the use of symbols and figures of speech is often indicated in the context (e.g., Matt. 13:13; John 6:63; Acts 10:17, 34–35). The safest way to interpret God's Word is to start from the assumption that God is capable of communicating accurately what He wants me to know and that His Word means just what it says, no matter how unnatural, "unmodern," or even bizarre it may appear to me.

MARK 9:14, 17, 18B, 23–25

> *And when he came to his disciples, he saw a great multitude about them, and the scribes questioning with them. . . . And one of the multitude answered and said, Master, I have brought unto thee my son, which hath a dumb spirit . . . and I spake to thy disciples that they should cast him out; and they could not. . . . Jesus said unto him, If thou canst believe, all things are possible to him that believeth. And straightway the father of the child cried out, and said with tears, Lord, I believe; help thou mine unbelief. When Jesus saw that the people came running together, he rebuked the foul spirit, saying unto him, Thou dumb and deaf spirit, I charge thee, come out of him, and enter no more into him.*

The presence of these disputing scribes is interesting. I believe that these scribes had enlisted the cooperation of the father of this boy with the stubborn debilitating spirit to test Jesus and His disciples. In its original presentation, this may not have been an appeal for help but a cynical attempt to embarrass publicly Jesus and His disciples.

Jesus then put the father on the spot. He made it clear there would be no healing of his son on the basis of false pretenses and skepticism but held out the hope of healing for his son on the basis of sincerity and trust. Immediately the man's fatherly instincts took over. He forgot about the scribes and appealed for help in doing whatever he must do for his son to be whole. Jesus responded to His sincerity and desperation—but quite pointedly not as a public display.

This is instructive. Jesus apparently does not respond to casual or cynical requests and challenges. On the other hand, His automatic instinct is to meet our acknowledged and genuine need in appropriate ways. When I turn to Him, acknowledge my own helplessness, confess my emotional investment, and trust Him completely, He will do exactly what is best for me.

MARK 9:29

And he said unto them, This kind can come forth by nothing, but by prayer and fasting.

I am not certain I understand all that this means, but I think the context indicates that Jesus was talking about the sincere prayer of the father, not the disciples (see previous devotional). Even Jesus Himself did not heal the boy until the father's attitude was right (v. 24; cf. Matt. 13:58, Mark 6:5).

This would fit perfectly with the observations on Mark 5:21–43, especially verse 36. If I know absolutely that God can answer my prayers and that He knows my heart attitude and desire, then I may express my request to Him in complete confidence. This confidence is not that He will always do what I ask but that He will always do what is best. This brings real peace.

MARK 9:30–31A

And they departed thence, and passed through Galilee; and he would not that any man should know it. For he taught his disciples, and said unto them, The Son of man is delivered into the hands of men, and they shall kill him.

Jesus understood all along that His purposes in coming to earth would culminate in His crucifixion. He also knew what the schedule was. He found it necessary to avoid publicity for the good things He had done and the truth He had taught because they incited the opposition of the religious establishment.

Too often, when we do good things or do the "right thing," there is disappointment over our not getting credit for it. Perhaps our motive is faulty; do we do good things just for the attention it may bring. Or perhaps we do not have a true understanding of the nature of sinful man. We need to realize that it is in the nature of the fallen human race, that any time I do the right thing or a good thing—especially if people happen to acknowledge and appreciate it—there is going to be someone who is envious, jealous, angry, and resentful (2 Tim. 3:12)!

The lesson here is that it is wise to do my best to do what is right as a matter of principle and to leave in God's hands the matter of whether I am recognized for it. I might even follow the example of Jesus and avoid recognition until that day when God chooses to say, "Well done."

MARK 9:33–34

And he came to Capernaum: and being in the house he asked them, What was it that ye disputed among yourselves by the way? But they held their peace: for by the way they had disputed among themselves, who should be the greatest.

How much of the "disputing" and criticizing among Jesus' disciples even today really has to do with "Who will be the greatest?" I need to be willing to speak up when matters of real substance need to be defended but to avoid getting involved in disputes over position and status.

MARK 9:33–35

And he came to Capernaum: and being in the house he asked them, What was it that ye disputed among yourselves by the way? But they held their peace: for by the way they had disputed among themselves, who should be the greatest. And he sat down, and called the twelve, and saith unto them, If any man desire to be first, the same shall be last of all, and servant of all.

We often tend to measure our importance by the head count of people we have "won" or the number of people we are over in some capacity. Are we ever going to be surprised when we stand before the judgment and find that our real importance will be measured by the head count of those to whom we have been an effective servant in some way!

MARK 9:36–37

And he took a child, and set him in the midst of them: and when he had taken him in his arms, he said unto them, Whosoever shall receive one of such children in my name, receiveth me: and whosoever shall receive me, receiveth not me, but him that sent me.

I think there is something profound here about the image of God in every human person. Pantheism is a lie, and God is a God of categories. There is a qualitative difference in a human being's rights and responsibilities as a child and that same person's rights and responsibilities as an adult. On the other hand, the person who is a child is no less a person than is any adult.

Christians who accept the biblical definition of personhood will have respect for every child's personhood as well as for his childhood. I do not believe we may demand maturity of children, but we are to encourage it and help them to cultivate it. At the same time, we must respect their full rights as a person carrying the image of God. And I most certainly believe this begins at conception!

MARK 9:37

> *Whosoever shall receive one of such children in my name, receiveth me: and whosoever shall receive me, receiveth not me, but him that sent me.*

There are two Greek words regularly translated "receive" in English (*lambano* and *dechomai*). The fact that one of them is found four times in this one verse makes it unavoidable to look at the meaning of these words to grasp what Jesus was saying. The word *lambano* means "taking" as opposed to rejecting or ignoring. *Dechomai*, on the other hand, means to receive with hospitality or honor as one would receive a guest or an ambassador. *Lambano* would describe receiving an ambassador or a specially appointed foreign dignitary at the border, examining his credentials and admitting him to the country; *dechomai*, then, would describe the red-carpet reception given in his honor as representative of a great king or country (1 Thess. 2:13).

A cognate of *dechomai* (*dechetai*) is used four times in this verse. Jesus said a child is to be received "in my name" and that doing so is equal to receiving "Him who sent Me." I believe Jesus was saying that every child sent into the world is a very special representative of God, in Whose image he is made (Gen. 1:26–28). What a privilege to be a parent. Or a teacher. And what a responsibility! And what a gross enormity is the sin of murdering the ambassador at the border through abortion.

I thank the Lord for the special privilege He has afforded me in the course of my life to work with so many wonderful persons when they were children and young people. What a joy and honor to be chosen to introduce them to the marvels of God's truth and God's world and to pray for them as they assume their responsibilities as His appointed representatives here.

MARK 9:38–40

And John answered him, saying, Master, we saw one casting out devils in thy name, and he followeth not us: and we forbad him, because he followeth not us. But Jesus said, Forbid him not: for there is no man which shall do a miracle in my name, that can lightly speak evil of me. For he that is not against us is on our part.

The Majority Text states verse 40 as a general principle: "For he who is not against you is on your side." Before issuing a stern warning in verse 42 concerning care in the use of our own influence, Jesus is suggesting we not waste our keen sense of biblical discernment correcting others who may not be in our "camp."

In today's confusion of cults and compromises, there is no question that young people and new Christians need direction in theologically sound beliefs and practices. But our warning young Christians and our attacking fellow Christians are not the same thing.

My own view is that a simple and positive statement of biblical faith needs only to be supplemented by our teaching (and by exampling) careful study and faithful obedience to God's Word. Young people and new Christians may need some clear theological guidance to get them started, but our primary purpose should be to facilitate their growing to be mature and discerning Christians on their own. I do not think this is best done by our telling them exactly what they must believe about everything but by our helping them to build a solid connection with God through their own study of His Word and to establish the habit of disciplined obedience to what God's Word commands.

MARK 9:43

And if thy hand offend thee, cut it off: it is better for thee to enter into life maimed, than having two hands to go into hell, into the fire that never shall be quenched.

Commentators tend either to tiptoe around verses like this or to overexplain them, usually using words such as *metaphor* or *hyperbole*.

My own view is that the key to the real meaning of Mark 9:43 (and vv. 45 and 47) is found in the mode of the single word translated "offend thee" (*skandalize*). It is subjunctive. In view of the general biblical principle of personal responsibility (e.g., Deut. 24:16), it should be clear that one's hand never "causes" one to sin nor does the foot (v. 45) or the eye (v. 47).

Jesus was using physical members as a familiar and understandable metaphor for voluntarily chosen spiritual and moral mindsets or attitudes that cause us to sin. The "members" that really need to be excised from our thought life and behavior are things such as "fornication, uncleanness, passion, evil desire, and covetousness, which is idolatry" as Paul tells us in Colossians 3:5 (cf. also Rom. 8:13). It is these kinds of voluntarily chosen attitudes that would cause us to sin in trampling upon innocent children to satisfy our own priority of selfishness and self-indulgence (v. 42).

My hands, eyes, and feet will behave themselves quite nicely and cause me no problems if I will just "cut off" the attitudes listed in Colossians 3:5.

> *Therefore put to death your members which are on the earth: fornication, uncleanness, passion, evil desire, and covetousness, which is idolatry. Because of these things the wrath of God is coming upon the sons of disobedience. (Col. 3:5–6 NKJV)*

MARK 9:49–50

> *For every one shall be salted with fire, and every sacrifice shall be salted with salt. Salt is good: but if the salt have lost his saltness, wherewith will ye season it? Have salt in yourselves, and have peace one with another.*

In seeking a personal meaning from these verses I found the commentaries of little help since most follow the monastic desert manuscripts and omit the reference to sacrifices. Following the Textus Receptus and noting the context, I believe Jesus may be making a profound and meaningful observation followed by an admonition consistent with the entire context starting at verse 33.

"For everyone will be seasoned with fire" may refer to the fact, observed in the literature of all cultures, that in a fallen world, everyone's "life scenario" will be tested by major tragic elements. No one escapes pain, disappointment, and disharmony. In the lives only of those who have sacrificed their inner demand for self-fulfillment to the higher demand of obeying God (vv. 33–35) may the short-range tragedies of life hold positive meaning and make sense as elements in the long-range plot of God's wonderful, loving, positive purposes.

But sacrifices must be salted (Lev. 2:13). This refers to Jesus' command to believers to maintain their distinctive testimony as the "salt of the earth" (Matt. 5:13). When faced with life's disappointments, I must not lose my saltiness by compromising the consistency of my obedience to biblical commands (Matt. 5:13) or hide the embarrassing tragic elements of my life from the sight of others (Matt. 5:14–17). By doing either, I may cancel the opportunity for my "life tragedies" to make a positive contribution to God's purposes in the lives of others in this world.

MARK 10

MARK 10:2–3

And the Pharisees came to him, and asked him, Is it lawful for a man to put away his wife? tempting him. And he answered and said unto them, What did Moses command you?

The Pharisees were not seeking truth or guidance; they were "testing Him." This is the kind of antagonistic question often asked of politicians because any answer will certainly offend someone. Politicians, of course, have become aware of this strategy and usually are skilled at talking their way around these questions and avoiding "taking sides." Among the Pharisees there were several well-defined schools of thought concerning lawfully divorcing one's wife, and these interlocutors aimed to force Jesus to fit into one or the other of their categories to make Him unpopular with those in other camps.

Jesus did not give a political answer. He was not afraid to make enemies of those with wrong opinions. On the other hand, He refused to "agree" or "disagree" on the basis of the Pharisee's categories. He started His answer to their question right where they should have started in seeking for truth in such a vital matter. He asked them to look into God's Word.

If I really need the truth about any subject related to real life, looking for a "school of thought" or an "expert" who says what I like or want to hear is not the right first step. I need to look with a receptive heart and an obedient attitude to the Word of God.

MARK 10:2–4

And the Pharisees came to him, and asked him, Is it lawful for a man to put away his wife? tempting him. And he answered and said unto them, What did Moses command you? And they said, Moses suffered to write a bill of divorcement, and to put her away.

At the time God led Moses to write this commandment, it would have been considered quite strict and very restrictive of the rights of men in the cultures of the surrounding areas. Men were allowed to kick out their wives indiscriminately and then tell any lie about them that they pleased. What God demanded of the Israelites was that a man put a written document in the hands of his wife (Deut. 24:1–5), accepting personal responsibility for the dissolution of the God-ordained relationship (Gen. 2:22–24). As an aside, this is just one more indication that the moral and religious life of the ancient Israelites was based on written rather than oral communication.

What Moses wrote was a permission granted by God as He weaned His people from the animalistic sexual habits of the Egyptians and introduced them to the spiritual and moral realities and blessings of His original creative design for marriage (cf. Exod. 20:14; Deut. 5:18; Mal. 2:16).

As a Christian today, with the power of the indwelling Holy Spirit, I may return to the original model for marriage (Matt. 19:8), which is a life-long relationship of one man and one woman. Period.

MARK 10:2–4

And the Pharisees came to him, and asked him, Is it lawful for a man to put away his wife? tempting him. And he answered and said unto them, What did Moses command you? And they said, Moses suffered to write a bill of divorcement, and to put her away.

The Pharisees never answered Jesus' question! Jesus was focused on the command (*eneteilato*) of the Creator while the Pharisees focused on the permission (*enetrepsen*) of the great religious leader. This is typical of people dealing with the question of divorce, even in our own day. Too many people who claim to know God do not really seek to conduct their married lives according to God's command but seek for permission from "Christian leaders" to live according to their own desires.

The divorce rate among evangelicals is about the same as that of atheists. This continues to be so—and to worsen—in spite of the fact that for the past few decades, Christian books and seminars on enriching marriage have multiplied exponentially.

We need to quit approaching this problem with a pharisaical bag of tricks and focus instead on God's commands. After all, God designed and created men, women, and marriage. When the chips are down, the thing it takes to hold my Christian marriage together is not increased intimacy as defined by the psychological experts but absolute integrity as defined by God's Word.

MARK 10:4–8

And they said, Moses suffered to write a bill of divorcement, and to put her away. And Jesus answered and said unto them, For the hardness of your heart he wrote you this precept. But from the beginning of the creation God made them male and female. For this cause shall a man leave his father and mother, and cleave to his wife; and they twain shall be one flesh: so then they are no more twain, but one flesh.

"But from the beginning of the creation" (cf. Matt. 19:8–9). This is the key phrase in understanding Jesus' teaching about the marriage relationship. Jesus was pointing out that God permitted (*epetrepsin*) before the cross behaviors in relation to marriage that were far short of the original creative model. But to God, the realities of the model were unchanged and the two persons had become permanently one in His eyes.

What God had allowed to unregenerate man was never in God's original plan, which has always remained exactly the same. Jesus clarified the permanence of the original model, because He Himself was about to open to the human race the possibility of regeneration. This meant that the temporary Mosaic adaptations and permissions would no longer be necessary or acceptable. Since Jesus' death on the cross for our sins, we may now have God the Holy Spirit living in our bodies. This makes it possible for the Christian, if he will accept the truth of God's Word and obey it, to live according to the original Edenic model.

God expects me as a Christian husband to live according to the original marriage model. My attitude and behavior toward my wife never has to be an unregenerate reaction to her (occasionally unregenerate) behavior but may be controlled by God's Spirit according to the truth of God's Word. For me, as a Christian, the original marriage model is not just the "ideal" but is the applicable and expected biblical model. It is God's command.

MARK 10:6–12

But from the beginning of the creation God made them male and female. For this cause shall a man leave his father and mother, and cleave to his wife; and they twain shall be one flesh: so then they are no more twain, but one flesh. What therefore God hath joined together, let not man put asunder. And in the house his disciples asked him again of the same matter. And he saith unto them, Whosoever shall put away his wife, and marry another, committeth adultery against her. And if a woman shall put

away her husband, and be married to another, she committeth
adultery.

Jesus said, "God 'made them male and female,'" and He said, "what God has joined together." When He said this, Jesus was saying that, like everything else in life, marriage is not about us; it is about Him (cf. Eph. 5:31–32).

A young man may decide for himself whether to try to make it in major league baseball. He may decide for himself which team to join. But once he has made these decisions, he finds there are rules, there is a baseball commissioner, and there are umpires. He is then expected to play by the rules.

In the matter of marriage, God is the baseball commissioner, His Word is the rulebook, and God's Holy Spirit is the umpire. I should play by His rules.

MARK 10:13–15

And they brought young children to him, that he should touch
them: and his disciples rebuked those that brought them. But
when Jesus saw it, he was much displeased, and said unto them,
Suffer the little children to come unto me, and forbid them not: for
of such is the kingdom of God. Verily I say unto you, Whosoever
shall not receive the kingdom of God as a little child, he shall not
enter therein.

Jesus' response to His disciples' rejection of those bringing little children was twofold. First, of course, He reinforced the lesson He had taught in 9:37 concerning the awesome responsibility of recognizing, respecting, and ministering to the full human personhood of little children.

Then Jesus utilized the lowly status assigned to children as they faced life with their open, curious, and learning attitude to teach His disciples an important lesson. He admonished His ambitious and sometimes self-important disciples that relating to God would require a humble, childlike, learning attitude. In this passage, the lesson is especially clear as we understand the phrase "kingdom of God" (*basileian tou Theou*) to refer to personal acceptance of God's rulership of our respective individual lives, rather than some vague institutional entity.

As I become older and I hope more mature, I need to remember that keeping my relationship to God fresh via unbroken fellowship with Him will not be possible without a humble and teachable attitude. I will never get so smart I do not need to learn more from God.

MARK 10:13–14

> *And they brought young children to him, that he should touch them: and his disciples rebuked those that brought them. But when Jesus saw it, he was much displeased, and said unto them, Suffer the little children to come unto me, and forbid them not: for of such is the kingdom of God.*

The disciples recognized, of course, that Jesus had a powerful ability to meet people's needs, based on a genuine concern and compassion for them. Unfortunately, the disciples' primary interest in Jesus' power was too often limited to what it could do for them and their own ambitions (Matt. 20:20–21; Mark 9:33–34; Luke 9:46). And whenever Jesus attempted to explain to them what His real motivation and ministry were, they quickly tried to redirect His thinking and His approach in somewhat more "practical" directions (Matt. 15:12; 16:22–23; Mark 8:32–33).

You can see, then, why the disciples would discourage doting mothers from bothering Jesus to bless their little children. Children didn't count. In that highly patriarchal society, neither women nor children had any influence; they didn't "vote." For this reason, the disciples did not want Jesus wasting His time with them.

But Jesus' motivation of care and compassion toward all people did not fit their categories at all. While they were fixated on personal ambition, Jesus was focused on human need. I should focus where Jesus focused.

MARK 10:14–16

But when Jesus saw it, he was much displeased, and said unto them, Suffer the little children to come unto me, and forbid them not: for of such is the kingdom of God. Verily I say unto you, Whosoever shall not receive the kingdom of God as a little child, he shall not enter therein. And he took them up in his arms, put his hands upon them, and blessed them.

Jesus "put His hands on them and blessed them." Children are little human persons. God's assignment for human beings, made in His image, is to be the responsible supervisors and stewards of His earth. His plan for doing this includes a very long period of growing, maturing, and learning. Unlike the animals, which mature rapidly and live almost exclusively by instinct, humans are meant to be governed by deliberate thought and by principled and responsible decision. Little persons coming into today's world need all the blessing they can get.

I am grateful to God for allowing me to spend much of my working life dealing with children and young people. For many years, I made it a practice to pray for my students by name daily. When I became an administrator, I prayed for the faculty members responsible for working directly with children and young people and encouraged them to pray for each of their students by name every day. I realize I can never know the full extent to which God may have answered my petitions over the years, but He has been gracious to lift the curtain on a few very interesting results of my prayers and testimony.

This should encourage me in "retirement" to remember in prayer those children and young persons facing life in this difficult world whenever God calls them to my attention.

MARK 10:17–18

And when he was gone forth into the way, there came one running, and kneeled to him, and asked him, Good Master, what shall I do that I may inherit eternal life? And Jesus said unto him, Why callest thou me good? there is none good but one, that is, God.

Jesus perceived right away that this young man worked hard at being a "good man" in order to please God (v. 20). The way he phrased his question to Jesus indicated he considered Jesus to be a success at being a "good man." He hoped therefore that Jesus could advise him about improving in being "good" so that he could please God and receive eternal life.

Before dealing with the man's question, Jesus dealt with his false assumptions. Jesus' question and observation in verse 18 pointed to two important truths: (1) Jesus' goodness was not a teachable human achievement but a natural aspect of His godhood, and (2) no one but God is "good enough" to have eternal life.

If I am to become all I was created to be in God's image, it will never be accomplished by a self-improvement program. I must confess my own failure and inability. I must accept the forgiveness of my sins through the death of Christ. Only then may I accept the gracious gift of the controlling power of the Holy Spirit to understand and obey His Word.

MARK 10:17

And when he was gone forth into the way, there came one running, and kneeled to him, and asked him, Good Master, what shall I do that I may inherit eternal life?

Apparently, the one kneeling before Jesus was a wealthy young Jewish man who was conscientious about obeying the laws and traditions of his faith (Matt. 19:18–22). His question reflected the Jews' understanding that there was life after death, that this life was everlasting, and that there was some connection between everlasting life and one's behavior here on earth. They had a lot of their facts right but misunderstood the relationship and sequence among those facts.

This young man did not realize that receiving everlasting life was not the result of "doing" something. Everlasting life does not come from successful "good behavior" but from confession of failure and acceptance of forgiveness. The connection with good behavior is that such behavior is a natural result of a relationship that exists only after confession of sin and acceptance of life everlasting as a free gift.

> *This is a faithful saying and worthy of all acceptance, that Christ Jesus came into the world to save sinners, of whom I am chief. (1 Tim. 1:15 NKJV)*

I am not saved because I deserve it or have earned it. I believe my greatest appreciation and enjoyment of the absolute assurance of eternal life come as I grasp accurately my total failure to deserve it.

MARK 10:19–21

> *Thou knowest the commandments, Do not commit adultery, do not kill, do not steal, do not bear false witness, defraud not, honour thy father and mother. And he answered and said unto him, Master, all these have I observed from my youth. Then Jesus beholding him loved him, and said unto him, One thing thou lackest: go thy way, sell whatsoever thou hast, and give to the poor, and thou shalt have treasure in heaven: and come, take up the cross, and follow me.*

The Ten Commandments are divided into two "tables" of laws. The first four laws define one's relationship to God as God; the remaining six regulate one's relationship to other people as human beings made in God's image. Jesus and a Jewish lawyer agreed that the first table of four laws, recognizing and worshiping God, was the "great" (Matt. 22:36–40), or "first," (Mark 12:28–34) commandment of God, and that the second table of six laws, dealing with human interrelations, was the second greatest, or derivative, commandment.

Jesus questioned this young man concerning the second table of the law, which he claimed to have kept. Jesus then challenged the man's claim by suggesting he demonstrate his commitment to God by being totally unselfish in relating to others. This would seem to be a logical expression of a complete commitment of obedience to the second table of God's law.

What Jesus said next was a powerful reinforcement of the implication of His first response to the young man's original question. When the young man had called Jesus "good," Jesus had pointed out that no one was "good" but God. After challenging His questioner to prove his claim of an obedient attitude toward God's commandments, Jesus expressed His own claim to be God by exercising the prerogative of God in commanding the young man to give up everything and follow Him.

My whole life, including possessions and positions, are God's property. I am authorized to dispose of them only as a steward, following the commands of God's Word.

MARK 10:21–22

Then Jesus beholding him loved him, and said unto him, One thing thou lackest: go thy way, sell whatsoever thou hast, and give to the poor, and thou shalt have treasure in heaven: and come, take up the cross, and follow me. And he was sad at that saying, and went away grieved: for he had great possessions.

"For he had great possessions." If this man had liquidated all his earthly possessions, realized millions of dollars, and had given it all away, the final result would be no different from possessing only five dollars and giving it all away. The fact that he possessed great wealth made this young man sad at the thought of giving it all away. This says nothing about possessing wealth but a great deal about one's attitude toward possessions.

Having been lovingly created by God in His own image to enjoy an eternal existence, this young man had limited his definition of who he was to his temporal (i.e., temporary) and merely physical possessions. What a shame!

God intends for me to enjoy the temporal aspects of His wonderful world as He chooses to bless me with His choice of possessions, relationships, experiences, and so forth. On the other hand, my sense of eternal personhood and security may be safely trusted only to my relationship with Him and His loving purposes for my life as revealed in His inerrant Word.

MARK 10:23–24

> *And Jesus looked round about, and saith unto his disciples, How hardly shall they that have riches enter into the kingdom of God! And the disciples were astonished at his words. But Jesus answereth again, and saith unto them, Children, how hard is it for them that trust in riches to enter into the kingdom of God!*

The native Greek manuscripts (and many others) make it clear that in verse 24 Jesus said that those who allow themselves to place their confidence and assurance in their wealth and what it can do for them will have great difficulty accepting the rulership of God. The really frightening implication comes from the apparent fact that verse 24 is the explanation for the meaning of verse 23. "Those that have" becomes synonymous with "those who trust in."

Jesus seems to be saying that it is virtually automatic that those who are wealthy will place such confidence in their wealth, that they simply cannot accept the fact of their total dependence upon God and place themselves under His rulership. This is, of course, quite understandable and natural. After all, why should I surrender control of my life to God when plan B is working so well for me?

This may serve as a warning. Nothing—that is nothing—besides accepting God's grace can bring me into the wonderful life for which I was created. Not wealth, not education, not position, not connections, not hard work, not "successful ministry." There is no plan B for enjoying the very best.

MARK 10:23

And Jesus looked round about, and saith unto his disciples, How hardly shall they that have riches enter into the kingdom of God!

Here, once again, we find a statement of Jesus that is made much clearer by our understanding that the "kingdom of God" (*basileia tou Theou* and cognates) does not refer to a vague institutional entity coterminous with the church or the nation of Israel. Jesus' statement concerning the difficulty experienced by those possessing riches in "entering the kingdom" describes well a personal crisis of decision. This description fits perfectly with the understanding that the "kingdom" (rulership) of God always refers to personal, individual acceptance of the control of God over one's life demonstrated by consistent obedience to His Word.

Nothing I possess in the way of material things or positions or accomplishments or relationships is ever more important than my knowing and obeying God's will as revealed in His Word.

MARK 10:24B–25, 27

But Jesus answereth again, and saith unto them, Children, how hard is it for them that trust in riches to enter into the kingdom of God! It is easier for a camel to go through the eye of a needle, than for a rich man to enter into the kingdom of God. . . . And Jesus looking upon them saith, With men it is impossible, but not with God: for with God all things are possible.

Verse 25 has been the subject of a plethora of creative eisegetical acrobatics. It means exactly what it says. It was meant to reinforce and underscore the meaning of the word *trust* (*pepoithotas*) in verse 24 and to prepare the disciples to understand and accept the literal truth of verse 27.

It is impossible for me to trust and obey God with the consistency I should without walking close to Him through the daily use of His inerrant Word. Only in this way is it possible for the author of that Word, God the Holy Spirit, to empower me to trust in Him alone so as to enter His kingdom by making Him the ruler (*basileian*) of my life.

MARK 10:27

> *And Jesus looking upon them saith, With men it is impossible, but not with God: for with God all things are possible.*

Jesus took advantage of a specific occasion to share a generally and universally applicable truth. On the other hand, it is significant that the specific situation had to do with money and material possessions. Jesus consistently warned that loving money could cut one off from many of the blessings of God (Matt. 6:24ff.; Luke 16:10–13). Material blessings are given to us to enjoy, but wealth is to be our servant to help us in being God's servant. It is not to be our master, to be served in place of our proper loving master, Who is God.

> *No one can serve two masters; for either he will hate the one and love the other, or else he will be loyal to the one and despise the other. You cannot serve God and mammon.* (Matt. 6:24 NKJV)

My confidence and my peace will be in God or in material wealth. It cannot be both. Only with the proper relationship to the power of God is it possible to master material blessings and serve God.

MARK 10:28–30

> *Then Peter began to say unto him, Lo, we have left all, and have followed thee. And Jesus answered and said, Verily I say unto you, There is no man that hath left house, or brethren, or sisters, or father, or mother, or wife, or children, or lands, for my sake, and the gospel's, but he shall receive an hundredfold now in this time, houses, and brethren, and sisters, and mothers, and children, and lands, with persecutions; and in the world to come eternal life.*

My own observation is that those who find themselves without some of the normal relationships of life because of their obedience to

God seem to have their lives enriched with more positive relationships among Christian brothers and sisters than they have time to enjoy.

MARK 10:31

> *But many that are first shall be last; and the last first.*

The context, both here (vv. 17–30) and in the parallel passage (Matt. 19:16–30) indicates Jesus is contrasting wealth, position, and influence in this world with position in relation to God in heaven. He appears to be talking about the priority of eternal values.

Eternal life starts when we become Christians, not when we die. In view of this, I like to think it possible for us to mature in the kingdom (rulership) of God and in our essentially eternal relationship to Him while still serving here on earth. The very real quality of our eternal relationship as it moves from "last" toward "first" will contrast sharply with those whose only measure of "success" in life is a fixation on visible, tangible, and measurable positions or possessions.

Living in God's Word will help me develop—here and now— criteria for reality and success that will not become totally invalid and outdated the minute I leave this physical world.

MARK 10:32–34

> *And they were in the way going up to Jerusalem; and Jesus went before them: and they were amazed; and as they followed, they were afraid. And he took again the twelve, and began to tell them what things should happen unto him, saying, Behold, we go up to Jerusalem; and the Son of man shall be delivered unto the chief priests, and unto the scribes; and they shall condemn him to death, and shall deliver him to the Gentiles: and they shall mock him, and shall scourge him, and shall spit upon him, and shall kill him: and the third day he shall rise again.*

Mark described Jesus' revealing to the disciples the things that were going to happen to Him several times before (8:31–32; 9:12,

31), and he would do so again (10:45). Yet they still didn't grasp it (cf. vv. 35–37).

How easy it is to see in others the tendency to hear and believe only what they want to hear and how much valuable truth people miss in this way. The fact that this kind of problem is so common may serve as a warning that any of us may fall prey to the same failing without realizing it. Obviously the antidote to believing dangerous falsehood is to saturate myself with the message of the Spirit of truth (John 14:6; 15:26). In order to be sure I do not miss facts important to my life and ministry through wishful thinking, I should make it my daily habit to read, believe, study, and obey the Word of God.

MARK 10:32A

And they were in the way going up to Jerusalem; and Jesus went before them: and they were amazed; and as they followed, they were afraid.

Jesus and the disciples were joining others in going up to Jerusalem for the Passover Feast. Apparently the disciples were "amazed" and "afraid" because they knew what a hornet's nest of opposition Jesus had stirred up among the religious leaders in Jerusalem. He had described to His disciples the treatment these leaders had in store for Him (Mark 8:31; 9:31) and on a previous occasion delayed His going to a Jerusalem feast in order to go up later privately (John 7:1–10). In spite of all His attempts to prepare them for the persecution and death He had come to "accomplish" (Luke 9:31), they still were not able to believe He would behave so contrary to human nature (Luke 18:34).

This is a warning that if I judge whether things are going well or "successfully" by my natural human standards, I may often be way off the mark in grasping what God is trying to accomplish. I need to facilitate the development of the mind of the Holy Spirit within me by reading, studying, and obeying His Word.

MARK 10:33–34

Behold, we go up to Jerusalem; and the Son of man shall be de-
livered unto the chief priests, and unto the scribes; and they shall
condemn him to death, and shall deliver him to the Gentiles: and
they shall mock him, and shall scourge him, and shall spit upon
him, and shall kill him: and the third day he shall rise again.

God is the master of language, and Jesus communicated the
truth precisely. It is interesting to observe the actors and their actions in this short pithy series of future tense verbs. Jesus is the
subject of the passive verb *delivered*, but the actor was Judas. The
high priests (Sadducees) and the scribes (Pharisees) were the actors
who condemned Him to death and delivered (same word as *deliver*
above) Him to the Roman authorities. The Romans were the actors
in mocking, scourging, spitting, and executing. But the subject of
the active verb *rise again* is Jesus Himself.

No matter how despicable the betrayal, no matter how passionate
and hateful the condemnation, and no matter how much power is behind the persecution, God will have the last word, and God can perform whatever miracles He pleases in order to accomplish His will.

MARK 10:35–38A

And James and John, the sons of Zebedee, come unto him, saying,
Master, we would that thou shouldest do for us whatsoever we
shall desire. And he said unto them, What would ye that I should
do for you? They said unto him, Grant unto us that we may sit,
one on thy right hand, and the other on thy left hand, in thy glory.
But Jesus said unto them, Ye know not what ye ask.

These are the same James and John to whom Jesus later said: "If
you abide in Me, and My words abide in you, you will ask what you
desire, and it shall be done for you" (John 15:7 NKJV).

What's the difference? And what should it teach me about prayer?
Jesus indicated in Mark 10 that James's and John's problem was that
there was something they did not know. In John 15, Jesus seems to

indicate that their problem of unanswered prayer could be solved if they would abide in Jesus by having God's Word abide in them.

I am to keep my mind focused on Jesus and His life rather than on me and my own life; I do this by reading and obeying His Word. This will bring my desires and requests in line with His loving purposes for me so that He can then give me my desires. After all, this is what He really wants to do, as it will fulfill me—and that will please Him.

MARK 10:38–39

> But Jesus said unto them, Ye know not what ye ask: can ye drink of the cup that I drink of? and be baptized with the baptism that I am baptized with? And they said unto him, We can. And Jesus said unto them, Ye shall indeed drink of the cup that I drink of; and with the baptism that I am baptized withal shall ye be baptized.

Jesus told these disciples they did not know what they were asking. Then He asked them a question. When they replied that they were able to drink Jesus' cup and endure Jesus' baptism, they still had no idea what they were saying. As Mark recorded this conversation under the direction of the Holy Spirit, the response of Jesus to the disciples' "We are able!" is meant as a commentary on the statement in verse 27: "With men it is impossible, but not with God; for with God all things are possible."

Both James and John later endured persecution. James was martyred (Acts 12:2), and John was imprisoned (Acts 4:3; 5:18, 26–27), threatened (Acts 4:21), beaten (Acts 5:40), and in his old age exiled to Patmos for his testimony (Rev. 1:9).

The encouragement here is that whatever God chooses to send or allow in my life is all purposeful and need not disturb my inner peace as it can never affect my relationship with Him with whom all things are possible.

MARK 10:42–44

But Jesus called them to him, and saith unto them, Ye know that they which are accounted to rule over the Gentiles exercise lordship over them; and their great ones exercise authority upon them. But so shall it not be among you: but whosoever will be great among you, shall be your minister: and whosoever of you will be the chiefest, shall be servant of all.

The message of Jesus here seems to be the same as it was on a previous occasion (Mark 9:34–36), but the word study here is even more interesting and revealing. Whoever wants to be great (*megas*) must become a "servant" (*diakonos*), but whoever wants to be first (*protos*) must be a "slave" (*doulos*).

The word *diakonos* describes one whose function is to do menial things for others. The word *doulos*, on the other hand, describes the permanent status of a slave who is to do whatever he is ordered to do. A dynamic translation into our modern language might be "Whoever wants to be important in Christian ministry must be available to help others be more important than he is, but whoever will not be satisfied unless he is number one does not own his own time and talents but must always be ready to do whatever God directs him to do for anyone."

This puts a whole new meaning on my purpose in life. If I wish to please and impress God, I cannot be concerned with pleasing and impressing other people with my own rights and importance, but I must always be available to serve anyone at any time in any way that God may choose to direct.

Jesus may have been describing beforehand the officers of the local church congregation. Those desiring to be useful to the church are, in fact, called "deacons" (*diakonos*) and serve the needs of the most humble of the congregation (Acts 6:1–6). Those who want to go first as shepherds are to be available to serve anyone at any time in almost any way. According to Paul, they are asking for more good work.

This is a faithful saying: If a man desires the position of a bishop, he desires a good work. (1 Tim. 3:1 NKJV)

MARK 10:44–45

And whosoever of you will be the chiefest, shall be servant of all.
For even the Son of man came not to be ministered unto, but to
minister, and to give his life a ransom for many.

The essential core of Christian truth starts with the fact that
God created me in His own image to live and to fellowship with
Him, but I have sinned and deserve to die and to be separated from
a holy God forever. The gospel, or good news, is that Jesus, Who
is God Himself, became a man and suffered everything my sin de-
serves so that I might become what I was created to be in God's
image—so that I might live and fellowship with God.

If I am restored to the image of God in which I was created, then
Jesus, the God-man, is my example of what God is like. As I become
more like Jesus, I become what I was created to be. In the passage
above, Jesus was trying to explain to His disciples the anomaly that
to become the real me I must become less like me and more like Him
(John 3:30). And the essential character of God in human flesh was
humble obedience in the service of others, even to the point of death
on the cross, since that was what we needed.

As I become more like Him, my life will be totally absorbed in
serving what others truly need, not necessarily what they deserve
and certainly not always what they want. Spiritual growth, then,
consists of becoming what I was created to be while overcoming the
selfish mess I have learned to be. It will become a pattern of giving
up my "self" to meet the needs of others. This is the example set for
me by Jesus, Who was (and is) God in human flesh.

MARK 10:46–48

And they came to Jericho: and as he went out of Jericho with his
disciples and a great number of people, blind Bartimaeus, the son
of Timaeus, sat by the highway side begging. And when he heard
that it was Jesus of Nazareth, he began to cry out, and say, Jesus,
thou Son of David, have mercy on me. And many charged him

that he should hold his peace: but he cried the more a great deal,
Thou Son of David, have mercy on me.

It is interesting to see that nearly all Jesus' recorded miracles were in response to someone who reached out, cried out, sought out, or in some way acknowledged a need and brought it to Jesus. Only rarely did Jesus initiate a contact to perform a miracle for someone, and even then He demanded a confession of need and helplessness (John 5:6–7).

As long as I feel that I can handle things or I depend on other people, institutions, resources, or methods to deal with my problems, I may not see His miracles on my behalf. Likewise, in praying for others, perhaps my first petition should be that God will graciously show them their need and helplessness (John 16:8–11).

MARK 10:46B–52

Blind Bartimaeus, the son of Timaeus, sat by the highway side begging. And when he heard that it was Jesus of Nazareth, he began to cry out, and say, Jesus, thou Son of David, have mercy on me. And many charged him that he should hold his peace: but he cried the more a great deal, Thou Son of David, have mercy on me. And Jesus stood still, and commanded him to be called. And they call the blind man, saying unto him, Be of good comfort, rise; he calleth thee. And he, casting away his garment, rose, and came to Jesus. And Jesus answered and said unto him, What wilt thou that I should do unto thee? The blind man said unto him, Lord, that I might receive my sight. And Jesus said unto him, Go thy way; thy faith hath made thee whole. And immediately he received his sight, and followed Jesus in the way.

Once again, it appears that the faith God honors is not a presumptuous faith that He will do exactly what we ask, but a childlike faith that He can do anything we ask, that He will do what is best for us, and that He will always keep His promises in exactly the way that will truly meet our real needs and enable us to follow Him more closely. This is the faith that brings a deep sense of gratitude and genuine inner peace.

> *Therefore, having been justified by faith, we have peace with God through our Lord Jesus Christ. (Rom. 5:1 NKJV)*

MARK 10:47–48, 51–52

> *And when he heard that it was Jesus of Nazareth, he began to cry out, and say, Jesus, thou Son of David, have mercy on me. And many charged him that he should hold his peace: but he cried the more a great deal, Thou Son of David, have mercy on me.... And Jesus answered and said unto him, What wilt thou that I should do unto thee? The blind man said unto him, Lord, that I might receive my sight. And Jesus said unto him, Go thy way; thy faith hath made thee whole. And immediately he received his sight, and followed Jesus in the way.*

There appears to be a logical and natural sequence here, which I believe illustrates what happens when we turn to Jesus for salvation from sin. The sequence goes like this: (1) we cry out for help, (2) we confess our need, (3) we place our faith in Him, (4) we are saved, and (5) we follow along the road where He is going.

There is a serious warning in the essential negative corollaries to these important axioms. (1) If I do not find myself intuitively and naturally wanting to follow in His ways, perhaps I should question whether I am really saved. (2) If I am not certain that I am saved, perhaps I have never truly placed my faith in Him for asking forgiveness of my honestly confessed sin and admitting I needed His help.

MARK 10:51

> *And Jesus answered and said unto him, What wilt thou that I should do unto thee? The blind man said unto him, Lord, that I might receive my sight.*

It was obvious that Bartimaeus was blind, and he had shouted persistently, "Have mercy on me!" (vv. 47–48). Jesus nevertheless requested that he be more specific in his request for mercy. This was quite in line with Jesus' typical pattern of ministry. He consistently responded to honest acknowledgments of need and confessions of helplessness.

It is important to pray, "Thy will be done," and to mean it. On the other hand, God encourages us to be specific in our prayers. He does not promise to do exactly what I ask, but He encourages me to ask exactly what it is I want or think that I need from Him.

MARK 10:52

And Jesus said unto him, Go thy way; thy faith hath made thee whole. And immediately he received his sight, and followed Jesus in the way.

Fascinating word studies. Seeing this incident as a picture of our salvation from sin is certainly legitimate, as the word translated "whole," ("healed" in other versions) is from *sozo*, which is translated "saved" in many passages in the New Testament (Luke 8:12; Acts 4:12; 16:30; Rom. 10:13).

The phrase "go thy way" translates one word, *'upage*, a general term that can mean anything from "go away" to "you are dismissed." In this case, I believe Jesus was saying, "The purpose for which you came to Me has been accomplished, now move on to the next step" (Heb. 6:1).

The spontaneous reaction of the formerly blind man was to follow Jesus "on the road" (*en te 'odo*). When this man was saved from his blindness, he did what he could not have done before: he observed where Jesus was going and moved in the same direction toward the same goal.

If I am saved from my sin, I am enabled to see Jesus' direction as I read His Word. I may now move with Him toward His goals.

MARK 11

MARK 11:1–2

*And when they came nigh to Jerusalem, unto Bethphage and
Bethany, at the mount of Olives, he sendeth forth two of his disciples, and saith unto them, Go your way into the village over
against you: and as soon as ye be entered into it, ye shall find a colt
tied, whereon never man sat; loose him, and bring him.*

Jesus told the disciples exactly where to go, exactly what they
would find there, and exactly what to do about it. Why do I worry
about "What will happen tomorrow?" Or "What's around the corner?" Or "What will happen if I do this—or that?"

If I am careful to know His will and to be obedient to Him, then
He always controls exactly what good things I will find around the
corner and will tell me exactly what to do about it. If I go into the
village He indicates, I will find the colt He knows is there; all I have
to do is loose it and bring it. The key is to read His Word with an
attitude of obedience on a regular basis. If I know His will and obey
His will, I can relax and trust His will.

MARK 11:1–6

And when they came nigh to Jerusalem, unto Bethphage and Bethany, at the mount of Olives, he sendeth forth two of his disciples, and saith unto them, Go your way into the village over against you: and as soon as ye be entered into it, ye shall find a colt tied, whereon never man sat; loose him, and bring him. And if any man say unto you, Why do ye this? say ye that the Lord hath need of him; and straightway he will send him hither. And they went their way, and found the colt tied by the door without in a place where two ways met; and they loose him. And certain of them that stood there said unto them, What do ye, loosing the colt? And they said unto them even as Jesus had commanded: and they let them go.

Only God knows how people will behave in any given situation. When the disciples loosed the colt, they did not know how people around them would react. They didn't have to. They knew what Jesus had told them to do and what He had told them to say, and they trusted Him. Jesus did not instruct them in how to untie knots or how to lead animals; that was their department. They knew only that they were to use their training and experience skills in obeying His instructions.

When we know we are obeying Him exactly, we can know that, however people react to our behavior, it will be what God intended. I need to be certain only that I am doing what He would have me to do and that I know how He would have me respond. Then I may be at peace about what I do and say and how people will react. My basic reference and authority for my behavior is God and His Word, not people's reactions.

The king's heart is in the hand of the Lord, like the rivers of water; He turns it wherever He wishes. (Prov. 21:1 NKJV)

MARK 11:8–10

And many spread their garments in the way: and others cut down branches off the trees, and strawed them in the way. And they that went before, and they that followed, cried, saying, Hosanna; Blessed is he that cometh in the name of the Lord: blessed be the kingdom of our father David, that cometh in the name of the Lord: Hosanna in the highest.

This whole picture indicates that Jesus was presenting Himself as the Messiah and was being enthusiastically welcomed. The spreading of branches, the use of the word *Hosanna* (which means "Help us now!"), and the reference to the "kingdom of David" (Ps. 118:25–26) all indicate this. When the people saw Him as One Who would do good things for them, they lionized Him, praised Him, and were ready to offer Him a position of religious and civil dignity and power (John 6:15).

Later, however, when Jesus made clear He was not only Messiah but is God with absolute power to rule, the people followed their religious leaders in rejecting His claims. Jesus was not rejected because His claims were not true but because they were not welcome. A messiah who would fulfill their contemporary desires was welcomed with great enthusiasm and fanfare; the Messiah Who is God and Who makes demands was rejected.

How much has changed? The reality of Jesus' godhood and the absolute authority of His Word are still not welcomed. While I cut the branches and shout "Hosanna," I need to remember that real peace and security come through recognizing His lordship and obeying His rulership.

MARK 11:11, 15–16

And Jesus entered into Jerusalem, and into the temple: and when he had looked round about upon all things, and now the eventide was come, he went out unto Bethany with the twelve. . . . And they come to Jerusalem: and Jesus went into the temple, and began to

> *cast out them that sold and bought in the temple, and overthrew the tables of the moneychangers, and the seats of them that sold doves; and would not suffer that any man should carry any vessel through the temple.*

It is popular to use this incident to justify human anger by interpreting Jesus' behavior on this occasion as an angry outburst. It was not. Jesus had arrived at the temple the previous evening after walking in one day all the way from Jericho. At that time, He had calmly surveyed the entire situation before retiring to Bethany to spend the night. He returned to the temple the following day and did what was appropriate about what He had seen the previous evening. In none of the accounts is there any mention of anger on His part (cf Matt. 21:12–13; Luke 19:45–46).

The Greeks had two words for anger. One of them (*orge*) meant a settled attitude of opposition, often issuing in revenge or judgment; the other (*thumos*) reflected a spontaneous uncontrolled outburst of resentment. Neither word was used at any time to describe Jesus. In John's account of an apparently earlier cleansing, it was Jesus' disciples who interpreted His action in the light of Psalm 69:9, which used a word indicating "envy." It seems they saw Jesus exercising a strong sense of responsibility and of proprietorship in regard to the proper use of His Father's house. (Those among us who have ever worked with cattle know what the "whip of small cords" was for.)

I am sometimes tempted to be angry about things that, in fact, deserve resentment and anger. I'm afraid that I cannot justify such a reaction or attitude on my part on the basis of Jesus' example. Anger does not seem to be compatible with real faith in God.

MARK 11:12

> *And on the morrow, when they were come from Bethany, he was hungry.*

Jesus was very God of very God, knowing all truth, prescient, and trustworthy in His omniscience. Yet, He was very man of very man, subject to the pangs of hunger, pain, weariness, and so forth. This is a great mystery. It is also a great truth. Whenever our minds attempt to understand or explain the truth concerning Jesus, the God-man, we become embroiled in apparent logical contradictions and in questions we cannot answer. Yet this fact is absolutely foundational to the reality of Christianity and to the whole truth concerning God, man, and the universe. Its recognition is the bedrock of true Christian theology, and its denial is the very basis for the definition of heresy.

The truth regarding the incarnation of God Himself in the person of Jesus, like the truth concerning the Trinity and the conundrum of free will vs. sovereignty, is apparently one of the great truths God did not equip the human mind to understand. It is something I must know and accept absolutely but I do not need to understand or explain at all. I am to recognize that, while knowledge is important and discernment is desirable, faith is absolutely critical.

My spiritual growth is not just growth in what I know about God or growth in what I understand about theology but is primarily growth in trusting God.

MARK 11:13–14, 20–22

> And seeing a fig tree afar off having leaves, he came, if haply he might find any thing thereon: and when he came to it, he found nothing but leaves; for the time of figs was not yet. And Jesus answered and said unto it, No man eat fruit of thee hereafter for ever. And his disciples heard it. . . . And in the morning, as they passed by, they saw the fig tree dried up from the roots. And Peter calling to remembrance saith unto him, Master, behold, the fig tree which thou cursedst is withered away. And Jesus answering saith unto them, Have faith in God.

I have heard and read many interesting comments and interpretations of this incident. I cannot "disagree" with those who see a picture of the hypocritical contemporary religious leaders of Jesus' day (note vv. 15–19). I also consider it quite legitimate to see here an illustration of individual Christians who have symbolic leaves but no real spiritual substance.

The most reliable "commentary" on the incident of the fig tree drew only one lesson from it: "Have faith in God!" My faith should not be placed in my own ability to produce visible results or in already impressively leaved "fig trees" but strictly in the Word of God.

MARK 11:15–17

> *And they come to Jerusalem: and Jesus went into the temple, and began to cast out them that sold and bought in the temple, and overthrew the tables of the moneychangers, and the seats of them that sold doves; and would not suffer that any man should carry any vessel through the temple. And he taught, saying unto them, Is it not written, My house shall be called of all nations the house of prayer? but ye have made it a den of thieves.*

The symbolic representation of the Jewish temple in this age is not the church house but the human body (1 Cor. 6:19–20). Our bodies are the sanctuary in which God the Holy Spirit conducts the worship of God the Father and God the Son. It is not a stretch to apply that truth to Jesus' reaction to what was going on in the temple.

God declared that His temple was to be a "house of prayer for all nations," yet the very court of the Gentiles was being prostituted to price gouging for the profit of the religious establishment. Likewise, our bodies, though designed and created by God and dedicated to carrying out His purposes in His earth (Gen. 1:25–28; 1 Cor. 6:13), are too often prostituted in many ways to other uses for our own pleasure and profit (1 Cor. 6:16–18). Jesus is not pleased.

If the very purpose for God's giving me a body is that I carry out His purposes, it follows that using my body to obey His Word and serve and worship Him is the way of fulfillment for me. I should not use my body in unscriptural pursuits and should surrender it to obey His Word as His instrument and His temple. I then find that

I am fulfilled more and more as exactly the person I was designed and created to be.

MARK 11:15, 18, 27–28

And they come to Jerusalem: and Jesus went into the temple, and began to cast out them that sold and bought in the temple, and overthrew the tables of the moneychangers, and the seats of them that sold doves . . . and the scribes and chief priests heard it, and sought how they might destroy him: for they feared him, because all the people was astonished at his doctrine. . . . And they come again to Jerusalem: and as he was walking in the temple, there come to him the chief priests, and the scribes, and the elders, and say unto him, By what authority doest thou these things? and who gave thee this authority to do these things?

The legitimate authority held by the chief priests and their allies was descended from Moses and Aaron, whom God had appointed to responsibility for directing Jewish worship. The response of these leaders when their authority was challenged stands in stark contrast to that of Moses.

When the position of Moses and Aaron was questioned by Korah and others (Num. 16), Moses fell on his face before God (Num. 12:3). After that, Moses challenged his questioners to a fair comparison of worship to reveal God's response and approval. God responded by justifying his obedient servant Moses and destroying the pretenders. Moses never found it necessary to protect, defend, or justify his position (Phil. 2:5–9).

The religious leaders of Jesus' day were quick to assert and defend their authority. On the other hand, they were more concerned with enforcing their own opinions (Mark 2:23–24, et al.) than in obeying and teaching God's Word (John 5:37–39). They were more concerned with maintaining popularity with the people (Mark 11:32) than with pleasing God (John 5:41–47).

I should be conscientious about carrying out any responsibility God gives me but leave in His hands the matter of recognition, response, or appreciation on the part of others.

MARK 11:15, 27–33

> *And they come to Jerusalem: and Jesus went into the temple, and began to cast out them that sold and bought in the temple, and overthrew the tables of the moneychangers, and the seats of them that sold doves. . . . And they come again to Jerusalem: and as he was walking in the temple, there come to him the chief priests, and the scribes, and the elders, And say unto him, By what authority doest thou these things? and who gave thee this authority to do these things? And Jesus answered and said unto them, I will also ask of you one question, and answer me, and I will tell you by what authority I do these things. The baptism of John, was it from heaven, or of men? answer me. And they reasoned with themselves, saying, If we shall say, From heaven; he will say, Why then did ye not believe him? But if we shall say, Of men; they feared the people: for all men counted John, that he was a prophet indeed. And they answered and said unto Jesus, We cannot tell. And Jesus answering saith unto them, Neither do I tell you by what authority I do these things.*

The religious authorities were responsible for the theological and spiritual protection of God's people and God's temple. In this capacity, they had the right to question Jesus' action in cleansing the temple. Jesus knew, of course, that their purpose in questioning His authority was not to protect the temple or the people but was solely to protect their own popularity and power. In His counterquestion, He forced them to admit they were not courageously protecting truth but were cravenly guarding their position with the people. They were not spiritual leaders but political poll watchers.

When I am placed in a position of teaching or leading in a congregation of God's people, I need to remember that I may answer to the congregation for my position of leadership but to God's Word for my teaching.

MARK 11:15

And they come to Jerusalem: and Jesus went into the temple, and began to cast out them that sold and bought in the temple, and overthrew the tables of the moneychangers, and the seats of them that sold doves.

The Old Testament gave clear instructions for worshiping God in the Passover sacrifice. A lamb from one's own flock was to be set aside on the tenth day of the month (Exod. 12:1–4). This gave several days to observe the animal and be certain it had no blemishes (Lev. 22:18–20; Deut. 17:1). Then the lamb was slain on the fourteenth of the month for the Passover worship observance.

As the Jewish people scattered abroad, it became cumbersome and inconvenient to sacrifice to God one's own property and to be certain it was top quality. The religious establishment in Jerusalem franchised businessmen to sell acceptable animals in the temple for cash, thus making it much easier than doing it in the way God had instructed them. This made worship more enjoyable and convenient for the Jewish people to the enrichment of the established religious leaders. The people were able to "worship" without much commitment or sacrifice, and the leaders drew larger and more satisfied crowds and made more money. In this way, everybody was happy—except God.

On behalf of His Father, Jesus rejected this cozy arrangement and once again made clear the priority of the Word of God over the adaptations and traditions of men. My guide for true worship should always be God's Word, not the attractive, convenient, "effective" methods or shortcuts offered by religious leaders.

MARK 11:17–18

And he taught, saying unto them, Is it not written, My house shall be called of all nations the house of prayer? but ye have made it a den of thieves. And the scribes and chief priests heard it, and sought how they might destroy him: for they feared him, because all the people was astonished at his doctrine.

The Jewish leaders who claimed positions of official authority felt their position threatened by the popularity of Jesus, which was based solely on His meeting people's needs and teaching God's truth. They were not interested in meeting needs or in learning and teaching God's truth, but in protecting their claim to power. Jesus' character and focus on ministry and truth did not allow Him to compromise with falsehood and dishonesty. He spoke the truth concerning their misuse of God's temple.

People in official positions of authority are sometimes less concerned with carrying out their responsibilities than in protecting their positions. They are made very uneasy by the popularity and influence that comes to people who meet needs and teach truth. Their response is almost never to cooperate in meeting needs or into dialogue in seeking truth. They usually engage in ad hominem tactics.

God's truth does not change. His Word is always truth. If I am truly committed to God and His truth, I cannot "go along to get along." I must follow Jesus' example in refusing to compromise and be willing to accept whatever consequence it is God's will for me to endure in order to remain true to His character and truth.

MARK 11:23–25

For verily I say unto you, That whosoever shall say unto this mountain, Be thou removed, and be thou cast into the sea; and shall not doubt in his heart, but shall believe that those things which he saith shall come to pass; he shall have whatsoever he saith. Therefore I say unto you, What things soever ye desire, when ye pray, believe that ye receive them, and ye shall have them.

*And when ye stand praying, forgive, if ye have ought against any:
that your Father also which is in heaven may forgive you your
trespasses.*

In most English translations of the Bible, there is a paragraph break between verses 24 and 25. I do not think it belongs there. The juxtaposition of verses 22–24 and verses 25–26 is not a coincidence. I believe the Holy Spirit had Mark place them just where they are because they are inseparably related.

One of the most important things I can do (must do) in order to have the faith to see my prayers answered is to give up the luxury of an unforgiving spirit. When verse 25 says, "If you have anything against anyone," there is no indication this means that I am just making things up because of my own hostile attitude. I may, in fact, have a really legitimate reason for resenting an egregious and unprovoked action or attitude on the part of someone. That doesn't matter. God wants me to have a forgiving attitude because He loves me and wants to honor my prayer and bless me. And the handle that opens the sluice gate of blessing is a forgiving spirit.

MARK 11:25–26

*And when ye stand praying, forgive, if ye have ought against any:
that your Father also which is in heaven may forgive you your
trespasses. But if ye do not forgive, neither will your Father which
is in heaven forgive your trespasses.*

Verse 26 is not found in some modern translations because it is missing from several of the desert monastery manuscripts. It is, however, found in dozens of others, including those from the Eastern Church, where Greek continued to be the living language of the church into the fifteenth century. It is clearly a part of what Jesus said (cf. Matt. 6:12, 14–15).

Our sins are forgiven before God and our relationship with Him is established when we repent and accept the death of Christ on our behalf (1 Cor. 15:1–3; 2 Cor. 5:21) and that this is effective once and for all eternally (John 10:28–30; Rom. 5:1). So, what is Jesus talking about here? I believe when Jesus began His statement by saying, "Whenever you stand praying," He was talking about our enjoyment of God's presence through our fellowship with Him.

This is consistent with the little letter of 1 John, the theme of which is having our joy fulfilled by our fellowship with Him (1 John 1:3–4) and which makes very clear that this fellowship and joy are dependent on our honest confession of sin (1 John 1:8–10). When we combine these two truths, we can see the full basis for fulfillment in life through fellowship with God. I may cultivate my permanent relationship with God into a daily fellowship with God through (1) my honestly confessing my own sins against God and (2) my forgiving others of their sins against me.

MARK 11:30–32

The baptism of John, was it from heaven, or of men? answer me. And they reasoned with themselves, saying, If we shall say, From heaven; he will say, Why then did ye not believe him? But if we shall say, Of men; they feared the people: for all men counted John, that he was a prophet indeed.

The chief priests and scribes had a right to know what John the Baptist had preached, to evaluate it, and to disseminate their conclusion among God's people (John 1:19). They were the established religious leaders and were thus responsible to protect God's people from false or misleading doctrines or practices. Unfortunately, as this passage makes clear, they were not discussing among themselves what might have been true about John but only what they said about him and what effect their statements might have on their own popularity and power with the people. There is no evidence their primary interest was in spiritual truth; they appear to have been concerned only with their own position and authority.

Essentially, the chief priests were casuists. Whatever worked in their favor or brought results that would advance or protect their interests was truth. As typical pragmatists, they believed that "if it works, it must be right." To them the ends justified the means—and the ends were measured by their own self-interests.

In obeying and serving God, I must avoid taking the attitude of those religious leaders. I must put truth before results that may make me look good. Many of God's "heroes of the faith" in Hebrews 11 failed to accomplish results favorable to themselves, but they did not abandon God's eternal truth because their eyes were fixed on God's eternal values. They are a far better example for me than religious leaders fixated on their own position and authority.

MARK 12

MARK 12:1–2

> *And he began to speak unto them by parables. A certain man planted a vineyard, and set an hedge about it, and digged a place for the winefat, and built a tower, and let it out to husbandmen, and went into a far country. And at the season he sent to the husbandmen a servant, that he might receive from the husbandmen of the fruit of the vineyard.*

Whenever the word *fruit* appears in any parable or figure of speech in the Bible, someone is sure to say, "The fruit of a Christian is another Christian." I do not find this to be consistent with Scripture. In this instance, Jesus was talking about the Jewish religious leaders, including those of His own day (v. 12). He was definitely not upbraiding them for lack of evangelism (Matt. 23:15) but for hypocrisy and self-promotion. The fruit God sought but did not receive from them, as Jesus and all the Old Testament prophets made clear, had to do with their attitude and behavior toward God and their fellow human beings.

This is consistent with the teaching of Jesus (John 15:1–17, esp. vv. 3, 10, 12, 14), of Paul (Gal. 5:22–25), and of the other apostles (Heb. 12:11; James 3:18; 1 Pet. 2; 1 John 2:3–11). The fruit God looks for from my life has to do with my obedience to His Word, including my attitude and behavior toward other people.

> But the fruit of the Spirit is love, joy, peace, longsuffering, kindness, goodness, faithfulness, gentleness, self-control. Against such there is no law. (Gal. 5:22–23 NKJV)

MARK 12:1–9

> And he began to speak unto them by parables. A certain man planted a vineyard, and set an hedge about it, and digged a place for the winefat, and built a tower, and let it out to husbandmen, and went into a far country. And at the season he sent to the husbandmen a servant, that he might receive from the husbandmen of the fruit of the vineyard. And they caught him, and beat him, and sent him away empty. And again he sent unto them another servant; and at him they cast stones, and wounded him in the head, and sent him away shamefully handled. And again he sent another; and him they killed, and many others; beating some, and killing some. Having yet therefore one son, his wellbeloved, he sent him also last unto them, saying, They will reverence my son. But those husbandmen said among themselves, This is the heir; come, let us kill him, and the inheritance shall be ours. And they took him, and killed him, and cast him out of the vineyard. What shall therefore the lord of the vineyard do? he will come and destroy the husbandmen, and will give the vineyard unto others.

God's people had rejected God's prophets, so God sent His Son, saying, "Respect my Son" (Mark 9:7). The reason we respect Jesus as God's Son is that God said to do so.

Refusing to believe that the historical Jesus is God in human flesh distinguishes heretical cults from Christian denominations. Church history teaches us that denying the deity of Jesus starts with questioning God's Word. Groups refusing to believe the voice of God through His Word eventually find they have no reliable basis for accepting the truth concerning His Son.

It is very easy to question individual denominational and evangelical leaders, both historical and contemporary. Ultimately my confidence in Christian truth, including the deity of Jesus, is based on the absolute accuracy of God's Word.

MARK 12:9–12

What shall therefore the lord of the vineyard do? he will come and destroy the husbandmen, and will give the vineyard unto others. And have ye not read this scripture; The stone which the builders rejected is become the head of the corner: this was the Lord's doing, and it is marvellous in our eyes? And they sought to lay hold on him, but feared the people: for they knew that he had spoken the parable against them: and they left him, and went their way.

In explaining the point of His parable, Jesus quoted from Psalm 118. He made clear that the rejection of the owner's son in the story was intended to illustrate the attitude and behavior of those rejecting His teaching and that God's Word had anticipated and prophesied this rejection.

Once again, we see Jesus responding to the religious authorities' fixation on their own position and authority in the proper practice of religion by appealing to the truth of the Word of God. As far as I know, Jesus never appealed to the Mishna or the various rabbinic traditions as authority but always to the written Old Testament. In doing this, Jesus often rejected historical traditions and the contemporary opinions of religious leaders regarding worship activities.

This means I may avoid "taking sides" in religious squabbles. On the other hand, I should not hesitate to obey God's Word. I am free to love everybody but should look only to God's Word as my guide and authority in worshiping and serving God.

MARK 12:10–11

*And have ye not read this scripture; The stone which the build-
ers rejected is become the head of the corner: this was the Lord's
doing, and it is marvellous in our eyes?*

"This was the Lord's doing." Once again we are faced with the
absolute sovereignty of God. The rejection of Jesus as prophesied in
Psalm 118 and His crucifixion as prophesied in Psalm 22 were "accomplished" (Luke 9:31) under the complete control of God.

God is in charge. Sometimes it may appear that wrong is win-
ning out over right, but God's Word indicates this is always temporary and is all a part of God's long-range control of all things. The
only area for which I am responsible and over which I have "control"
is whether I pray and obey. If I have the peace of knowing I have
done all God asks of me, I can be at complete peace about God's
handling of all His enemies, including even Satan himself.

*Surely the wrath of man shall praise thee: the remainder of wrath
shalt thou restrain. (Ps. 76:10)*

MARK 12:10–11

*And have ye not read this scripture; The stone which the build-
ers rejected is become the head of the corner: this was the Lord's
doing, and it is marvellous in our eyes?*

This quotation from Psalm 118 was given by Jesus as the explanation or point of the parable about the destruction of the thiev-
ing and murderous stewards of the vineyard. It made clear that the
meaning of the parable could be seen in real contemporary events
as an application of truth from God's Word in the Old Testament.
The religious leaders understood Jesus' point much better than they
would like to have (v. 12).

There is a principle here for me to learn. Contemporary events,
especially in spiritual and church life, cannot be best understood
by analysis that uses the "wisdom" of the world's current experts

or modern methods. If I wish to grasp the true meaning of what's going on in my world, I need to become more familiar with the eternal and unchanging wisdom of the Word of God.

MARK 12:10–11

And have ye not read this scripture; The stone which the builders rejected is become the head of the corner: this was the Lord's doing, and it is marvellous in our eyes?

This quotation from the Old Testament is consistent with Jesus' occasional references to the first being last and the last first. There is a theme running through God's Word concerning the complete reversal of the order of things. And why not? Unregenerate man, though made in God's image, has intuitively ordered the affairs of this world in rebellious and counterproductive ways.

When we find that God's people who obey God's Word are repeatedly out of step with contemporary normal human activities, standards, and attitudes, it does not mean that God or His people are naturally contrary or behind the times. The eternal God does not change to please people—nor just to displease people. God is the "definition" of what is right, and His Word is the instruction book for normal standards of living and arranging our affairs. In an unregenerate world, it is perfectly natural to find God out of step and to expect Him to change and reverse things when His Word is obeyed and His power is released.

If I want to live a normal human life, I must look to God and His Word for standards and directions and purposefully ignore much of the guidance offered by my contemporary human world.

And do not be conformed to this world, but be transformed by the renewing of your mind, that you may prove what is that good and acceptable and perfect will of God. (Rom. 12:2 NKJV)

MARK 12:10–11

And have ye not read this scripture; The stone which the build-ers rejected is become the head of the corner: this was the Lord's doing, and it is marvellous in our eyes?

The passage from Psalm 118, from which Jesus quoted, is so obviously a prediction of the events and significance of Passion Week, the rejection and crucifixion of Christ, it is amazing that the Jewish scholars missed it—and still miss it.

The previous verse tells us that God sees our need and He becomes our salvation. The word translated "salvation" is from the root Hebrew word from which the name "Jesus" is derived:

I will praise You, For You have answered me, And have become my salvation. (Ps. 118:21 NKJV)

The following verse indicates that the day of these events, while appearing to be a tragic time, would be a day to occasion great rejoicing:

This is the day the Lord has made; We will rejoice and be glad in it. (Ps. 118:24 NKJV)

The final verse of the psalm then calls for recognition that all these matters are the prime manifestation of the mercies of God toward His people:

Oh, give thanks to the Lord, for He is good! For His mercy en-dures forever. (Ps. 118:29 NKJV)

I have always liked to apply Psalm 118:24 to every day, day by day. But the only reason I may rejoice and be glad in any given day is because of what God the Son did on that special day in dying for my sins to become my salvation.

And she shall bring forth a son, and thou shalt call his name Jesus: for he shall save his people from their sins. (Matt. 1:21)

MARK 12:12–13

And they sought to lay hold on him, but feared the people: for they knew that he had spoken the parable against them: and they left him, and went their way. And they send unto him certain of the Pharisees and of the Herodians, to catch him in his words.

"So they left Him and went away" (NKJV). But notice how quickly they were back again in another attempt to neutralize Jesus' influence. They still "feared the multitude." People whose position of importance and sense of security are dependent on the whims of "the multitude" are never really at peace. These religious leaders found it necessary to continue their efforts against Jesus because of their fear of their position with the fickle crowd.

While the religious leaders resorted ultimately to dishonest schemes, multiplied illegalities, and Roman violence to eliminate Jesus, they were agitated by a sense of fear and insecurity throughout the procedures and continued to be so afterward (Matt. 27:62–66). Jesus, on the other hand, endured persecution, torture, and death while maintaining a sense of inner peace and victory (Luke 23:46; John 19:11, 30).

If I am to have the inner peace for which I was created and redeemed, I must rest my sense of personhood, purpose, and peace in my relationship to God and His Word and never allow them to be dependent on the attitudes or actions of other people.

MARK 12:13–17A

And they send unto him certain of the Pharisees and of the Herodians, to catch him in his words. When they were come, they say unto him . . . Is it lawful to give tribute to Caesar, or not? Shall we give, or shall we not give? But he, knowing their hypocrisy, said unto them, Why tempt ye me? bring me a penny, that I may see it. And they brought it. And he saith unto them, Whose is this image and superscription? And they said unto him, Caesar's.

> *And Jesus answering said unto them, Render to Caesar the things that are Caesar's, and to God the things that are God's.*

One interesting observation here is that Jesus' ultimate answer to the question was the same answer the Herodians would have given: "Pay the taxes." His reasons, however, were based on biblical principles.

Throughout the Old Testament, it is made clear through Moses and all the prophets that God controls civil governments, He often used them to discipline His own people, and He commanded His people to live in peace and harmony when under foreign governments. The Old Testament also recognized in many places the simple fact that, subject to God's overall sovereignty, governments control wealth. More specifically, it is civil governments that control rare metals and mint coins.

Jesus' reply forced the Pharisees to acknowledge that God, in His wisdom and for His own reasons, had placed them under governance by the Roman Empire. As long as the Romans minted the coins, they were in charge. It was the responsibility of God's people to live in peace and harmony and obey the laws as long as they were left free to worship God and obey His Word.

MARK 12:13–14

> *And they send unto him certain of the Pharisees and of the Herodians, to catch him in his words. And when they were come, they say unto him . . . Is it lawful to give tribute to Caesar, or not?*

"Is it lawful?" This raised a question that is still with us regarding the relationship of God's people to the civil government. Neither the Herodians nor the Pharisees were genuinely seeking help in answering this difficult question. Their purpose was to "catch him in his words."

They already had their minds made up. The Herodians would say, "Yes, taxes should be paid." Of course, the Herodians were politically and financially dependent on the Romans, who collected the taxes. The Pharisees insisted it was not "lawful" for God's people to pay their money to a government not believing in God; nevertheless they paid the taxes. This protected their reputation as religious leaders who were jealous for the honor of God while keeping them out of trouble legally. Whichever answer Jesus gave would alienate Him from one group or the other.

A political answer would have been one composed to skirt the question and avoid offense to either party while mouthing popular platitudes. How would we have answered? When I am faced with these kinds of questions, do I compose my answer on the basis of its reception by the interrogators? Or on the basis of my own personal advantage? Or my reputation? Or do I seek to base my answer and my actions on biblical principles and the truth of God's Word?

MARK 12:13

And they send unto him certain of the Pharisees and of the Herodians, to catch him in his words.

This was not the only time the Pharisees and Herodians, natural enemies, cooperated against Jesus (Matt. 22:15–16; Mark 3:6). The Pharisees considered the Jewish Herodians traitors for cooperating with the occupying Romans, while Herodians saw the Pharisees as religious fanatics threatening civil peace and order. Both were bothered by Jesus' teaching and popularity.

Jesus taught that the written Word of God was the only basis for religious and spiritual authority and that it always took priority over both traditional and contemporary religious opinions and practices. This threatened the Pharisees. The secularized Herodians, on the other hand, had serious problems with Jesus' insistence that all human government answers to God, exercises civil power only by God's permission, and should obey God's Word.

The truth of the Word of the sovereign and only creator God will always pose a threat to illegitimate pretensions of civil and religious authorities. God's people must follow the example of God's

Son and not compromise with either Pharisees or Herodians. I really have no choice but to believe God and recognize His Word as truth in the face of authority claims, either secular or religious.

MARK 12:17

And Jesus answering said unto them, Render to Caesar the things that are Caesar's, and to God the things that are God's. And they marvelled at him.

Following up on the thought from the previous devotional, this statement of Jesus underscores the fact that there are things that most distinctly belong to God and over which the civil government has no rights of governance. After all, God established the institution of civil government among men for their good (Rom. 13:1–7; 1 Pet. 2:13–14). While God allows man to exercise his free will in operating this institution, God still has sovereign control of all government affairs and does not place within the province of the civil government authority over the relationship of man to his Maker.

Every legitimate power my government exercises over me comes from God. I am to submit to its laws in obedience to Him (Eph. 5:21), but my personal relation to God does not fall within the area of the government's business.

MARK 12:17

And Jesus answering said unto them, Render to Caesar the things that are Caesar's, and to God the things that are God's. And they marvelled at him.

"And they marveled at him." Of course they marveled! Jesus had used Pharisee logic to reach Herodian conclusions. This left both parties speechless. The Pharisees insisted God had the last word in determining human behavior (and since Pharisees represented God, their rules must be obeyed). The Herodians, as pure secular pragmatists, couldn't have cared less what kind of sophistic religious logic one used; they just insisted the taxes were to be paid.

Jesus totally agreed that God had the final word on everything but pointed out that God said to pay the taxes.

There are two important implications for me today in Jesus' words. First, He made it clear that God indeed has the final word, but the ultimate way to know God's will is not to consult and obey religious leaders but to consult and obey God's Word. The second implication is perhaps more critical for today. The civil government may not govern how I worship God simply because it has arrogated to itself the authority to do so. Quite the contrary, it is God Almighty Who determines how I am to relate to the civil government.

MARK 12:18–19, 24

> *Then come unto him the Sadducees, which say there is no resurrection; and they asked him, saying, Master, Moses wrote unto us, If a man's brother die, and leave his wife behind him, and leave no children, that his brother should take his wife, and raise up seed unto his brother. . . . And Jesus answering said unto them, Do ye not therefore err, because ye know not the scriptures, neither the power of God?*

The little conundrum the Sadducees presented to Jesus was based on the Old Testament Levirate marriage law (Deut. 25:5–6). It was probably used often in their disputes with the Pharisees regarding the resurrection. Jesus pointed out their real problems: they were quoting an isolated Scripture and they were giving it an interpretation that contradicted the clear unambiguous meaning of other passages of Scripture.

When I am sincerely seeking guidance from God's Word, the best commentary on God's Word is God's Word. I may not give any Scripture passage a "private interpretation" (2 Pet. 1:20–21) to suit my desires or my arguments in violation of the obvious meaning of other clear passages in His Word.

MARK 12:18, 24

Then come unto him the Sadducees, which say there is no resurrection; and they asked him, saying . . . And Jesus answering said unto them, Do ye not therefore err, because ye know not the scriptures, neither the power of God?

Sadducees were the politico-religious ruling class. They were responsible for the temple in Jerusalem, they furnished the high priests, and they cooperated with the Romans in their attempts to keep the religious practices of the Jews in line with the purely secular civil and military rule of the Roman Empire. Theologically, they were materialists and were quite skeptical of anything supernatural. The Sadducees were distinguished from the Herodians, who made no profession of religion, and from the Pharisees, strong traditionalists and were much less flexible about religious beliefs and practices. Today, Sadducees would be called conservative politically and liberal theologically. While being careful not to offend the Romans, they were often forced to work in cooperation with the Pharisees, who were aware of the supernatural and much more popular with the common people.

There are few people more dense about the basic facts concerning God, man, and the universe than those who cling to the forms and practices of religion but do not grasp the realities of spiritual (and moral) truth. The Sadducees were just as threatened by Jesus' popularity as the Pharisees and Herodians. Since they perceived that His popularity with the common people would increase as He embarrassed the Pharisees and Herodians, they decided it was time to get this matter under control. They were quite confident they could handle this unsophisticated and uneducated supernaturalist with logical and rhetorical conundrums.

One thing this little exchange tells me is that when I have to deal with the politically worldly-wise and their theological sophistries, mere religious tradition will not offer much real protection. I must defer always to the ultimate authority of the Word of God.

MARK 12:19

*Master, Moses wrote unto us, If a man's brother die, and leave
his wife behind him, and leave no children, that his brother should
take his wife, and raise up seed unto his brother.*

The Sadducees were quoting the Levirate marriage law from
Deuteronomy 5. It is unlikely that Moses, though extremely well
educated for his day, had detailed knowledge of the microscopic operation of the process of mitosis. He did not realize the distinctive
origin and function of somatic cells and germ cells. He could not
have known that the germ cells, or sperm, in a man's body developed
right from the beginning as a human unborn baby in a hermetically
separated process from the somatic (general body) cells. God, of
course, knew all about the processes of cell development in minute
detail.

In an adult man, the germ cells, though obviously developed by
various body (somatic) cells do not share the exact gene or chro-
mosomal pattern of that man's body cells but are derived from his
parents. This means that the gene pools of full brothers carry the
inheritance pattern from the same parents. If full brothers joined in
marriage with the same woman, the offspring would come from the
same gene pools. This is why Moses could write that a man could
"raise up offspring for his brother." As man has learned more about
himself and his world, he is increasingly enabled to follow the un-
erring logic of God's Word in greater detail. Repeatedly, science justifies the confidence of those who believe in the inerrancy of God's
Word.

What all this biological esoterica says to me is that I can believe
the words of God. It is not smart for me to presume to correct or
explain "mistakes" in the Bible on the basis of my human logic or
knowledge. And it is also not wise to take seriously those who do so;
God's Word is not "just a book."

MARK 12:24

And Jesus answering said unto them, Do ye not therefore err, because ye know not the scriptures, neither the power of God?

Jesus was precise in pointing out the two things the Sadducees did not know (*eidotes* = "grasp" or "understand"). They did not understand the nature of the Old Testament Scriptures, so they did not understand the power of God.

The Sadducees had just demonstrated (vv. 19–23) that they saw the Old Testament as a document to be questioned rather than believed and as a source of "proof-texts" to be adapted for their own topical and theological arguments. Jesus' answer to them (vv. 26–27) clarified the fact that the Old Testament is the Word of God expressed exactly in words chosen by God.

It was precisely because they did not accept the literal meaning of the words of God's Word that they did not see the power of God at work. The Sadducees were very familiar with power. But they knew only the power that human beings exercised through civil government by political and military means. Because they did not believe the Old Testament, they never saw the controlling hand of God behind all possession and exercise of any form of power. Though they were "religious leaders," they were actually humanists and materialists, and, as such, they were blind to the reality of spiritual truth, including, of course, the resurrection.

God's Word will explain and clarify for me the real meaning behind many of the things I see in this world in the light of important truths that I cannot see on my own. God's Word makes things "make sense."

MARK 12:26–27

And as touching the dead, that they rise: have ye not read in the book of Moses, how in the bush God spake unto him, saying, I am the God of Abraham, and the God of Isaac, and the God of

Jacob? He is not the God of the dead, but the God of the living: ye
therefore do greatly err.

This is an amazing passage of Scripture. This Greek in the quote
of God speaking from the bush is a translation of Exodus 3:6 and
is uncannily accurate and precise. Neither can be translated exactly
into English.

The point Jesus was making to the Sadducees was that Abraham, Isaac, and Jacob had to be alive somewhere at the time God
made this statement to Moses; the verb is not past tense! Interest-
ingly enough, in both Hebrew and Greek, it is not exactly present
tense either. The words "I . . . the God" are given an exclusive promi-
nence (not merely emphasis) in this sentence, which seems to communicate not merely the present tense condition of Abraham, Isaac,
and Jacob when the statement was made to Moses but God's eternal
existence as the God of His people. Hallelujah!

MARK 12:27

He is not the God of the dead, but the God of the living: ye there-
fore do greatly err.

In its immediate context, this statement conveyed to the Sadducees the fact that Moses, whom they claimed to believe, taught
plainly the fact of a resurrection by quoting God as saying Abraham, Isaac, and Jacob were still living in Moses' day.

The full depth of meaning behind this simple pronouncement,
however, is unfathomable by the human mind. Here is the key to the
meaning of the expulsion from the garden with its "tree of life." Here
is the underlying key to the meaning of Hebrews 11. Here is the
simple but powerful fact behind many other Scripture passages:

In him was life; and the life was the light of me. (John 1:4)

I am come that they might have life, and that they might have it
more abundantly. (John 10:10)

Most assuredly, I say to you, he who hears My word and believes in Him who sent Me has everlasting life, and shall not come into judgment, but has passed from death into life. Most assuredly, I say to you, the hour is coming, and now is, when the dead will hear the voice of the Son of God; and those who hear will live. For as the Father has life in Himself, so He has granted the Son to have life in Himself. (John 5:24–26 NKJV)

And I give unto them eternal life; and they shall never perish, neither shall any man pluck them out of my hand. (John 10:28)

MARK 12:28

And one of the scribes came, and having heard them reasoning together, and perceiving that he had answered them well, asked him, Which is the first commandment of all?

This scribe, a Pharisee (Matt. 22:34–35), asked Jesus to identify the foundational law on which all (*panton*) God's laws were based (Matt. 22:40). He was not implying that God's laws might be in conflict or competition with one another so that one might cancel another.

This confirms the principle that God's Word is true and harmonious throughout, and I may not make a "private" interpretation of any passage to the cancellation of the clear meaning of any other passage.

MARK 12:29–31

And Jesus answered him, The first of all the commandments is, Hear, O Israel; The Lord our God is one Lord: and thou shalt love the Lord thy God with all thy heart, and with all thy soul, and with all thy mind, and with all thy strength: this is the first commandment. And the second is like, namely this, Thou shalt

love thy neighbour as thyself. There is none other commandment
greater than these.

To follow on the previous devotional, it helps in grasping the
meaning of "the first of all the commandments" if we read also Matthew's description of this incident: "On these two commandments
hang all the law and the Prophets" (Matt. 22:40 NKJV).

This does not mean that my loving God before other things
trumps all the other commandments but that it includes all the
other commandments. I think a corollary would be that if I find my
thought life or lifestyle violates the letter or spirit of any of God's
commands, I am not basing my life on the right premises. "Trying"
to discipline myself to obey God by my own self-will is not the solution; I start by loving God before all other things.

Truly loving God starts with believing and accepting His overwhelming love for me (John 3:16; 15:13). This passage indicates
that, as God's love fulfills me, it will then issue in His love for others
flowing out through me in attitude and action.

MARK 12:32–34

And the scribe said unto him, Well, Master, thou hast said the
truth: for there is one God; and there is none other but he: and
to love him with all the heart, and with all the understanding,
and with all the soul, and with all the strength, and to love his
neighbour as himself, is more than all whole burnt offerings and
sacrifices. And when Jesus saw that he answered discreetly, he
said unto him, Thou art not far from the kingdom of God. And
no man after that durst ask him any question.

I can learn something from this scribe. The New Testament use
of *basileia* and its many cognates means "rulership" rather than the
archaic (especially for Americans) "kingdom." Its meaning usually,
as here, refers to the personal choice of an individual to accept and
enjoy God's rulership of his life.

This being true, what Jesus said to this scribe tells me that an important step in accepting God's rulership of my life is to recognize God's love and to respond by returning His love. Such a response on my part—as an individual—is more important than whatever I may do in public religious activity. A key symptom of my truly loving God is to find myself loving other people with God's love.

MARK 12:35–37

And Jesus answered and said, while he taught in the temple, How say the scribes that Christ is the Son of David? For David himself said by the Holy Ghost, The Lord said to my Lord, Sit thou on my right hand, till I make thine enemies thy footstool. David therefore himself calleth him Lord; and whence is he then his son? And the common people heard him gladly.

"And the common people heard him gladly." What Jesus said in the temple on this occasion was typical of His teaching of God's truth: it was a straightforward exposition of an Old Testament text. "And the common people heard him gladly." How about that?

This accords with my own experience and observation. It encourages me to believe that the Holy Spirit will draw people to God's truth. People really want to have God's Word clearly explained to them. I do not need to employ a contemporary, slick presentation and entertainment methods to draw people to hear the teaching of God's Word.

MARK 12:35–37A

And Jesus answered and said, while he taught in the temple, How say the scribes that Christ is the Son of David? For David himself said by the Holy Ghost, The Lord said to my Lord, Sit thou on my right hand, till I make thine enemies thy footstool. David therefore himself calleth him Lord; and whence is he then his son?

The fact is that Jesus ascended in the flesh to heaven and sits at the right hand of God the Father as described in Psalm 110, which Jesus quoted here. This fact is a key part of Christian truth; it is referred to or alluded to at least nineteen times in the New Testament. The right-hand position was one of power (Matt. 20:20–21; Rev. 5:1, 7) and of influence (Rom. 8:32–34). Psalm 110, which Jesus here identified as a Davidic psalm, is one of the most important messianic passages in the Old Testament.

Jesus' point here was not only that the Messiah was descended from David but also that this passage, from the pen of David himself, made it clear the Messiah was also David's Lord, which would require that He be God. For the Jewish leadership to oppose the Messiah was not only traitorous but also heretical and blasphemous.

The comfort in this for me is found in Romans 8:32–34. Jesus' primary activity at the Father's right hand, while He awaits the time to assume all the power that is His (Rev. 5), is to intercede for His stumbling followers here on earth (John 16:7). Hallelujah!

MARK 12:36

> For David himself said by the Holy Ghost, The Lord said to my Lord, Sit thou on my right hand, till I make thine enemies thy footstool.

I have never had any problem believing the doctrine of the Trinity of the Godhead, but I used to think that actually proving it from the Bible was an interesting challenge. No more. The more I study God's Word, the more I find myself "stumbling" over the Trinity repeatedly in the process of simply reading for meaning. Whenever a passage of God's Word links two of the members of the Trinity, more often than not, I will find the other person of the Godhead "lurking" within a verse or two before or after.

The passage above is typical. Jesus pointed out that God the Holy Spirit inspired David to predict in the Old Testament—centuries of human time before it actually occurred—that God the Father would make the God of David literally a descendant of David in the person of the Messiah. Amazing!

MARK 12:38–39

And he said unto them in his doctrine, Beware of the scribes, which love to go in long clothing, and love salutations in the marketplaces, and the chief seats in the synagogues, and the uppermost rooms at feasts.

I do not believe this passage was placed by the Holy Spirit in the New Testament (along with others, Matt. 23:1ff.; Mark 8:15; Luke 20:45–47; John 8:42ff.) so that those in the Christian religious hierarchy in later centuries could criticize those in the Jewish religious hierarchy of the first century. It is here as a stern warning to Christians to avoid adopting the same attitudes and practices that motivated much of the religious leadership among the Jews of Jesus' day.

One of the reasons I like the Bible-based congregational polity in church government is that it does not officially call for an authoritative organizational hierarchy, either at the local or denominational level. Unfortunately this does not mean that "big-shotism" at the denominational level and claims of clerical authority at the local level do not happen. They do. They simply confirm God's wisdom in placing these warnings of Jesus in the New Testament, which is the inerrant charter of His church.

This is a warning for me when I find myself thrust into leadership responsibilities, either behind the scenes or in the more up-front roles. Opportunities to serve God in these capacities do not give me more importance to God nor more authority in His church than faithful Christians who live godly Bible-based lives, serve and bless one another, and point others to Jesus without ever taking on leadership roles.

MARK 12:38–40

And he said unto them in his doctrine, Beware of the scribes, which love to go in long clothing, and love salutations in the marketplaces, and the chief seats in the synagogues, and the uppermost rooms at feasts: which devour widows' houses, and for a pretence make long prayers: these shall receive greater damnation.

"For a pretense make long prayers." This has the hallmark of rank hypocrisy and was roundly and rightly condemned by Jesus. But think about it: it is extremely difficult for any of us to pray aloud or word the prayer for a group without being very conscious of the impression we are making on other people.

We feel a legitimate obligation to speak in language that is clear and understandable to other people while trying to be honest and transparent in communicating worshipfully to God. This is not easy to do without catering to the expected response of other people and the impact we are making on behalf of our own position and reputation.

In this kind of situation, I need to give top priority to "connecting" honestly with God, while giving only secondary consideration to draw others into my communication with God and my attempt to express the common group message to Him. It might also help if I keep in mind Jesus' use of the word *long (makra)* in His description of the scribes' hypocrisy.

MARK 12:38–40A

And he said unto them in his doctrine, Beware of the scribes, which love to go in long clothing, and love salutations in the marketplaces, and the chief seats in the synagogues, and the uppermost rooms at feasts: which devour widows' houses.

The devouring of widows' houses by the use of laws of "Corban" (Mark 7:11) went out with the destruction of the temple and the Diaspora of the Jewish nation. No longer are the equitable Old Testament laws of inheritance circumvented so that widows and orphans starve in order that religious leaders can afford "long robes . . . the uppermost rooms at feasts" and so forth. Such things as these are not done by the church in the way it was by the Jews. Not exactly.

On the other hand, much of the work of God in the ministry of His church is supported by the sacrificial tithes and gifts of couples and widows on limited income. These tithes and gifts are then "laundered" through church financial management practices so that churches and denominational leaders feel no twinge of conscience about the way the money is spent supporting an expensive or ostentatious lifestyle by those charged with carrying out God's work.

Whenever I find myself responsible for determining the spending of "God's money," I must remind myself that it is God's money, given—often sacrificially—by God's people to support God's work.

MARK 12:41–44

And Jesus sat over against the treasury, and beheld how the people cast money into the treasury: and many that were rich cast in much. And there came a certain poor widow, and she threw in two mites, which make a farthing. And he called unto him his disciples, and saith unto them, Verily I say unto you, That this poor widow hath cast more in, than all they which have cast into the treasury: for all they did cast in of their abundance; but she of her want did cast in all that she had, even all her living.

The more one reads economic theories, postmortems, and predictions, the more one realizes that unregenerate man does not truly understand, and certainly cannot control, the operation of the "economic laws" of macroeconomics, which appear to affect powerfully the personal microeconomic welfare of everyone. As we read the theories of libertarians, monetarists, supply-siders, socialists, Keynesians, and so forth we find no one mentioning the "economic law" of tithing and giving. I have yet to read an economist who pointed out that investing at least one-tenth of one's income in the recognition and worship of God is an important key to microeconomic peace and security. Pity!

MARK 12:41–44

And Jesus sat over against the treasury, and beheld how the people cast money into the treasury: and many that were rich cast in much. And there came a certain poor widow, and she threw in two mites, which make a farthing. And he called unto him his disciples, and saith unto them, Verily I say unto you, That this poor widow hath cast more in, than all they which have cast into the treasury: for all they did cast in of their abundance; but she of her want did cast in all that she had, even all her living.

Jesus did not mention the actual amount most worshipers put into the treasury. What He noted was the percentage of income given to the Lord as a reflection of the attitude of the givers. Jesus did not count the money in the temple treasury but the amount left in the pockets of God's people after they gave. The greatest joy of giving comes from the confident peace of helpless dependence upon a loving Father, Who never fails me.

I like the observation of a dear saint I once knew who gave sacrificially to God's work. He said, "Pay no attention to those who say, 'Give until it hurts.' If it hurts, you have not yet given enough; you must continue giving until it feels good." While our organizational and institutional giving goals are important, I believe my personal goal in giving should be a goal of joyful worship and trust.

MARK 12:41A

And Jesus sat over against the treasury, and beheld how the people cast money into the treasury.

Back (way back) when I was a young pastor in a little country church, I considered it "unspiritual" to concern myself with the giving habits of church members or to preach often on tithing and giving. Then I read that "Jesus sat over against the treasury" and that He observed and commented on the attitude and actions of worshipers in the area of their personal financial relationship to the Lord.

I also noted in my own life the close relationship between joyful giving and peaceful trusting. I concluded that returning to God from the material blessings of life was an essential element in worship, spiritual growth, and Christian joy. Ignoring this means of grace leads to distortion and lack of balance in my personal relationship to God. To neglect to share this truth with others is to fail to encourage an important and essential element in spiritual growth and blessing.

To fail to preach and witness regarding the importance of tithing and giving is to sin against sincere Christian brethren who need to know how to grow in the joy of their relationship to the Lord.

MARK 12:41A

And Jesus sat over against the treasury, and beheld how the people cast money into the treasury.

I suspect Jesus still sits opposite the treasury and observes how I put money into the treasury. When I do so, I believe I am (1) acknowledging God's ownership of all He has allowed me to possess, (2) expressing gratitude to Him for all the material and financial means with which He has blessed me, and (3) expressing confidence that He will always continue to give me all that I truly need.

When I "cast money into the treasury" with these attitudes, it can become a joyful (*'ilaron*; 2 Cor. 9:7) and worshipful experience. When I fail to put into God's treasury with the right attitude, I should not be surprised that all my attempts at a truly joyful worship experience are incomplete, distorted, and spiritually unfulfilling.

MARK 13

MARK 13:1–2

*And as he went out of the temple, one of his disciples saith unto
him, Master, see what manner of stones and what buildings are
here! And Jesus answering said unto him, Seest thou these great
buildings? there shall not be left one stone upon another, that shall
not be thrown down.*

The temple of Herod was huge! This building complex had been
under construction for many years and was nearing completion. Its
decorations and appearance were breathtaking and unparalleled in
the known world, and its dimensions dominated the skyline of the
city of Jerusalem. To hear Jesus calmly describe its total destruction
must have amazed the disciples who heard Him.

There are things in our situational, institutional, and material
world that seem to be so big, so powerful, so permanent that we
take them for granted as a natural part of the way things are—and
always will be. When such things change radically, or even disap-
pear entirely, it shakes us to the core as it seems to alter the whole
basis of truth and reality in our little world. God, however, is never
"shook up."

God is also never surprised. He knows long before they happen
all the details of every possible change in our environment. Nothing

changes Him or His truth or the inevitable unfolding of His on-going will and purposes. What a comfort to know He is my heavenly Father and is always concerned for my welfare—quite independent of any circumstances, conditions, or situations. Praise the Lord!

MARK 13:1–2

And as he went out of the temple, one of his disciples saith unto him, Master, see what manner of stones and what buildings are here! And Jesus answering said unto him, Seest thou these great buildings? there shall not be left one stone upon another, that shall not be thrown down.

The disciples were impressed with the magnificent size and appearance of Herod's temple. Jesus understood that this physical structure, whose design and purpose were specifically related to the worship of God, was nevertheless just a physical structure. When not sincerely used for its intended purpose, it became irrelevant and, in fact, was shortly to be destroyed.

God has been gracious to the Christian (and quasi-Christian) organizations of Europe and the Western Hemisphere in allowing many of their beautiful, gigantic, and ingenious church structures to remain intact while becoming irrelevant. Many magnificent cathedrals may still be enjoyed as objects of aesthetic beauty and examples of human genius, persistence, and organizational ability while the religious organizations associated with them are spiritually dead and the numbers of people utilizing them for "worship" activities has radically diminished.

As a Christian, I believe my primary concern should be for spiritual reality rather than physical impressiveness. Any necessary and adequate physical facilities should be supplied according to the spiritual needs of congregations and of outreach and service ministries. Such facilities should be functional and useful for spiritual purposes and not designed or built merely to impress people or to support the pride of an organization or the ego of a person.

MARK 13:3–6

And as he sat upon the mount of Olives over against the temple, Peter and James and John and Andrew asked him privately, Tell us, when shall these things be? and what shall be the sign when all these things shall be fulfilled? And Jesus answering them began to say, Take heed lest any man deceive you: for many shall come in my name, saying, I am Christ; and shall deceive many.

What they were asking about privately was Jesus' prediction of the destruction of the temple. They wanted inside information on how to anticipate these events and to predict them by reading the signs of the times.

The first thing Jesus said in answering their question was "There will be plenty of 'signs' made available for those who are fixated on knowing the future but don't believe any of them!"

Good lesson. The Bible is full of information about the end times; this information is not given so I may know when end-time events will occur but that I may be ready whenever they occur.

MARK 13:5–8, 14–20

And Jesus answering them began to say, Take heed lest any man deceive you: for many shall come in my name, saying, I am Christ; and shall deceive many. And when ye shall hear of wars and rumours of wars, be ye not troubled: for such things must needs be; but the end shall not be yet. For nation shall rise against nation, and kingdom against kingdom: and there shall be earthquakes in divers places, and there shall be famines and troubles: these are the beginnings of sorrows. . . . But when ye shall see the abomination of desolation, spoken of by Daniel the prophet, standing where it ought not, (let him that readeth understand,) then let them that be in Judaea flee to the mountains: and let him that is on the housetop not go down into the house, neither enter therein, to take any thing out of his house: and let him that is in the field not turn back again for to take up his garment. But woe to them that are with child, and to them that give suck in those days! And pray ye that your flight be not in the winter. For in those days shall be affliction, such as was not from the beginning of the creation which God created unto this time, neither shall be. And except that the Lord had shortened those days, no flesh should be saved: but for the elect's sake, whom he hath chosen, he hath shortened the days.

The two long passages establish context, but, in reality, verses 4–33 (and Luke 21:7–33) are all needed as context for what is here. I believe that verses 14–18 (and Luke 21:23a), referring to the fall of Jerusalem in AD 70, belong to Jesus' first response to the disciples' question in verse 4 (and Luke 21:7). They are a part of Jesus' warning not to interpret intervening events to mean the ultimate end has come (v. 5ff.; Luke 21:8ff.).

Verse 19 (and Luke 21:24b) is transitional and introduces Jesus' description of the real "end times." In verse 19, the phrase translated "for in those days" (*gar ʿai ʿemerai ekeinai*) is unique in the New Testament. Unlike all other passages so translated (v. 17), there is no preposition, and the word translated "days" (*ʿemerai*) is in the nominative case. An accurate translation might be "for those days shall be."

This may be a warning against automatically assuming any current events, however cataclysmic, are certainly signs of the second coming. My primary fixation should be on living in fellowship with Jesus here and now rather than on guessing about dates and details of His future coming.

MARK 13:7–9

And when ye shall hear of wars and rumours of wars, be ye not troubled: for such things must needs be; but the end shall not be yet. For nation shall rise against nation, and kingdom against kingdom: and there shall be earthquakes in divers places, and there shall be famines and troubles: these are the beginnings of sorrows. But take heed to yourselves: for they shall deliver you up to councils; and in the synagogues ye shall be beaten: and ye shall be brought before rulers and kings for my sake, for a testimony against them.

Jesus was saying to His disciples that the natural outworkings of unregenerate human nature, on whatever personal or corporate scale, are what is to be expected in this age. Such things are not necessarily to be seen as signs that God is moving in any specific end-time events.

It is true that Scripture says a great deal about Jesus' second coming because God wants me (1) to be assured that Jesus will return and (2) to be warned and motivated to be ready at any time. On the other hand, there are also many passages, such as this one, that warn us not to become fixated on our own knowledge of specific future events. Too many things in God's Word need my attention in cultivating my relationship with Him and in knowing how to minister on His behalf that I do not need to invest a lot of my time, energy, and focus on seeking special knowledge of the details of future events.

MARK 13:8

For nation shall rise against nation, and kingdom against kingdom: and there shall be earthquakes in divers places, and there shall be famines and troubles: these are the beginnings of sorrows.

These words of Jesus, which the Holy Spirit had Mark record as a look at the future, are so accurate and up-to-date that it is startling. A more literal translation of the inerrant original would say, "Race will rise up (to rule) over race (*egerthesetai gar ethnos ep' ethnos*) and government (to rule) over government (*basileia epi basilieian*)." This sounds like a preview of modern newspapers and television news—without the liberal bias.

This is just one more reassurance that what I read in God's Word is accurate and reliable. I can believe all of it and rest my life upon its truth. Hallelujah!

MARK 13:9

But take heed to yourselves: for they shall deliver you up to councils; and in the synagogues ye shall be beaten: and ye shall be brought before rulers and kings for my sake, for a testimony against them.

Jesus predicted that His followers would be opposed and persecuted by "councils" (*sunedria*), a word usually referring to the Sanhedrin, the supreme Jewish religious court and ruling religiopolitical body in Jerusalem. This word occurs over twenty times in the New Testament, most of them in the book of Acts. The Sanhedrin worked hand in glove with the Roman government and joined the Romans in discouraging and persecuting those Jewish religious movements that questioned the civil government's claim to control religious practice.

Jesus correctly predicted that His followers would suffer at the hands of the Sanhedrin (*sunedrion*; Acts 4, 5, 6, 22, 23, 24). I should not be surprised to find the same kind of opposition and persecution of true followers of Jesus in my own day. Wherever you find opposition to the true biblical teaching that human governments have no right to define or regulate the worship of almighty God, you most often find some religious establishments, institutions, and leaders that are themselves in bed with the government while mouthing about separation of church and state.

While maintaining an irenic spirit and avoiding conflict, I must never compromise the plain fact that the truth of God and the worship of God should always take precedence over the exercise of power by any human civil (or religious) authorities.

MARK 13:12–13

Now the brother shall betray the brother to death, and the father the son; and children shall rise up against their parents, and shall cause them to be put to death. And ye shall be hated of all men for

my name's sake: but he that shall endure unto the end, the same
shall be saved.

"And ye shall be hated." We live in a day when relationships are considered the ultimate value in life—to the point of idolatrous worship. The contemporary assumption is that if I am hated, especially by many people, something must be done! It is expected that I will do whatever I possibly can and will change myself in whatever way is required so that I might restore relationships and avoid being hated.

Even complete and consistent obedience to the Word of God is sometimes considered extreme and needs to be modified if it hurts people's feelings to such an extent that they dislike us and our relationship is affected.

Jesus indicated that His true followers would naturally grate against the grain of the kosmos world order. He said that we should expect to be hated "for my name's sake" (cf. 2 Tim. 3:12). My hating others can cut me off from my fellowship with God (1 Cor. 14:20; Eph. 4:31; Col. 3:8; James 1:19–20; 1 Pet. 2:1, etc.), but being hated should not in any way affect the peace and joy of my relationship to God. Having good human relationships may be enjoyed, but human relationships are not to be worshiped.

MARK 13:12–13

Now the brother shall betray the brother to death, and the father
the son; and children shall rise up against their parents, and shall
cause them to be put to death. And ye shall be hated of all men for
my name's sake: but he that shall endure unto the end, the same
shall be saved.

This speaks to two important truths. The first is a warning that God alone is totally and unfailingly to be trusted to love me at all times. While personal and family relationships and corporate Christian fellowship may be enjoyed as elements of my Christian life, my only reliable "significant other" is God. It is the only relationship on which I can totally depend and always "let my whole weight down" with complete trust and confidence.

The other truth I see in this passage (vv. 9–13) is that an eternal point of view is the only perspective from which I may grasp the full reality of human life. No matter what the immediate circumstances of my life on earth, nothing can be permanently unfortunate or tragic since my relationship to God means I will endure to the end of this earthly life and will ultimately be saved from all its problems and limitations to live in blissful fellowship with Him forever. Hallelujah!

MARK 13:21–23

> And then if any man shall say to you, Lo, here is Christ; or, lo, he is there; believe him not: for false Christs and false prophets shall rise, and shall shew signs and wonders, to seduce, if it were possible, even the elect. But take ye heed: behold, I have foretold you all things.

This passage apparently warns about specific events and persons appearing in the end times ("Then"; *tote*, cf. v. 19). On the other hand, I believe Jesus meant it to be applicable generally to all times and places ("any man," *tis*).

When anyone claims to be—or represent—a person especially anointed of God to rule over His people, I believe this passage from God's Word authorizes me, "Do not believe it." Such a person is a false messiah. I think the same command applies when anyone claims to be—or represent—an authorized source of God's truth, independent of His written Word. Such a person is a false prophet. Until Jesus returns, God's truth and God's commands for me come from God's Word.

MARK 13:24–25, 28–29

But in those days, after that tribulation, the sun shall be darkened, and the moon shall not give her light, and the stars of heaven shall fall, and the powers that are in heaven shall be shaken. . . . Now learn a parable of the fig tree; When her branch is yet tender, and putteth forth leaves, ye know that summer is near: so ye in like manner, when ye shall see these things come to pass, know that it is nigh, even at the doors.

The illustration of the fig tree was used by Jesus to say that in God's scheduled time in the "seasons" of the life of the earth, there will come the proper time for Christ's second coming. It will occur on God's millennial calendar as surely as fruit bearing occurs on His annual calendar.

Jesus' statements were obviously not included in the inerrant Scriptures for the sake of the disciples or for the people of their generation. The astronomical phenomena described, have in fact, not happened in any intervening generation since New Testament times. If God's Word is true—and it is—these things are yet future. One day they will occur (v. 31).

This is one more warning to me, consistent with the context, that I cannot predict end-time events on the basis of human activities alone. Until absolutely unprecedented astronomical events begin to occur, the primary focus of my Christian life should be on fellowship with Him and ministry to His people and others, not on details of prophecy!

MARK 13:24–25, 29–31

But in those days, after that tribulation, the sun shall be darkened, and the moon shall not give her light, and the stars of heaven shall fall, and the powers that are in heaven shall be shaken. . . . So ye in like manner, when ye shall see these things come to pass, know that it is nigh, even at the doors. Verily I say unto you, that

this generation shall not pass, till all these things be done. Heaven
and earth shall pass away: but my words shall not pass away.

When Jesus said that "this generation" (*genea 'aute*) should not pass until everything is fulfilled, it is obvious He did not mean the generation of the apostles. Some scholars believe *genea* does not mean a genealogical unit or time span but refers to ethnic identity of the Jewish race, God's chosen earthly people; this is most certainly possible.

My own view is that it refers to the generation that experiences the beginning of the astronomical phenomena described in verses 24–25. Consistent with the context, Jesus was speaking to those who would observe in the latter days events of such unprecedented nature and magnitude that they appeared to cancel out the normal unfolding of God's order of things. He was saying, "No matter what happens in the future, God's plans and purposes will not fail to unfold according to God's schedule and exactly according to God's Word!"

MARK 13:24–27

But in those days, after that tribulation, the sun shall be darkened, and the moon shall not give her light, and the stars of heaven shall fall, and the powers that are in heaven shall be shaken. And then shall they see the Son of man coming in the clouds with great power and glory. And then shall he send his angels, and shall gather together his elect from the four winds, from the uttermost part of the earth to the uttermost part of heaven.

When I try to "read" current events at the level of human political or military developments for signs of the second coming, I need to remind myself of passages such as this one from the mouth of Jesus. God, of course, does not provide us with a "scientific" description of astronomical events from His own point of view. We wouldn't understand it if He did. But even from a human, earthly, phenomenological perspective the events described here will obviously affect things beyond our spherical earth and well beyond any human activity.

If a pretribulation rapture occurs, and I think it will, Christians will see only the bare beginnings of these cataclysmic happenings, and the "elect" are the Jewish people rather than the church. There is an invitation here to adopt an attitude of humility in any "understanding" I have about the second coming. What is called for is trusting belief in what the Word of God actually says rather than abstruse speculation about what it might mean. God does not intend for me to invest a large portion of the brief time and limited intellectual abilities He allots to me on earth trying to fill in a lot of details He has not chosen to share.

MARK 13:28–29, 35–37

> Now learn a parable of the fig tree; When her branch is yet tender, and putteth forth leaves, ye know that summer is near: so ye in like manner, when ye shall see these things come to pass, know that it is nigh, even at the doors. . . . Watch ye therefore: for ye know not when the master of the house cometh, at even, or at midnight, or at the cockcrowing, or in the morning: lest coming suddenly he find you sleeping. And what I say unto you I say unto all, Watch.

God's promises and God's calendar can always be depended on to operate without fail, even when He does not choose to share with us all the details we would like to know. That is the way God works and it gives us the opportunity to exercise faith in God. The illustration Jesus used from nature told the disciples—and tells us—that God's millennial calendar will work as certainly as His annual fruit-bearing calendar. The eschatological cycle is like the fruit-bearing cycle: (1) the fact is certain, (2) there may be a few "signs" or indications that it is unfolding on schedule, but (3) the details and exact dates are in God's hands, and (4) we are admonished to be ready at any time.

For instance, when the Holy Spirit impregnated the Virgin Mary, and the announcement came from God via Gabriel, God's gestational calendar was set in motion. The fact of the first coming of Jesus via the virgin birth was then certain. Mary's weight gain, discomfort, and possible false labor pains gave hints that it was imminent, but neither Mary nor Joseph (nor the innkeeper nor the shepherds) knew precisely when it would happen.

Likewise the second coming. Jesus' resurrection and ascension, along with His earlier discourses about these matters with His disciples, plus the specific promise from the angels (Acts 1:10–11), guarantee that God's calendar for the second coming has been set in motion but leave the exact details and date in God's hands—and not in ours. This is an opportunity to exercise faith. It is also an opportunity to obey Jesus' command to watch and be ready.

"Christ has died; Christ has risen; Christ will come again."

MARK 13:31

Heaven and earth shall pass away: but my words shall not pass away.

In our materialistic world, the Bible is viewed as a book on religion. Religion is seen as an emotional or psychological luxury or crutch not entirely in touch with solid, permanent physical and material reality. However, the message found in this passage, coming directly from the mouth of Jesus, should help us put things in perspective.

Jesus makes it very clear that the material world is subject to cataclysmic changes and is anything but stable and eternally reliable. There are conditions under which the material universe can become very unstable and evanescent. The Bible, on the other hand, being the Word of the eternal God, is not subject to change under any imaginable circumstances. That's any circumstance of any kind!

It shouldn't take a rocket scientist to calculate for me where I should place my trust or on what foundation I should build my life.

MARK 13:31

Heaven and earth shall pass away: but my words shall not pass away.

Modern skepticism about God's Word is not really modern at all. In every generation, unbelievers have had their own unique rationale for denying and avoiding eternal but uncomfortable truths of the holy Scriptures.

In the first and second centuries, God's truth was "supplemented" by combining it with Jewish tradition, Greek philosophy, or Eastern mystery religions. In the Middle Ages, the written Scriptures were "corrected" and "interpreted" by updating pronouncements of truth by a particular church. In early modern times, discoveries and theories of certain scientists claimed to prove the Bible outdated. Within the last couple of centuries, more scholars have tried to confuse the issue of the eternal truth of God's Word by questionable theories about the formation history of the Old Testament and of the manuscripts of the New Testament.

What has always eventually become outdated (though often not timely discarded) are theories that question the truth of God as revealed in His Word. This encourages me to read, believe, and obey God's Word even though the currently fashionable skeptics—both outside and inside the church—may call me "old-fashioned."

MARK 13:31

Heaven and earth shall pass away: but my words shall not pass away.

This is a wonderful truth. When I read, believe, and obey God's Word, I am cooperating with God's eternal program. What an awesome thought.

Read God's Word—contact eternal truth

Study God's Word—absorb eternal realities

Obey God's Word—participate in eternal operations

Touch the Bible—touch eternity

MARK 13:32–33

> *But of that day and that hour knoweth no man, no, not the angels which are in heaven, neither the Son, but the Father. Take ye heed, watch and pray: for ye know not when the time is.*

I should respond to the fact of the second coming of Christ with neither curiosity nor wild speculation. Jesus said God expects my responses to be "take heed" (*blepete*), "watch" (*agrupneite*), and "pray" (*proseuchesthe*).

Blepete means to keep my eyes open and be aware of what is going on around me. This, of course, requires that I be familiar with the light of God's Word so that I can see the reality behind the events and circumstances around me. The word *agrupneite* means to be awake and not asleep. I need to be living in the world of spiritual reality and not in a dream world induced by closing my eyes to God's truth. To pray (*proseuchesthe*) means to worship God and look to Him alone to meet all my true needs.

If I do these things anticipating the second coming of Christ, I will lead a fulfilled and useful life now and be ready for His return if it should occur in my earthly lifetime. Sitting at the gate puzzling over minor details of the airline schedule neither hurries the plane nor prepares me for boarding.

> *And every man that hath this hope in him purifieth himself, even as he is pure. (1 John 3:3)*

MARK 13:34–35A

> *For the Son of man is as a man taking a far journey, who left his house, and gave authority to his servants, and to every man his work, and commanded the porter to watch. Watch ye therefore: for ye know not when the master of the house cometh.*

The word translated "watch" in verse 33 is *agrupneite*; it is from *agrupneo* and is a command not to sleep. The word *watch* in verses

34–35—and verse 37 as well—is *gregoreite* from *gregoreo*. This is a command to be aroused to a pitch of continuous alertness.

Too often our attitude is to concern ourselves exclusively with the activities, attitudes, and standards of our contemporary earthly scene. Concerns about otherworldly, silent, invisible, and spiritual matters are postponed to the future realm of our eternal, heavenly existence. After all, we live in a physical and material earth, and it is easy to procrastinate about the reality of anything that does not promise some material advantage or appeal to our physical senses.

Jesus was specific and emphatic. He warned us that our knowledge of tomorrow, including end-time events, is not sufficient to justify letting our spiritual guard down and immersing ourselves in the contemporary appeal to the physical. God expects me as His child to be always keenly aware of my relation to my heavenly Father and His business on earth, even when these silent and invisible realities offer no worldly advantage or physical sensual appeal:

> No one engaged in warfare entangles himself with the affairs of this life, that he may please him who enlisted him as a soldier. (2 Tim. 2:4 NKJV)

MARK 13:35–37

> Watch ye therefore: for ye know not when the master of the house cometh, at even, or at midnight, or at the cockcrowing, or in the morning: lest coming suddenly he find you sleeping. And what I say unto you I say unto all, Watch.

Had the little boy perched on the kitchen counter with his hand in the cookie jar been aware that his mother was at that very moment walking into the room, he would no doubt not have been so occupied. Our behavior is controlled by our personal desires as they are conditioned by our awareness and understanding of significant facts in our circumstances. The little boy's behavior ought to have been controlled by his mother's loving instructions not to eat sweets between meals. This is not just a moral "ought to"; it would have been the way of health and happiness for the little boy.

Jesus was explaining in this passage that the fact of His second coming could be a motivation to live our lives in the way they were designed to be lived. I was created in the image of God for a life of joy and happiness. But this joy and happiness come only as a by-product of the life of obedient fellowship with God for which I was designed. I should keep my hand out of the cookie jar of disobedience because I live my life always under the watchful eye of a loving God, Who will one day come back and draw me into the reality of blissful eternal fellowship with Him.

MARK 13:37

And what I say unto you I say unto all, Watch.

"And what I say unto you (*'umin*—pl.), I say unto all (*pasin*—pl.), Watch (*gregoreite*—pl., imperative)." The word translated "watch" carries an absolute and intense implication. It indicates much more than an occasional monitoring or an incidental activity. It calls for unblinking vigilance and total focus (Matt. 26:40; Mark 14:37; Col. 4:2; Rev. 3:3).

How do I live my life on a daily basis while maintaining a vigilant attitude toward the second coming of Christ? This calls for keeping in mind that my primary purpose in life, obedient fellowship with God, will one day be totally fulfilled. In the meantime, I am to live day by day in the penumbra of that fellowship. How do I do this?

The answer is found in the circumstances under which Jesus gave this command and in His subsequent conversations with these disciples. In this verse, Jesus clearly gave a command to all but gave it in the course of a private conversation with His disciples. It seems obvious to me that this laid on the disciples a responsibility to communicate Jesus' message to later generations of His followers (2 Pet. 1:12–21). This is consistent with Jesus' message to His disciples and His prayer in their presence at the last supper (John 14:25–26; 15:25–27; 16:13–15, especially 17:20; 2 Tim. 3:12–17).

The way I am able to live my daily life to the fullest in the light of Jesus' second coming is to connect daily with the message of truth the disciples left for me in God's written Word.

MARK 14

MARK 14:1–2

After two days was the feast of the passover, and of unleavened bread: and the chief priests and the scribes sought how they might take him by craft, and put him to death. But they said, Not on the feast day, lest there be an uproar of the people.

The people in this picture, who did not hesitate to use dishonesty and to take innocent human life but who were so concerned about what people thought of them, were the religious leaders. They were supposed to lead God's people in worshiping and obeying God, but they were much more concerned with what the people might say than what God had said. Like some modern politicians, they were more responsive to polls than to truth. They were casuists who believed that the end justified the means.

Unregenerate human nature can sometimes be found alive and well in those who hold positions of leadership among God's people. A really important lesson, of course, would be to keep this in mind when I find myself thrust into such a position. A critical part of doing God's work is doing it God's way. I will never be able to accomplish things that truly please God when I resort to methods—no matter how effective or impressive—that do not please God.

MARK 14:3–5

And being in Bethany in the house of Simon the leper, as he sat at meat, there came a woman having an alabaster box of ointment of spikenard very precious; and she brake the box, and poured it on his head. And there were some that had indignation within themselves, and said, Why was this waste of the ointment made? For it might have been sold for more than three hundred pence, and have been given to the poor. And they murmured against her.

Socialists and other materialists often point to money, time, and energy that are used for religious purposes as a waste. They insist that such resources would be better invested in tangible things and financial returns. Yet when we look at those countries and cultures that are, in fact, materially prosperous and the subject of envy by others, we most often see their hills and valleys and their city streets dotted with Christian churches and places of worship (as well as with hospitals and schools and missions ministering to the poor). Since man was created for obedient fellowship with God, why should we be surprised to find that seeking and cultivating that fellowship leads to positive results in other important areas of human life?

And does knowing these facts theoretically and theologically affect the way I actually spend my own time and resources? Every day? All the time? Today? Right now?

MARK 14:3–7

And being in Bethany in the house of Simon the leper, as he sat at meat, there came a woman having an alabaster box of ointment of spikenard very precious; and she brake the box, and poured it on his head. And there were some that had indignation within themselves, and said, Why was this waste of the ointment made? For it might have been sold for more than three hundred pence, and have been given to the poor. And they murmured against her. And Jesus said, Let her alone; why trouble ye her? she hath wrought a good work on me. For ye have the poor with you always,

*and whensoever ye will ye may do them good: but me ye have not
always.*

There is nothing wrong with giving to the poor. The Old Testament is full of commands and admonitions about caring for the poor. They are provided for in the Law (Exod. 23:6–11; Lev. 19:10; 23:22; 25:35–39; Deut. 15:7–11; 24:14–15). Care for the poor is found over twenty-five times in Psalms and over fifteen in Proverbs and is also found in Isaiah, Jeremiah, Ezekiel, Daniel, Amos, and Zechariah. In almost every case, however, it is clear that the command to treat the poor with equity and generosity is addressed to individuals rather than to villages, nations, or any other civil governments.

*He who oppresses the poor reproaches his Maker, But he who
honors Him has mercy on the needy. (Prov. 14:31 NKJV)*

Jesus' rebuke was consistent with the Old Testament approach. He was not advising a government on its use of tax money, or even a church on the use of gifts and tithes. Jesus was addressing a group of individual hypocrites. He admonished them to care for the poor on their own initiative ("whenever you wish") but to leave other people to follow their own conscience in the disposition of their resources. Jesus gave no comfort to those who wish the government to "soak the rich" to enrich the bureaucrats and pander to the poor.

MARK 14:3

*And being in Bethany in the house of Simon the leper, as he sat at
meat, there came a woman having an alabaster box of ointment
of spikenard very precious; and she brake the box, and poured it
on his head.*

"Very costly" (NKJV). This woman (Mary, sister of Martha) took something of intrinsic value and wasted it in an act that "accomplished nothing" and brought no return to anyone. The entire value of her investment was gone and she had nothing to show for it but that she had called attention to Jesus and that she had expressed publicly her devotion to Him. What she did demonstrated total disregard for valuable time, energy, and resources invested in the expensive oil of spikenard. This cavalier attitude was impractical and irrational and showed poor stewardship of possessions and resources that had been entrusted into her care.

I fear that until I spend so much time with God and His Word (John 12:3; Luke 10:39, 42) that I develop this same twisted set of values, I may miss out on much of the blessing of joy and fulfillment for which God created me and redeemed me.

> And she had a sister called Mary, who also sat at Jesus' feet and heard His word. ". . . . But one thing is needed, and Mary has chosen that good part, which will not be taken away from her." (Luke 10:39, 42 NKJV)

MARK 14:4–5, 7

> And there were some that had indignation within themselves, and said, Why was this waste of the ointment made? For it might have been sold for more than three hundred pence, and have been given to the poor. And they murmured against her. . . . For ye have the poor with you always, and whensoever ye will ye may do them good: but me ye have not always.

People who talk about wanting to "help the poor" with someone else's resources are always suspect. Jesus' reply was succinct and to the point. He said, in effect, "There are plenty of poor at all times for you to help; go right ahead" or "Nothing is keeping you from helping the poor." This woman's "misuse" of her resources, which she had every right to do, did not have any relationship to their use of their own resources.

Jesus was pointing to their hypocrisy. In a sense, He was saying, "After you have used up your own resources to help the poor—who are always available for you to help—then you may be in a position to give this woman advice about the use of her resources." My own behavior must be consistent with my professed principles before I am qualified to teach these principles to others.

MARK 14:4–6, 10

And there were some that had indignation within themselves, and said, Why was this waste of the ointment made? For it might have been sold for more than three hundred pence, and have been given to the poor. And they murmured against her. And Jesus said, Let her alone; why trouble ye her? she hath wrought a good work on me. . . . And Judas Iscariot, one of the twelve, went unto the chief priests, to betray him unto them.

Judas felt that his hard work, financial skills, and sacrificial service were not properly appreciated. He previously suspected this and therefore had felt no twinge of conscience in helping himself to money from the treasury (John 12:6). Jesus' seemingly irrational and improvident reaction to Judas' sensible suggestion about the use of the fragrant oil (John 12:4) was the final straw. It became obvious that this religious teacher to Whom he had attached his future hopes and plans was going nowhere. Judas was for getting out at a time and in a way that would "cut his losses" and be to his financial benefit.

This passage is very convicting if we really think about it. How do I react when God calls on me to minister faithfully, effectively, and sacrificially without commensurate recognition or remuneration? Or pro bono? When people do not "appreciate me," am I tempted to betray and attack the ministry?

MARK 14:4–7

And there were some that had indignation within themselves, and said, Why was this waste of the ointment made? For it might have been sold for more than three hundred pence, and have been given to the poor. And they murmured against her. And Jesus said, Let her alone; why trouble ye her? she hath wrought a good work on

me. For ye have the poor with you always, and whensoever ye will
ye may do them good: but me ye have not always.

As is so often the case, those advocating caring for the poor are
the ones who will be personally enriched by this redistribution of
wealth (John 12:4–6). There are, and always have been, several kinds
of "poor." There are the indigent poor, who, for some reason have no
resources or access to resources. There are the working poor, who
have limited access to resources because of lack of well-remunerated
work skills in their location and situation. Then there are the lazy
poor, who refuse to apply their skills to accessing resources through
work as God intended (Gen. 3:17–19). Unfortunately, among all
three groups, there are dependent and demanding poor, who expect
others to access resources on their behalf and give to them.

The existence of this last type of poor people is one reason Jesus
encouraged personal and individual, rather than corporate and
organizational, decisions and actions in helping the poor. When
people share their own hard-earned money or property, they are
often much more generous but sometimes much more hesitant than
institutions caring for the poor. They are more discerning because
(1) they are more personally involved and (2) because they are more
familiar with the situation of the poor they are helping than an im-
personal source of funding, with resources obtained from third persons by force of law or by highly organized appeals.

In order for Jesus' system to work, we must be productive, caring, discerning, and responsible. My "giving to the poor" should be
based on my knowledge and application of principle as well as on
emotion, and never on the basis of guilt imposed by those with a
personal interest in the resources involved.

MARK 14:6, 8–9

And Jesus said, Let her alone; why trouble ye her? she hath
wrought a good work on me. . . . She hath done what she could: she
is come aforehand to anoint my body to the burying. Verily I say
unto you, Wheresoever this gospel shall be preached throughout

*the whole world, this also that she hath done shall be spoken of for
a memorial of her.*

By custom, the privilege of formally preparing a body for burial belonged to the women who were close to the deceased. In the case of Jesus, the women went to an empty tomb. The only woman who got to exercise the customary privilege was Mary. Perhaps Mary alone knew that Jesus was soon to die because Mary truly listened when Jesus spoke (Luke 10:39–42).

Jesus, of course, knew He was to be crucified; He knew that Mary understood this and knew that the others—including His disciples—did not understand. He also knew that Mary's act would be recognized and memorialized in the Gospels for later generations (Matt. 26:6–13; John 12:2–8).

Nothing surprises God. He sees and appreciates all that I do for Him. It is not necessary for others to know or understand, though occasionally God will let others recognize if it will honor Him and bless them.

MARK 14:10–11

And Judas Iscariot, one of the twelve, went unto the chief priests, to betray him unto them. And when they heard it, they were glad, and promised to give him money. And he sought how he might conveniently betray him.

In this picture we have people who believe that by spending money they can obtain anything they want. We have also a man who is willing to give up anything asked of him in order to get more money. In both cases, money is considered to be the ultimate value, trumping all other considerations.

Money is only a means of expressing value. Money is just a medium of exchange. It has no intrinsic value of its own. Nevertheless, my use of money acknowledges and betrays my own inner value system. I should let the Holy Spirit show me what my attitude toward money says about me.

MARK 14:12–13

And the first day of unleavened bread, when they killed the pass-over, his disciples said unto him, Where wilt thou that we go and prepare that thou mayest eat the passover? And he sendeth forth two of his disciples, and saith unto them, Go ye into the city, and there shall meet you a man bearing a pitcher of water: follow him.

The man the disciples met was apparently going about his daily life, carrying out some chore or work detail, and Jesus knew exactly what he was doing. Jesus knows and is interested in my daily life. He cares about the way I spend my time. All my activities, including those having nothing to do with church or spiritual matters, are of interest to Him. He wants them all to be done in a way that brings glory to God, blessing to others, and fulfillment to me.

As I go about my mundane business, I should be prepared at any time to be interrupted in my daily activities by opportunities to do something that is special for Him. This will not seem an inconvenience if I always remain conscious of the fact that He knows and cares about all that I am doing and wants to bless me.

MARK 14:12

And the first day of unleavened bread, when they killed the pass-over, his disciples said unto him, Where wilt thou that we go and prepare that thou mayest eat the passover?

It seems clear from this and other Scriptures (vv. 14, 16; Matt. 26:17–18; Luke 22:7–8, 13) that this meal was the Jewish Passover meal, instituted just before the exodus from Egypt as described in Exodus 12. For this symbolic meal, the primary food consumed was a lamb. Yet none of the New Testament descriptions of the events at this meal as observed by Jesus and His disciples mentions the lamb.

The Passover meal, established in Egypt and celebrated in Pales-tine for almost fifteen hundred years, was symbolic. Its fulfillment was the death of Jesus, the sacrificial Lamb provided by God, Whose death causes the death angel to "pass over" His followers so that our sins are forgiven and we have eternal life. Jesus knew that this crucial event was about to occur. Jesus used the occasion to introduce the true meaning of the real event, and to institute the symbolic meal, which was to look back to the real thing the way the Jewish Passover meal had looked forward to it. It seems clear that the same divine reality that this Jewish Passover meal anticipated, the Christian "Lord's Supper" memorializes.

It seems significant that the two disciples chosen by Jesus to prepare this last Passover meal were Peter and John (Luke 22:8). It was John who described Jesus as the "Lamb of God," and it was Peter who said (to me and you):

> Knowing that you were not redeemed with corruptible things, like silver or gold, from your aimless conduct received by tradition from your fathers, but with the precious blood of Christ, as of a lamb without blemish and without spot. (1 Pet. 1:18–19 NKJV)

MARK 14:13–15

> And he sendeth forth two of his disciples, and saith unto them, Go ye into the city, and there shall meet you a man bearing a pitcher of water: follow him. And wheresoever he shall go in, say ye to the goodman of the house, The Master saith, Where is the guestchamber, where I shall eat the passover with my disciples? And he will shew you a large upper room furnished and prepared: there make ready for us.

We do not know why the upper room was furnished and ready. We can be reasonably certain Jesus had not made any arrangements known to His disciples beforehand because of the way the disciples found the right house by simply following a man who was carrying a pitcher. What we do know is that as soon as His disciples indicated Jesus' need for the room, the master of the house immediately relinquished it to Him.

Those of us who claim to be His followers could follow this man's example. When Jesus' ministry needs something that I possess, do I immediately and spontaneously relinquish my claim to it so it is available for His use?

MARK 14:18–21

And as they sat and did eat, Jesus said, Verily I say unto you, One of you which eateth with me shall betray me. And they began to be sorrowful, and to say unto him one by one, Is it I? and another said, Is it I? And he answered and said unto them, It is one of the twelve, that dippeth with me in the dish. The Son of man indeed goeth, as it is written of him: but woe to that man by whom the Son of man is betrayed! good were it for that man if he had never been born.

Personal loyalty is a positive character trait; it should be acquired and practiced, but loyalty to principle and truth are of greater importance. Yet loyalty to truth and principle for the Bible-believing Christian are, in a way, an intensely personal kind of loyalty.

When a conflict appears between loyalty to a human person and loyalty to the truth of God, my personal relationship with God and my knowledge of His Word become the deciding factor. Loyalty to God takes top priority.

MARK 14:22–25

And as they did eat, Jesus took bread, and blessed, and brake it, and gave to them, and said, Take, eat: this is my body. And he took the cup, and when he had given thanks, he gave it to them: and they all drank of it. And he said unto them, This is my blood of the new testament, which is shed for many. Verily I say unto

*you, I will drink no more of the fruit of the vine, until that day
that I drink it new in the kingdom of God.*

When Jesus said, "This is my body," He was obviously using
a figure of speech because His actual body was alive before them
handling the bread and the cup. This was confirmed by John as he
quoted Jesus' earlier explanation for similar words: "The words that
I speak to you are spirit" (John 6:63 NKJV).

Jesus was quite deliberate in choosing the bread and cup instead
of the roast lamb that was before Him. The slain lamb was only
a symbol of the real sacrifice to be offered once for all the following day. The slaying of a symbolic sacrificial animal was no longer
needed or appropriate. Jesus wanted to emphasize this fact as He
instituted a memorial meal with bread and juice (nowhere does the
Bible say what was in the cup (*poterion*—Matt. 26:27; Mark 14:23;
Luke 22:20; 1 Cor. 11:25–28). He wanted His followers to remember His death but to understand clearly that they were not offering
to God a repeat of His once-for-all-time death for our sins (Heb.
7:27; 9:12, 26–28; 10:8–12; 1 Pet. 3:18).

When I sin, there is nothing I can offer to God but full honest
confession, as the sacrificial price has been fully paid by my Savior
once-for-all (1 John 1:9–2:2). Hallelujah!

MARK 14:25

*Verily I say unto you, I will drink no more of the fruit of the vine,
until that day that I drink it new in the kingdom of God.*

Please pardon the Greek and theology, but this little word study,
if valid, has a special significance for us. The phrase "I drink it new
in the kingdom of God" is *pino kainon en te basileia tou theou.* The
Greek word *kainon* means "new" in the sense of freshness rather
than age. I think it entirely possible, since Jesus used the designa-
tion "fruit of the vine," He meant that in the future of which He
spoke, the fruit of the vine would not ferment.

This could mean that in God's proper order of things ("the kingdom of God") fermentation and other entropic signs of aging are not known. Jesus' reference might easily describe the Edenic world and possibly apply to some extent also to the entire antediluvian milieu. This would explain the long ages of the early generations of humans and the unexpected effect of fermented wine on Noah (Gen. 9:20–21).

This would reinforce my belief that my eternal fellowship with God (and possibly His millennial reign on earth) will not be subject to the deteriorating effects of aging with which we live in this age. Just think! No arthritis, no osteoporosis, no loss of energy, no macular degeneration. Also, no need for refrigeration, no spoiled food, no tofu; the possibilities are endless. You would think, as a saved man, I would look to the future with a silly grin of eager anticipation on my face at all times.

MARK 14:27–28

And Jesus saith unto them, All ye shall be offended because of me this night: for it is written, I will smite the shepherd, and the sheep shall be scattered. But after that I am risen, I will go before you into Galilee.

The entire word picture in this passage is that of a shepherd with His flock of sheep. When Jesus said He would "go before" (*proaxo*) them into Galilee, He was describing what a shepherd did. Unlike other common livestock, sheep are not driven; they are led. The shepherd would always "go before" the sheep. As long as the sheep followed the shepherd, they would be safe and provided for.

This speaks directly to me as a "follower" of Jesus. I am not an independent operator for God. God does not need my brilliant plans or schemes, nor does He need for me to "follow my dreams." All God requires is that I follow Him closely and not wander off, recognizing that He is the shepherd and I am just a sheep. Without Him, I would "stumble" and would become "scattered."

MARK 14:27–29

> *And Jesus saith unto them, All ye shall be offended because of me this night: for it is written, I will smite the shepherd, and the sheep shall be scattered. But after that I am risen, I will go before you into Galilee. But Peter said unto him, Although all shall be offended, yet will not I.*

The two primary things the shepherd's presence and leadership provided for his sheep were protection and sustenance. The presence of a strong and caring shepherd gave the sheep a sense of security. He was their defender against enemies more powerful than they (1 Sam. 17:34–37; Ps. 23:4; Isa. 40:10–11; Jer. 31:10–11). Likewise, it was the responsibility of the shepherd—not the sheep—to know or to discover the location of pasturage. As the sheep followed their shepherd, they were led to quiet refreshing waters and wholesome nourishing food (1 Chron. 4:39–40; Pss. 23:1–2; 79:13; 95:7; 100:3; Ezek. 34:14–15).

Peter was saying, "I do not need the shepherd to protect me. I am not afraid of the enemy because I can make it on my own" (cf. John 18:10). Peter had to learn that he was just a sheep as he cowered before the powerful enemy (Mark 14:66–72). Peter was also saying, "I do not need a shepherd to provide for me; I can take care of my own needs." Peter learned he was just a sheep as he toiled all night at his own chosen profession with a "good company" and earned nothing (John 21:1–11).

This should help me to remember that I am just a stupid, helpless sheep, not a sharp and independent operator. But this is OK because God is my shepherd. God does not need for me to defend Him or to provide for His work. All He asks is that I follow Him and obey Him.

MARK 14:27–30

And Jesus saith unto them, All ye shall be offended because of me this night: for it is written, I will smite the shepherd, and the sheep shall be scattered. But after that I am risen, I will go before you into Galilee. But Peter said unto him, Although all shall be offended, yet will not I. And Jesus saith unto him, Verily I say unto thee, That this day, even in this night, before the cock crow twice, thou shalt deny me thrice.

A dear friend responded to my devotional thoughts from verses 27–29, indicating that there may be an important quantitative message as well as a qualitative warning in this word picture. I think this is true. The sheep following closest to the shepherd are the safest, while those following at a distance are more likely to be in danger. Being close to the shepherd is our only real security.

Peter was quick to exalt and worship Jesus with religious activities (Mark 9:5), to give honor to the words of Jesus (John 6:68), to identify himself as a committed believer (Mark 10:28), to declare the deity of Christ (Matt. 16:16), to correct Jesus' "pessimism" about His messianic future (Matt. 16:21–23), and to defend Jesus with passion (John 18:10). What Peter did not do was to maintain his focus on Jesus and obey His command to pray while others slept (Matt. 26:38–43). In the passage above, Peter refused to believe the convicting words of Jesus, especially concerning his own weakness.

I certainly should have no problem seeing how I ought to apply the truth of the life of Peter to my own life, to heed the warning to follow my shepherd more closely, to believe His Word, and to obey His commands.

MARK 14:31

But he spake the more vehemently, If I should die with thee, I will not deny thee in any wise. Likewise also said they all.

"They all said likewise." Peter apparently was looked to as a leader by the other disciples. There is no question that people will follow the leadership of someone who knows what he is doing and does not hesitate to move ahead in a good cause without regard for his own welfare. Unfortunately, most people will default on their responsibility to know what they should do and will, instead, follow someone who appears to know what he is doing and speaks with enthusiasm or passion.

Peter did not know what he was talking about. He should have listened to the words of Jesus and kept his mouth shut. But he did not hesitate to speak up, and he seemed so sure of himself. All the other disciples jumped to follow Peter's leadership and example when they too should have been listening to Jesus.

I see two lessons here. (1) It is obvious that I should always look to God and His Word for guidance, leadership and example. This is especially true when there is confident leadership and example being offered and "all are saying likewise." (2) I believe there is also a warning here about my own example and leadership. We live in a time when the contemporary culture (including church culture) has become fixated on the subject of "leadership," and everyone wants to study and exercise leadership. While I should not refuse the ministry of leadership when it is thrust upon me, I should hesitate to exercise it at every opportunity. Leadership in God's work is an awesome responsibility, and I do not want to run the risk of emulating Peter by leading people in the wrong direction.

MARK 14:32–34

And they came to a place which was named Gethsemane: and he saith to his disciples, Sit ye here, while I shall pray. And he taketh with him Peter and James and John, and began to be sore amazed, and to be very heavy; and saith unto them, My soul is exceeding sorrowful unto death: tarry ye here, and watch.

The words translated "sore amazed" (*ekthambeisthai*), "very heavy" (*ademonein*), and "exceeding sorrowful" (*perilupos*) are all very strong words. They were chosen to describe the inner feelings of Jesus in reaction to what was happening and what was about to happen.

There is so much we do not understand about the absolute deity and absolute humanity of Jesus. Many heresies have attempted to fit these amazing facts into categories of human logic. As the eternal and infinite theanthropic *God*-man, Jesus knew ahead of time all that was happening to Him as the sins of humanity (including my sins) were being placed on Him in preparation for His undergoing the human persecution and torture and the divine rejection those sins deserve. But as the God-*man*, He was now actually experiencing these events within the framework of finite time, and powerful emotions were the result.

As I think about this, I need only to understand that all this was for me. An intellectual analysis of it would be futile, but a simple realization of its depth of reality is a powerful reassurance of God's infinite and unfailing love for me. Hallelujah!

MARK 14:35–36

> And he went forward a little, and fell on the ground, and prayed that, if it were possible, the hour might pass from him. And he said, Abba, Father, all things are possible unto thee; take away this cup from me: nevertheless not what I will, but what thou wilt.

As God the Son, Jesus was and is coexistent, coeternal, and co-equal with God the Father. He was very God of very God. When Jesus, the *God*-man spoke to God the Father, He was speaking to a fellow member of the infinite and eternal Godhead.

But Jesus was also very man of very man. So when Jesus, the God-*man*, addressed God the Father as "Abba, Father," He was addressing God the Father as His literal, earthly (biological) Father. There is so much we do not understand about this. It is, however, reassuring to me when I deal with my own very human thoughts and reactions. With God the Holy Spirit living in my body (1 Cor. 6:19) empowering me to be all I was created to be in fellowship with

God, neither my thought life nor my behavioral lifestyle need be controlled by a human emotional roller coaster. It is possible to experience the reality of the full range and depth of human emotions and yet remain inwardly calm and confident and outwardly self-disciplined.

MARK 14:38

Watch ye and pray, lest ye enter into temptation. The spirit truly is ready, but the flesh is weak.

I often receive e-mails from various Christian and conservative organizations that urge me to sign petitions, to write to my congressman, to use my influence—and of course, to contribute to their vital activities on behalf of good and against evil. I can begin to feel pressured to worry about my world "going to hell in a hand basket" on every issue. Yet when I pray about these things, God often points me to Scripture passages such as this one (cf. Matt. 26:41; 1 Thess. 5:6), which, in fact, do appear to command me to "watch" (*gregoreite*) with a sort of tense and unblinking vigilance.

I am not to relax and depend on a matrix of "Christian culture" to protect me and my country and my loved ones from trials and temptations. God has chosen for me to be born in the best possible country for enjoying the material blessings of life. He has also, however, plopped me down here in interesting and challenging times. There are plenty of problems and evils to be concerned about! He has also chosen to place me in a democratic republic, where I am not only responsible for obeying the civil government (Rom. 13:1ff.) but am also responsible to be a vital part of the civil government.

The thing that relieves the tension of these responsibilities is Jesus' command in this and similar passages: "Watch and pray." As I spend time with God, read His Word, share my concerns with Him, and believe His promises, it makes carrying my God-assigned responsibilities just another aspect of walking in peace with Him. Obeying the command to pray, then, removes the tension from the command to watch. It strengthens the willingness of the spirit and overcomes the weakness of the flesh.

MARK 14:38

Watch ye and pray, lest ye enter into temptation. The spirit truly is ready, but the flesh is weak.

The primary motive of the non-Christian life is a natural self-interest. After I become a Christian, I find myself at least occasionally wanting to do the right thing in defiance of my natural desires. My problem is that I am often not able to follow these promptings of the Holy Spirit within me. My natural selfish desires are accustomed to reinforcement by my ingrained habits and my familiar lifestyle.

Jesus was pointed and straightforward in providing me with the secret to success in this struggle to do what pleases God rather than pandering to my own self-indulgence and familiar habits. His command was "Watch and pray." My watching requires a principled decision and disciplined action in putting priority on God's will. No longer does life have to be a desperate struggle about me; it can be the peaceful and meaningful existence it was meant to be about Him.

Watching also requires that I know the meaning of the things I see in my "watching." It requires light as well as eyesight and attention. It demands that I reinforce the power of the indwelling Holy Spirit to control my attitude and lifestyle by reading, studying, and obeying the Holy Spirit's book. Overcoming the weakness of my flesh and empowering my spirit's desire to obey His Spirit starts with personal, private, daily Bible study and prayer.

MARK 14:41–42

And he cometh the third time, and saith unto them, Sleep on now, and take your rest: it is enough, the hour is come; behold, the Son of man is betrayed into the hands of sinners. Rise up, let us go; lo, he that betrayeth me is at hand.

Judas himself never laid a hand on Jesus. He did not witness against Him at His trial nor rise up in opposition to Him or express any views contrary to the truth that Jesus taught. The word translated "betrayer" (*paradidomi*) means simply to "hand over" or to commit something into the hands of another. The factor that makes its use pejorative is the character of the person or institution into whose "hands" (*cheiras*) a thing is entrusted.

The thing entrusted to God's church and to those who lead and teach in the church is the truth of God, specifically the Word of God as written for us by the apostles under the guidance of the Holy Spirit. I think this means that it is not enough for me always to identify with Jesus and the Bible and to say only good things about the Bible. I must also be careful—"watch and pray"—in regard to those to whom I am willing to commit the translation, interpretation, and teaching of the Word of God for my study and use. For me to commit such an awesome responsibility to persons or institutions that have "missed the mark" is, I believe, a form of betrayal.

MARK 14:43

And immediately, while he yet spake, cometh Judas, one of the twelve, and with him a great multitude with swords and staves, from the chief priests and the scribes and the elders.

The religious authorities (*archiereon*), with their academic experts in law and tradition (*grammateon*) and their Sanhedrin colleagues in religious rulership and right of judgment (*presbuteron*), were recognized as the sophisticated experts in matters of theology. Yet here they were sending to arrest Jesus this rabble (*ochlos*) with their military weapons (*machairon*) and crude sticks of wood (*xulon*).

Regardless of theology, people who are not truly born again do not understand the nature and appeal of the simple gospel truth. The fact that God Almighty is just as infinite in love as He is in power "does not compute" in the calculations of theological politics and academic sophistication. When they are threatened by the truth of God's Word, such hierarchies regularly resort to the use of the crudest sort of ad hominem weapons. Because of the appeal of the Word of God to the spiritually needy, God's children are often feared and attacked as "power brokers" by those eager to hold political position and to exercise emotional power over people. I am to expect this and not be disturbed or surprised by it.

> *Yea, and all that will live godly in Christ Jesus shall suffer persecution.* (2 Tim. 3:12)

MARK 14:44–45

> *And he that betrayed him had given them a token, saying, Whomsoever I shall kiss, that same is he; take him, and lead him away safely. And as soon as he was come, he goeth straightway to him, and saith, Master, master; and kissed him.*

A kiss is supposed to be an outward expression of a genuine inner emotion or commitment. To kiss as a calculated act when there is no true message of affection is lying and hypocrisy. When I communicate, either privately or publicly, my words and actions should always be genuine and not an act calculated to impress.

MARK 14:46–47

And they laid their hands on him, and took him. And one of them that stood by drew a sword, and smote a servant of the high priest, and cut off his ear.

What the guards and rabble were doing to Jesus was outrageous. Peter was outraged! He responded to the crude show of force of Jesus' enemies with a crude show of force of his own. His immediate and instinctive response to this outrageous and violent physical attack on Jesus was to put his life on the line with a strong and violent physical counterattack.

After all, Peter was "doing God's work" (for Him). Both logic and sincere commitment agreed that what he did was the right thing. When it came to "serving God," Peter was right there! When it was time to "watch and pray," however, Peter had been asleep at the switch (vv. 37–41). This may explain why Peter's instinctive and effective "service" for God was actually counterproductive in accomplishing God's true purposes.

I should be walking close to Jesus, looking to Him for direction, obeying His Word (v. 38), then trusting Him to accomplish His will. Likewise, as I teach and preach God's Word, I do not need to lay guilt trips on God's people about serving God. I believe that it is enough if I teach people by example and exegesis to read God's Word, to believe God's Word, to obey God's Word, and to trust God—that is, to "watch and pray."

MARK 14:48–49

And Jesus answered and said unto them, Are ye come out, as against a thief, with swords and with staves to take me? I was daily with you in the temple teaching, and ye took me not: but the scriptures must be fulfilled.

Jesus was pointing out the hypocrisy of those arresting Him. These were the officials charged by position and vocation with preserving and disseminating the truth of God. In order to "play their role" publicly, they could not arrest Jesus as He was teaching God's truth in the temple. Instead, they attacked Him secretly and crudely at night. In doing so, they confessed their fear and hatred for His message, which was the truth of God.

Jesus indicated that, by their identifying God's Word with criminality, they were actually fulfilling the very Word of God they were attempting to suppress. Their blatant and hypocritical opposition to God's Word was all in vain. While they were gloating over their clever and successful arrest of Jesus, God's Word was being justified and God's purposes were being inexorably fulfilled by the very way in which their true character was revealed.

This should be an encouragement to me when I see clever and underhanded opposition to God's Word being mounted by those in positions of great authority and popularity. God is still on the throne. Patronizing Jesus' message in the temple and then attacking and arresting Him personally in the garden did not hinder the operation of God's will and purposes.

MARK 14:51–52

And there followed him a certain young man, having a linen cloth cast about his naked body; and the young men laid hold on him: and he left the linen cloth, and fled from them naked.

I have read several reports from people who have seen the film *The Passion*. These reports contain very little description of the content of the film but a great deal about the emotional reaction of the viewers. I suppose this is to be expected in this age of existential self-absorption and the worship of personal feelings. The word *passion* has become the current fetish word that is expected to give ultimate meaning and purpose to life—including even Christian life and ministry.

Peter expressed his passion of loyalty to Jesus, putting his life on the line by an attack on the vastly superior and well-armed force arresting Jesus. On the other hand, the "young man" in the verse above (traditionally Mark) expressed his passion of fear by abandoning Jesus and fleeing the scene. There was an obvious contrast between the reaction of these two. But the behavior of both expressed their "passion." And both were wrong!

My relationship to God is by no means emotionless. Worshiping Him ignites a deep and genuine emotional commitment. This emotional commitment does not need to be "worked up" or "facilitated" because it is the genuine product of a very real relationship. Like any real relationship, my relationship with God requires quality (= quantity) time spent in personal private fellowship with Him. My public "worship" based on anything else, regardless of the passion involved, is just as meaningless as Peter's foolish attack or Mark's cowardly (but prudent) flight.

Since God is God, true worship moves quickly from listening to Him to obeying Him—with or without passion. I hope it is not too simplistic to observe that worship starts with relationship, is cultivated through fellowship (= personal time), and eventuates in obedience. Emotions may—or may not—be involved at any or all steps in this development.

MARK 14:53–54

> *And they led Jesus away to the high priest: and with him were assembled all the chief priests and the elders and the scribes. And Peter followed him afar off, even into the palace of the high priest: and he sat with the servants, and warmed himself at the fire.*

This was a gathering of the Sanhedrin, the legislature and supreme court of the Jewish nation, attended by its staff of academic and legal experts. They were meeting to assume the right to adjudicate matters pertaining to God and His relationship to human beings. Human civil governments still do this. It is still illegitimate usurpation.

Unfortunately, those of us claiming to follow Jesus are sometimes still found "right in the courtyard" of the world's presumptuous legal system, warming ourselves at their fire. That is also illegitimate.

MARK 14:54, 66–68

And Peter followed him afar off, even into the palace of the high priest: and he sat with the servants, and warmed himself at the fire. . . . And as Peter was beneath in the palace, there cometh one of the maids of the high priest: and when she saw Peter warming himself, she looked upon him, and said, And thou also wast with Jesus of Nazareth. But he denied, saying, I know not, neither understand I what thou sayest. And he went out into the porch; and the cock crew.

This can be a warning that I may be about to get in trouble when I attempt to make myself more comfortable by associating with those who serve the enemies of Jesus.

MARK 14:55–62

And the chief priests and all the council sought for witness against Jesus to put him to death; and found none. For many bare false witness against him, but their witness agreed not together. And there arose certain, and bare false witness against him, saying, We heard him say, I will destroy this temple that is made with hands, and within three days I will build another made without hands. But neither so did their witness agree together. And the high priest stood up in the midst, and asked Jesus, saying, Answerest thou nothing? what is it which these witness against thee? But he held his peace, and answered nothing. Again the high priest asked him, and said unto him, Art thou the Christ, the Son of the Blessed?

And Jesus said, I am: and ye shall see the Son of man sitting on the right hand of power, and coming in the clouds of heaven.

When there was no legitimate charge against Him, Jesus was not obligated to give an answer. He said nothing since there was nothing to say. When asked a direct and legitimate question concerning His claim to messiahship, however, He gave a straightforward and unequivocal answer. At that point, there should have been a trial to "try" whether His claim was true. Instead, the Sanhedrin defaulted on its judicial responsibility and turned Jesus over to the Romans for execution. This put the Sanhedrin on trial, and God Himself demonstrated that Jesus' claims to messiahship and deity (v. 62) were absolutely true by His resurrection from the dead.

The Jews and the Romans treated Jesus as if He were not the Son of God—but He is! It is my privilege to live in the light of the fact that Jesus was the Son of God. By taking His Word seriously to the point of simple obedience, I may demonstrate to my world that the Sanhedrin was mistaken; the historical Jesus was—and is—God Almighty in human flesh.

MARK 15

MARK 15:1–5

> *And straightway in the morning the chief priests held a consultation with the elders and scribes and the whole council, and bound Jesus, and carried him away, and delivered him to Pilate. And Pilate asked him, Art thou the King of the Jews? And he answering said unto him, Thou sayest it. And the chief priests accused him of many things: but he answered nothing. And Pilate asked him again, saying, Answerest thou nothing? behold how many things they witness against thee. But Jesus yet answered nothing; so that Pilate marvelled.*

Once again we see Jesus claiming, without hesitation or equivocation, that He is the Messiah. At the same time, He refused to answer, or even to acknowledge, the irrelevant accusations. This is a good example for me, as His follower. I may also ignore the irrelevant ad hominem distractions while insisting on the truth of the core of the gospel message: Jesus, Who was—and is—God in human flesh, died for my sins according to the Word of God (1 Cor. 15:3–4).

MARK 15:3–5

And the chief priests accused him of many things: but he answered nothing. And Pilate asked him again, saying, Answerest thou nothing? behold how many things they witness against thee. But Jesus yet answered nothing; so that Pilate marvelled.

Neither the number nor the seriousness of the accusations charged against Jesus by the Sanhedrin were in any way relevant since they were patently false. False accusations are always irrelevant.

What was—and is—relevant is the list of many and grievous sins charged against Jesus by God the Father. They were my sins! Jesus accepted them voluntarily and paid the price for them on my behalf. Jesus was able to do this for me because He had no sins of His own chargeable against Him. God's Word makes very clear the sinlessness of Jesus and the irrelevance and falsity of all charges against Him as a reassurance to me that Jesus was qualified to assume the burden of all my very real sins and that they are paid for, forgiven, and gone.

MARK 15:6–8

Now at that feast he released unto them one prisoner, whomsoever they desired. And there was one named Barabbas, which lay bound with them that had made insurrection with him, who had committed murder in the insurrection. And the multitude crying aloud began to desire him to do as he had ever done unto them.

It makes no more sense to release a criminal who should be locked up than it does to lock people up arbitrarily for no reason. The institution of civil government was ordained by God (Gen. 9:5–7; Rom. 13:1–7; 1 Pet. 2:13–17). But in the hands of unregenerate men, it has often become an irrational exercise in arbitrary power. The Roman control of the Jewish lands had become an unstable and antagonistic hostility-dependency relationship between government and governed, in which the atmosphere of hate created by raw power exercised over an irrational and fanatic population would be punctuated and relieved by irrational "favors," such as releasing a notoriously dangerous character on popular demand.

Historically, true governments of law and equity (as distinguished from governments of naked power or mere political manipulation) have been established and maintained only by peoples with cultures based on genuine belief in a supernatural religion with clear-cut moral standards. Theoretically, then, a population dominated by a "critical mass" of born-again believers, and including many "cultural Christians," should be able to establish a government favorable to equity and prosperity. This theory was justified and demonstrated in North America for about two hundred years. This would mean that what our country needs today is not just a political conservatism but a real revival of Bible-based Christianity.

MARK 15:7–11

And there was one named Barabbas, which lay bound with them that had made insurrection with him, who had committed murder in the insurrection. And the multitude crying aloud began to desire him to do as he had ever done unto them. But Pilate answered them, saying, Will ye that I release unto you the King of the Jews? For he knew that the chief priests had delivered him for envy. But the chief priests moved the people, that he should rather release Barabbas unto them.

These people followed their religious leaders, who would rather be at the mercy of a rabble-rousing murderer than tolerate a Messiah, Who insisted they needed to be saved from their sins.

I should examine more closely the religious leaders I choose to support and follow. If they talk more about human religious opinions and popularity of worship methods than about sin and its consequences, they might be leading God's people in false and counterproductive directions. This certainly speaks to me as I teach God's Word. I have a responsibility to insist that Jesus came to save His people from their sins—but only as we acknowledge our sins and turn to Him. If people always "enjoy" my teaching God's truth,

I may not be presenting the same Jesus these people of Jerusalem and their leaders so emphatically rejected.

MARK 15:12–15

And Pilate answered and said again unto them, What will ye then that I shall do unto him whom ye call the King of the Jews? And they cried out again, Crucify him. Then Pilate said unto them, Why, what evil hath he done? And they cried out the more exceedingly, Crucify him. And so Pilate, willing to content the people, released Barabbas unto them, and delivered Jesus, when he had scourged him, to be crucified.

When I read this passage and its parallel passages, especially Matthew 27:24, it strikes me as typical of the way we humans behave. We rarely accept responsibility for our own sins; we pass the buck of guilt to someone else. Pilate knew that Jesus was innocent. He had the responsibility—and the authority—to release Him. Yet, to placate the Jewish religious leaders and to ingratiate himself with Emperor Tiberius (and distance himself from his disgraced political patron, Sejanus), he had an innocent man crucified. He acknowledged none of these unworthy motives and laid all the blame on the Jews.

This reminds me of the prototype of human buck passing by Adam in the Garden of Eden: "The woman whom You gave to be with me, she gave me of the tree" (Gen. 3:12 NKJV). While the Jews rejected their Messiah and must answer to God for it, they are no more guilty of the death of Jesus than Eve was for Adam's sin in disobeying God by eating of the forbidden fruit.

When I sin, the key to my return to fellowship with God and fullness of joy is honest and full confession of my own sins of attitude and action (1 John 1:4, 8–10).

MARK 15:12–15

And Pilate answered and said again unto them, What will ye then that I shall do unto him whom ye call the King of the Jews? And they cried out again, Crucify him. Then Pilate said unto them, Why, what evil hath he done? And they cried out the more exceedingly, Crucify him. And so Pilate, willing to content the people, released Barabbas unto them, and delivered Jesus, when he had scourged him, to be crucified.

It is true that Jesus as the Messiah was rejected by the official religious leaders of the Jewish nation and by the early morning pickup crowd in Jerusalem on Passover. But the decision to crucify Jesus was made by Pilate, official representative of the Gentile civil government.

Pilate acknowledged that Jesus was innocent (Matt. 27:24; Luke 23:4, 14; John 19:4, 6) and decided to crucify Him anyway. Then he tried to shift the blame to the Jews for his dastardly and illegal action. Pilate was the prototype for historical anti-Semitism: (1) he represented a Gentile-dominated secular civil government, (2) he did not accept God's truth for himself, and (3) he blamed the Jews for the death of Christ.

Whether and however God may wish to deal with the presumption of the first century Jewish leadership in attempting to transfer their assumed guilt to their descendants (Matt. 27:25) is strictly between God and His chosen people. It is my privilege as well as my responsibility as a Christian to love God's chosen earthly people, to share the gospel with the "Jew first" (Rom. 1:16), and to pray for the peace of Jerusalem.

MARK 15:15–19

And so Pilate, willing to content the people, released Barabbas unto them, and delivered Jesus, when he had scourged him, to be crucified. And the soldiers led him away into the hall, called Prae-torium; and they call together the whole band. And they clothed him with purple, and platted a crown of thorns, and put it about his head, and began to salute him, Hail, King of the Jews! And they smote him on the head with a reed, and did spit upon him, and bowing their knees worshipped him.

This is typically the way the unregenerate world receives the pure truth of God and any who identify with God's truth without compromise. First, the religious and intellectual leaders are frightened by the truth because so many people are drawn to its obvious harmony with the way man was created to be; this undermines the dishonest and hypocritical posturing by which these leaders hold the loyalty of the people. Then, the pandering poll watchers who exercise governmental power exercise that power against God's truth to placate the opinion makers and their conformist followers. Finally, the politically correct rabble pile on in the crudest ways to express disapproval with mockery and sarcasm.

This all sounds contemporary. God's truth does not change and the reaction of unregenerate man does not change; improved civilization and "culture" make no difference.

My own response should be a commitment to stick with God's truth and God's Word in the face of whatever form of opposition and pressure is brought to bear on me. When God's enemies attack me, it does not mean that God has abandoned me and certainly does not mean I should abandon Him or compromise His truth.

MARK 15:21

And they compel one Simon a Cyrenian, who passed by, coming out of the country, the father of Alexander and Rufus, to bear his cross.

John tells us that Jesus began the trip from judgment to execution bearing His own cross (John 19:17). Apparently, the agony of the garden, the all-night "trials," and the mocking, flogging, and torture had left Jesus physically weakened so that He had to have someone else actually carry His cross. It was still Jesus' cross; Simon the Cyrenian was not crucified on that cross.

What was borne by the condemned from the place of judgment to the place of crucifixion was the patibulum, or crosspiece of the cross. Its weight was carried fully upon the shoulder and not dragged on the ground as is so often misrepresented in illustrations and reenactments. It was carried publicly as a symbol or acknowledgement that the person had been judged unworthy to live on earth any longer and was on his way to have his life denied to him by execution. Carrying the crosspiece was a confession of sin and unworthiness.

When Jesus told (each of) His followers to "deny themselves" and take up their (own) cross (Matt. 16:24; Mark 8:34; Luke 9:23), it had nothing to do with dragging our unique burdens and problems in life. Jesus used this as an accurate symbol of our confessing our sin and unworthiness as we praise God that Jesus bore that cross to Calvary and there suffered the death we deserve for our sins. Hallelujah!

MARK 15:22–23

> *And they bring him unto the place Golgotha, which is, being interpreted, The place of a skull. And they gave him to drink wine mingled with myrrh: but he received it not.*

Why would the Roman soldiers offer Jesus a painkiller before subjecting Him to the agonizing death of crucifixion?

The Romans executed people they considered troublemakers to eliminate them from the population, thus making the population more orderly and easier to control. They used the especially painful and agonizing method of crucifixion for the same reason. They were not getting revenge by making their prisoner suffer; the Romans used crucifixion in a very public place as an example. They wanted to make sure others would not be tempted to live as the troublemaker had lived. In this way, they kept the population under control.

God's truth has a way of turning man's logic upside down. Jesus was not a troublemaker and Jesus' death on the cross was not just an example. Jesus' death was punishment for my sins, and Jesus was willing to suffer all the pain and agony my sins deserve. In the wisdom of God, Jesus was crucified so that I could live as Jesus lived in harmony with God's order (Gal. 5:24) under the control of the Holy Spirit (Gal. 5:22–23). Hallelujah!

MARK 15:25–26

And it was the third hour, and they crucified him. And the superscription of his accusation was written over, THE KING OF THE JEWS.

We live in a culture that has turned our mastery of the physical world into an environment of artificiality, demanding personal convenience and pursuing the satisfaction of our personal desires. At the same time, we have become obsessed with things labeled "reality" and "X-treme" in the pretend worlds of sports and entertainment.

Are we ready to deal with the full truth of the impact on our personal world of the unparalleled "reality" and "X-tremity" of the moment in history that occurred at Calvary? This was not just a play. It did not depend upon acting skills or special effects for an impact on the jaded emotions of a sophisticated audience. In the reality drama of crucifixion, Satan performed at the nadir of his X-treme hatred and destructiveness, and God responded at the apex of His divine life-giving love. The genuine spiritual reality of the crucifixion puts the lie to a religion of convenience and entertainment catering to my contemporary lifestyle and propped up by play acting and the manipulation of sight and sound to titillate and arouse mere emotions.

The extent to which this ultimate moment of "X-treme reality" affects my life is not completed or measured by the emotions it may evoke in me as I think about it. The real test of "reality" is the disciplined consistency with which I seek to know and to do the will of the One Who demonstrated the reality and the X-tremity of His love for me at Calvary.

MARK 15:26

And the superscription of his accusation was written over, THE KING OF THE JEWS.

Pilate did not attempt to build up the importance of Jesus to call attention to Jesus. Knowing perfectly well he was executing an innocent man, Pilate used the occasion to protect and further his own political career by pretending to eliminate a threat to the stability of the Roman Empire by a claimant to the Jewish throne.

The amazing and ironic thing is that what Pilate had inscribed on the cross was the absolute and critical truth. It was a confession that Pilate, as representative of the Gentile governmental power, was anti-Semitic and was being used as the tool of Satan to try to eliminate God's Messiah. God has a way of controlling the behavior of men so that their actions fit His plans and purposes totally without their knowledge and often against their will.

The lesson is not to panic when things in my world do not make sense or when they seem to be going wrong or when evil people appear to have the upper hand. If my own life is in line with God's will and purposes, I am on the right side and God will make things work out to His glory and my blessing in the long run.

Surely the wrath of man shall praise thee: the remainder of wrath shalt thou restrain. (Ps. 76:10)

And we know that all things work together for good to those who love God, to those who are the called according to His purpose. (Rom. 8:28 NKJV)

MARK 15:27–28

And with him they crucify two thieves; the one on his right hand, and the other on his left. And the scripture was fulfilled, which saith, And he was numbered with the transgressors.

When we read, believe, study, and obey God's Word, it brings us into a life of joy (1 John 1:4) and fulfillment (John 10:10). It may also make those around us uncomfortable. Will those who are discomfited by our Christian lifestyle say, "Your life has placed us under conviction, so we are going to persecute you because you have a good testimony for God?" No, that is not what will happen! We will be called fanatics and right-wing extremists and accused of being mean-spirited, old-fashioned, legalistic, and narrow-minded troublemakers. (John 16:1–3). We will be lied about and accused of whatever crimes and sins come to the mind of those who choose to persecute us.

Jesus was condemned for blasphemy (Matt. 26:65; Mark 14:64) and executed among criminals as a troublemaker and pretender (Matt. 27:37; Mark 15:26; Luke 23:38; John19:19). Why should I be surprised or disappointed when my enjoying the Christian life to the fullest is criticized and I am accused of attitudes and actions that are the product of angry and dishonest minds. When I turned my whole life over to God, it included my reputation. When I am really at peace with God, it doesn't matter what accusations and charges may be brought against me by other people. Only God is authorized to issue—and to sign—my report card.

MARK 15:29–31

And they that passed by railed on him, wagging their heads, and saying, Ah, thou that destroyest the temple, and buildest it in three days, save thyself, and come down from the cross. Likewise also the chief priests mocking said among themselves with the scribes, He saved others; himself he cannot save.

The word *save* (*sozo*) has taken on a specialized theological meaning in the church because of the wonderful fact of salvation from sin and its consequences accomplished at Calvary. Before Calvary, however, the word *sozo* was used in a more general sense to mean "rescue" in many contexts. What the religious leaders were apparently saying was "He is reputed to have rescued people from many kinds of sickness and even death (Luke 7:11–15; John 11:39–44), yet He cannot now rescue Himself from death by crucifixion."

Once again, we can see the truth of God flipping human wisdom on its head (1 Cor. 1:20–21). Jesus could, of course, have easily saved Himself at any point in this tragic scenario (Matt. 26:53), but His whole purpose in coming to earth was not to fulfill any of His personal human desires but to obey and fulfill the Father's will (Matt. 26:54). This purpose had been decided long before (Gen. 3:15) and clearly announced just before His birth (Matt. 1:21). The irony is that by not saving Himself from death, He accomplished—once for all—salvation from eternal death for all mankind who will exercise their God-given free will to accept His rescue from their hateful and deadly enemy: their own sins.

The implication for me is obvious. I should praise God for the death of Jesus. I should thank Him for having rescued me, and I should stay continually in close fellowship with Him through His Word to exercise and enjoy the God-given victory over my enemy, accomplished on the cross by Jesus.

MARK 15:29–31

> *And they that passed by railed on him, wagging their heads, and saying, Ah, thou that destroyest the temple, and buildest it in three days, save thyself, and come down from the cross. Likewise also the chief priests mocking said among themselves with the scribes, He saved others; himself he cannot save.*

The people of Jerusalem and their religious leaders assumed that if Jesus actually had authority to exercise the power of God, He would exercise it for His own benefit in the physical and material world of the five senses. They were progenitors of the "Name-it-claim-it" gospel of wealth.

People who are naturalists and materialists assume that if "real" power is present and is exercised, they can see and feel it with their five senses. They do not perceive the truth concerning spiritual power. They do not understand the fact of the inner peace that is independent of any outward circumstances. Quiet and invisible obedience to the will of God does not exist for them. True spiritual activity does not count when it does not affect them in their physical world.

Jesus could easily have come down from the cross, but He did not. He could have ordered a force of at least ten thousand angels and summarily destroyed them all. There was a very real reason He did not do any such thing but hung on the cross and suffered. He was obeying the will of His Father in accordance with the Word of God. He was, in fact, dying for my sins. Jesus' death was not "just an example" but was a very real and a very powerful accomplishment. On the other hand, in submitting to the Father's will and ignoring the circumstances, He did set for me a perfect example for my own attitude and actions as I believe and obey the Word of God.

MARK 15:31–32

> *Likewise also the chief priests mocking said among themselves with the scribes, He saved others; himself he cannot save. Let Christ the King of Israel descend now from the cross, that we may see and believe. And they that were crucified with him reviled him.*

Mark (cf. also Matt. 27:44) tells us that both of the criminals crucified with Jesus began their session on the cross by reviling Jesus. Luke, however, relates the story of one of the criminals repenting and calling on Jesus to remember him and Jesus responding by assuring this criminal a place in paradise:

> *Then one of the criminals who were hanged blasphemed Him, say-*
> *ing, "If You are the Christ, save Yourself and us." But the other,*
> *answering, rebuked him, saying, "Do you not even fear God, see-*
> *ing you are under the same condemnation? And we indeed justly,*
> *for we receive the due reward of our deeds; but this Man has done*
> *nothing wrong." Then he said to Jesus, "Lord, remember me when*
> *You come into Your kingdom." And Jesus said to him, "Assur-*
> *edly, I say to you, today you will be with Me in Paradise." (Luke*
> *23:39–43 NKJV)*

In view of what Luke tells us, why would the Holy Spirit make a point of having both Matthew and Mark inform us that the repentant thief started by reviling Jesus along with the others? I believe these two criminals were representative—or types—of the whole human race. The entire human race is divided into only two categories: (1) saved from sin and (2) lost in sin. The repentant thief is a type of Christian in this age. To be saved from sin, we must first acknowledge that we deserve to die for our sins. We then acknowledge that Jesus is the sinless Lord of all creation, qualified to die for our sins. We can then repent and call upon Him and expect His response in accepting us into eternal fellowship with Him. Hallelujah!

MARK 15:33–34

> *And when the sixth hour was come, there was darkness over the*
> *whole land until the ninth hour. And at the ninth hour Jesus cried*
> *with a loud voice, saying, Eloi, Eloi, lama sabachthani? which is,*
> *being interpreted, My God, my God, why hast thou forsaken me?*

The trinity of the Godhead is a mysterious truth. It is just as mysterious as it is true. There is much we do not understand about God the Father's "forsaking" Jesus when Jesus hung on the cross. Among the things we do not know for certain is just how long this "forsaking" lasted.

What we do know is that Jesus was placed on the cross about 9 AM modern time, that there was darkness from noon to 3 PM, and that about 3 PM, Jesus cried, "My God, My God, why have You forsaken Me?" He then cried with a loud voice, apparently declaring His work finished (John 19:30) and committing His spirit to the Father (Luke 23:46). So, as the Light of the World hung on a cross, it was dark for three earth hours, followed by the cry regarding forsaking.

Whatever "time" was involved in Jesus' experience, it was adequate to suffer for my deserved separation from God the Father for eternity and to cancel all my punishment once for all. Hallelujah!

> So when Jesus had received the sour wine, He said, "It is finished!" And bowing His head, He gave up His spirit. (John 19:30 NKJV)

MARK 15:34

> And at the ninth hour Jesus cried with a loud voice, saying, Eloi, Eloi, lama sabachthani? which is, being interpreted, My God, my God, why hast thou forsaken me?

Even the person who has not accepted the death of Christ for his sins can discern the hand of God in nature and enjoy the reflection of God's presence in His handiwork (Ps. 19:1–3). In addition, the fact and character of the Creator is imprinted within our consciousness as we have been created in His image (Rom. 1:18–21). The fact that even a person lost in sin, living in a world marred by sin, lives a generally positive experience is attested by the way human beings cling to this earthly life.

The truth is that this earthly experience, with its blessings, the capacity to enjoy those blessings, and the ever-present opportunity to accept the forgiveness of sins and full fellowship with God is as close to God as the unregenerate person will ever get. The cry of Jesus, "My God, My God, why have You forsaken Me?" came when He was mysteriously separated from the Father (and survived because of His sinlessness). It is the cry of the unsaved person as he is called from this earth to eternity and realizes his chance to become what he was created to be and to enter fellowship with God is gone forever.

How grateful I should be that Jesus experienced that separation on my behalf and I will never face that kind of moment.

MARK 15:34–36

And at the ninth hour Jesus cried with a loud voice, saying, Eloi, Eloi, lama sabachthani? which is, being interpreted, My God, my God, why hast thou forsaken me? And some of them that stood by, when they heard it, said, Behold, he calleth Elias. And one ran and filled a spunge full of vinegar, and put it on a reed, and gave him to drink, saying, Let alone; let us see whether Elias will come to take him down.

They did not listen carefully to what Jesus said. This made it possible to believe He had said something He did not say, which, in turn, made it possible to "prove" Him wrong. People should listen more carefully when *God* speaks. People still try to make the Bible say things it does not so they may deny its truth.

The lesson should be obvious. I should study the Word of God carefully to know accurately what it says so that I may obey it accurately.

MARK 15:34

And at the ninth hour Jesus cried with a loud voice, saying, Eloi, Eloi, lama sabachthani? which is, being interpreted, My God, my God, why hast thou forsaken me?

All during His life as a human being, Jesus, the God man, had addressed God the Father as "Father." But here on the cross, Jesus was bearing in Himself the sins that separate me from a holy God. His addressing His Father as "God" rather than "Father" reflected the mysterious fact that He was somehow separated from the Father on account of my sins.

Along with all creation, I must always recognize God as God (Rom. 14:11; Phil. 2:10). However, as I confess my sinfulness and accept the gift of Jesus' dying for my sins, then I may also address almighty God as my "heavenly Father." Hallelujah!

MARK 15:37

And Jesus cried with a loud voice, and gave up the ghost.

The one word translated by the phrase "breathed His last" (NKJV) (*exepneusen*) is so translated by most modern versions. However, it is translated in the King James Version "gave up the ghost." There is a reason for this difference between these two most faithful translations. The word *exepneusen* is based on the Greek word *pneuma*, which can mean either "breath" or "spirit." In this passage, "gave up the ghost [i.e., spirit]" might be a better translation. On the other hand, exactly the same word is used in verse 39 to describe the observation of the Roman centurion, who would likely note only the physical phenomenon of breathing His last.

God, of course, is the master of language and communication. I suspect that He meant for us to see elements of both ideas in this description of what Jesus did as He cried with a loud voice. As He breathed His last physically, he dismissed His spirit from His body on His own initiative. Jesus, as God, had total control of both the physical and spiritual realms. What we are to understand from the report of the apostles in the Scripture (John 15:26–27) and what the centurion saw "on the ground" are one and the same occurrence (cf. Gen. 2:7). All reliable versions, though they differ among themselves, translate the word *exepneusen* consistently in verses 37 and 39.

The personal lesson for me once again is to see and rejoice in Jesus' control of all things. Even when He appears to be helpless, He is working all things for the glory of God and the blessing of His people. If Jesus had complete control of His own physical "death,"

He can certainly handle any problems He allows to come into my life. Praise the Lord!

MARK 15:37–38

> *And Jesus cried with a loud voice, and gave up the ghost. And the veil of the temple was rent in twain from the top to the bottom.*

In the symbolism of the Old Testament tabernacle and of the temple, the holiest place, or holy of holies, represented the very presence of God Himself. It clearly represented His presence in the midst of His people but separated from all the people, including the priests, by the holy veil. No one was allowed to enter this representation of the holy presence except the Jewish high priest, and he only one day a year and only with blood to atone for His sins and the sins of God's people.

The symbolic meaning of the veil itself, however, was not revealed until the death of Jesus in the New Testament. When Jesus died, the veil was ripped in two and the holy of holies was made wide open to all. The rip in the veil started at the top and extended all the way to the bottom; the finger of God Himself thus opened the invitation for man into His holy presence. In this way, He revealed that the veil represented the human body of Jesus, the God-man, Whose suffering and death opened the way for us into God's presence.

> *Having therefore, brethren, boldness to enter into the holiest by the blood of Jesus, by a new and living way, which he hath consecrated for us, through the veil, that is to say, his flesh. (Heb. 10:19–20)*

This is very convicting. If I fail to accept this invitation to spend time in God's presence, then Christ's suffering and death in my place were in vain. I am wasting the gift of God's holy invitation. Even if I spend my time serving Him as the priests did in the outer holy place with the candlestick, the shewbread, and so forth but do not first spend quality (i.e., quantity) time in the now opened holy of holies in God's presence, there is a real sense that Jesus' death means nothing to me. My first response to God's gracious invitation to salvation through the blood of Jesus is to spend time in His holy presence.

MARK 15:37

And Jesus cried with a loud voice, and gave up the ghost.

The fact that Jesus was able to shout with a "loud voice" (*phonen megalen*) just before breathing His last breath is significant. Jesus did not expire from the torture and exposure on the cross. Jesus had accomplished (Luke 9:31), on account of His innocence, survival of the momentary separation from His Father. His job was done (John 19:30). It was time to leave.

So who killed Christ? The Jews? Without question their leaders rejected their Messiah and betrayed Him to the Romans. The Romans? Most certainly Pilate ordered Him executed, despite knowing He was innocent. Our sins? It was our sins that made it necessary for the Father to "forsake Him" (v. 34) so that Jesus took our death sentence of separation from the Father, which is spiritual death.

But, physically, who killed Christ? I believe the answer is no one did because no one could! Jesus accomplished our spiritual death and survived, and left. The stage was set for the resurrection. Hallelujah!

MARK 15:39

And when the centurion, which stood over against him, saw that he so cried out, and gave up the ghost, he said, Truly this man was the Son of God.

What, or how much, the centurion meant by this observation we cannot know. He may have been a Gentile "God fearer" (Acts 11:22, 34–37), who was attracted to Judaism to a greater or lesser extent and familiar with Old Testament prophecy and theology. On the other hand, he may have been a rank heathen with a nominal knowledge of the Greco-Roman pantheon of semihuman gods and semidivine human beings.

We do know that a Roman centurion was not an ignorant novice in the matter of death by crucifixion. He had seen the torture and persecution Jesus had endured and observed the way He dealt with it and how He shouted loudly and stopped breathing. He had seen this very physical man endure very physical torture and suffering, and the thing that had impressed him was the evidence that there was very clearly a nonphysical, supernatural, and divine dimension or connection involved in this man's suffering and death. Once again, we see God wring from a person in official position a very specific acknowledgment of an important and relevant truth (cf. Mark 15:26; John 11:50; 18:14).

If a Roman centurion could perceive the unique deity of the historical Jesus, then those of us who profess Christianity and study theology are without excuse if we treat Him as merely a divine fetish or serve Him as an avocation while focusing our lives on our own interests. My own attitude and behavior should reflect the reality of Jesus' deity and of His rulership over all my affairs.

MARK 15:43

Joseph of Arimathaea, an honourable counsellor, which also waited for the kingdom of God, came, and went in boldly unto Pilate, and craved the body of Jesus.

Joseph was apparently a man of wealth (Matt. 27:57), a very honored (*euschemon*) member of the Sanhedrin (*bouleutes*; cf. Luke 23:50), and a secret believer in Jesus (John 19:38). He had to take courage to request the body of Jesus because it would unveil the secrecy of his belief and reveal his discipleship to the religious leaders. This would, in turn, destroy his position of honor, likely lose him his seat on the Sanhedrin, and possibly even threaten his personal wealth.

When the chips were down, however, this "secret" disciple showed more courage and consistency than the recognized "leader" of Jesus' disciples (Mark 14:30, 68, 72).

So how about me? Would I ever allow advantages, recognitions, and honors granted me by those who are not the friends of God to inhibit me from revealing the depth, reality, or narrowness of my trust in the Lord Jesus?

MARK 15:44–45

> *And Pilate marvelled if he were already dead: and calling unto him the centurion, he asked him whether he had been any while dead. And when he knew it of the centurion, he gave the body to Joseph.*

The "swoon" theory, so popular with theological liberals and other unbelievers, is disproved by the failure of those strongly motivated to do so to produce a body—dead or alive. It is also clearly disproved by the official report to his superior of a Roman centurion. It is likely this centurion was the best qualified person to judge and recognize physical life and death to be found anywhere within a hundred miles of Jerusalem.

Jesus' body was physically *dead* when removed from the cross. Recognizing this fact is necessary for a real understanding of Christian salvation from sin. Having endured the spiritual death of forsaking by the Father because of our sins, Jesus then voluntarily left His body so that it was dead, and, appropriately, was buried. At the predicted and scheduled time, Jesus then repossessed His body so that it became alive. The resurrection is proof that Jesus did not die for His own sins, since He had none, but endured spiritual death for our sins and survived because of His sinlessness. The resurrection, then, is a guarantee that our sins are paid for, forgiven, and gone.

> *Who was delivered for our offences, and was raised again for our justification. (Rom. 4:25)*

MARK 15:46

And he bought fine linen, and took him down, and wrapped him in the linen, and laid him in a sepulchre which was hewn out of a rock, and rolled a stone unto the door of the sepulchre.

"Which was hewn out of a rock." Why was Jesus not buried in an ordinary cave, tomb, or dug grave? There was a reason God arranged to have Jesus' body buried in a tomb quarried (*lelatomemenon*) out of solid bedrock (*petras*). In order to demonstrate His supernatural control of all aspects of physical and spiritual life, God had Jesus' body declared dead by an acknowledged expert in such matters (vv. 44–45) and buried in a place impossible to access by human effort in the time (thirty-seven hours plus or minus) available and under the circumstances prevailing (on a high Sabbath and under Roman guard).

There was no way a dead body was going to come to life and escape the tomb except by the power of almighty God. This means my salvation from the punishment that my sins deserve is guaranteed by that same eternal, supernatural power (Rom. 4:25). Hallelujah!

MARK 16

MARK 16:1–2

> *And when the sabbath was past, Mary Magdalene, and Mary the mother of James, and Salome, had bought sweet spices, that they might come and anoint him. And very early in the morning the first day of the week, they came unto the sepulchre at the rising of the sun.*

According to custom, the women among those closest as family and friends of the deceased had the responsibility and privilege of preparing the body for burial. These women, and others with them, were doing the normal thing in exercising their right to dwell upon the suffering and death of a precious loved one as they cleaned and spiced the body. In the case of Jesus, they never had the opportunity to dwell upon His suffering and death in preparing the dead body for burial; the only one to exercise this privilege was Mary the sister of Martha (Matt. 26:12; Mark 14:8; John 12:7).

The most significant fact about Jesus' torture, suffering, crucifixion, and "forsaking" by the Father was the fact that He rose from the dead. As Christians, we should never forget what it cost the Son of God to rescue us from the punishment we deserve, and we should not hesitate to share this good news boldly with others. The awful and once-for-all death of Jesus is the beginning of something wonderful and eternal for us.

But it is only the beginning. There is a temptation to fixate on Jesus' suffering and death and ignore the fact and significance of the resurrection. The true Christian life does not consist of repeatedly confessing and dwelling on our sins and Jesus' suffering and sacrifice. The true purpose of God will be carried out in my life as I thank God for what Jesus did and then immerse myself in obedience to His teaching and in the resultant enjoyment of the eternal resurrection life His death provides for me.

MARK 16:5–7

> And entering into the sepulchre, they saw a young man sitting on the right side, clothed in a long white garment; and they were affrighted. And he saith unto them, Be not affrighted: Ye seek Jesus of Nazareth, which was crucified: he is risen; he is not here: behold the place where they laid him. But go your way, tell his disciples and Peter that he goeth before you into Galilee: there shall ye see him, as he said unto you.

The "young man" (neaniskon) talking to this group of women was undoubtedly an angel (angelos = messenger) of God. On God's behalf, he delivered the good news about Jesus' resurrection. Notice what an effective and efficient communicator God is. In short, almost cryptic, but information-filled words and phrases, God's messenger laid out all the facts the women needed to know.

There was no fanfare, no exaggeration, and no overdramatization. There was no attempt to "impact" their emotions with this "powerful" message; in fact, the angel's first words were "Calm down" (me ekthambeisthe).

Then, having delivered God's good news of the resurrection, God's messenger commanded them to share these facts with Jesus' other followers. If I get the facts straight and communicate them accurately and effectively, I have done what God would have me to do; I have no responsibility to "high pressure" people or to use special methods designed to "reach" them by pandering to their emotions. I am to get God's message straight in my own mind, then deliver it to others just the way God gave it to me (1 Cor. 15:3–4). This sounds very much like careful study of God's inerrant message followed by clear, simple, exegetical teaching and preaching.

MARK 16:6–8

> And he saith unto them, Be not affrighted: Ye seek Jesus of Nazareth, which was crucified: he is risen; he is not here: behold the place where they laid him. But go your way, tell his disciples and Peter that he goeth before you into Galilee: there shall ye see him, as he said unto you. And they went out quickly, and fled from the sepulchre; for they trembled and were amazed: neither said they any thing to any man; for they were afraid.

The original reaction of (some of) the women was clear disobedience to the command from God to share the truth with other followers of Jesus. The reason (*gar*) for this disobedience is that they had already disobeyed the very first command given them by God's messenger. He had said, "Do not be alarmed." Yet they trembled, were amazed, and were afraid.

It is interesting how many other disobediences follow as we disobey by fearing in spite of the fact that God "has not given us a spirit of fear, but of power and of love and of a sound mind" (2 Tim. 1:7). Peter's hypocritical behavior in Antioch (Gal. 2:11–13) is a perfect example. The Jewish converts from Jerusalem wanted sincerely to be Christians—and to be considered Christians—yet were unwilling to change their pre-Christian lifestyle to conform to gospel truth. Peter, though a leader among them, conformed to their prejudice and inflexibility, fearing (*phoboumenos*) their opinion of him.

Do I put priority on conforming my life courageously to God's Word, or do I let fear cause me to conform to the opinions of my contemporaries?

MARK 16:9–14

Now when Jesus was risen early the first day of the week, he appeared first to Mary Magdalene, out of whom he had cast seven devils. And she went and told them that had been with him, as they mourned and wept. And they, when they had heard that he was alive, and had been seen of her, believed not. After that he appeared in another form unto two of them, as they walked, and went into the country. And they went and told it unto the residue: neither believed they them. Afterward he appeared unto the eleven as they sat at meat, and upbraided them with their unbelief and hardness of heart, because they believed not them which had seen him after he was risen.

Jesus rebuked His disciples for not believing a really fantastic story told them by a very few people about His rising from the dead after a horrible death and a very secure burial. Why would He rebuke them for being skeptical about such an incredible story as that? The reason, of course, is that He himself had clearly predicted that it would happen.

Jesus had taught many things that were "over the heads" of the disciples spiritually. They had filtered the meaning of His words through the screen of their own experience, observation, and judgment. That He meant exactly what He said did not register with them when His words violated their own understandings. Jesus rebuked them for rejecting His word on the basis of their own human judgment.

I should believe the Word of God, even—perhaps especially—when it does not fit into my human wisdom and learning.

MARK 16:15–16

And he said unto them, Go ye into all the world, and preach the gospel to every creature. He that believeth and is baptized shall be saved; but he that believeth not shall be damned.

Those who teach baptism regeneration read into the second phrase of verse 16, "He who believes but is not baptized will be condemned." This, of course, is not true.

But those of us who recognize that it is not true may be so busy explaining what the verse clearly does not mean that we do not examine carefully what it does mean. After we confess our sinfulness and accept the death of Jesus as punishment for our sins, one of our first opportunities to be obedient to God in our new life is to accept public baptism as a confession of our sinfulness and a testimony to our salvation by faith in Jesus.

Obedience to God can never save us from the eternal punishment we deserve because we cannot be perfectly obedient to all His will, but obedience to the Word of God is certainly a critical part of spiritual growth as we are being saved from the mess we have made of our lives to become all that God created and redeemed us to be. Submitting to public baptism is a first important step in this "salvation" growth. As a Baptist who understands the beauty of the truth of eternal security, I should not neglect to teach also the beauty of obedience. Obedience can be an important proof of the genuineness of belief (James 2:18).

MARK 16:15

And he said unto them, Go ye into all the world, and preach the gospel to every creature.

This passage is roughly parallel to Matthew 28:19, which commands the making of disciples, and Acts 1:8, which commands witnessing. But there seems to be more here. Jesus commanded them to "preach the gospel to every (*pase*) creature (*ktisei*)." *Ktisei* is from *ktisis*, which means a created thing. We are somehow to declare the ultimate removal of the curse from all creation.

Because He sinned, Adam lost his fellowship with God, and this placed the whole created earth under the curse (Gen. 3:17–19). As we accept forgiveness of our sin through the death of Jesus, we can be restored to our fellowship with God. Our maintaining this fellowship with God through Christ somehow declares to all creation that the curse has been defeated and all creation will ultimately be redeemed even as we have been. For man, God's sinful but redeemed image, to fellowship continually with a Holy God is proof that God is still in charge and that the state of debility of creation is temporary and God can and will restore all things. As I truly and faithfully fellowship with God, I become a part of His message of hope to all creation (cf 2 Pet. 3:1–9).

MARK 16:17–18

> And these signs shall follow them that believe; in my name shall they cast out devils; they shall speak with new tongues; they shall take up serpents; and if they drink any deadly thing, it shall not hurt them; they shall lay hands on the sick, and they shall recover.

These verses are a problem to some because they try to make them mean that every one of these miracles will happen to every believer on every occasion. Jesus, however, said only that these will follow as signs to those whom He was speaking as they (1) went into all the world and (2) preached the gospel (v. 15). And indeed we do find these sorts of things occurring in the book of Acts.

Such things can also follow as signs to those who go into their world in later generations and share the truth of God. But there is no guarantee that every sign will occur in the life of every believer on all occasions. There is certainly no indication that any of these may be ordered at our option on any occasion.

The comfort and assurance for me is that as I make it my business to be wherever God places me and share His truth accurately, any miracle He ordains is available at any time He deems it necessary to His purpose in my life. As I have followed Him, I have, in fact, seen a number of interesting things happen that defy natural explanation, sometimes appearing to violate natural physical laws and often violating laws of statistics and "coincidence." This does not guarantee that I may not die a martyr's death or die from snakebite in God's will and time, but it does guarantee that any miracle God needs to accomplish His will and purpose and my blessing and fulfillment are available to Him at any time.

MARK 16:19–20

So then after the Lord had spoken unto them, he was received up into heaven, and sat on the right hand of God. And they went forth, and preached every where, the Lord working with them, and confirming the word with signs following. Amen.

Mark, reflecting the teaching of Peter (John 14:25–26), locates Jesus the same place as other New Testament writers (Matt. 26:64; Mark 14:62; Luke 22:69; Acts 2:33–34, 7:56; Rom. 8:34; Eph. 1:20; Heb. 1:13; 10:12; 1 Pet. 3:22). The juxtaposition of these two verses is significant. It is the intercession of Jesus before the Father for our sins that makes it possible for the Holy Spirit of God to dwell in unholy human beings and empower us to serve God's purposes on earth.

As I fellowship with God and obey His Word, it is the power of the Holy Spirit and the intercession of the Lord Jesus that makes anything spiritually worthwhile occur. Anything wrought by any other means is wood, hay, and stubble, no matter how religiously impressive it may appear to me or others.